GREAT FARCES

THE PERMANENT THEATRE SERIES

GREAT FARCES

Edited by Robert Saffron

With an Introduction by Samuel Spewack

COLLIER BOOKS, NEW YORK

COLLIER-MACMILLAN LTD., LONDON

Library of Congress Catalog Card Number: 65–26450

FIRST EDITION 1966

The Macmillan Company, New York

Collier-Macmillan Canada Ltd., Toronto, Ontario

Printed in the United States of America

ACKNOWLEDGMENTS

Lysistrata, by Aristophanes. An English version by Dudley Fitts. Copyright 1954, by Harcourt, Brace & World, Inc.; © 1962 by Dudley Fitts. Reprinted by permission of the publishers.

Le Bourgeois Gentilhomme, by Molière, translated as *The Proper Gent* by Henry S. Taylor. Reprinted by permission of Ginn & Co. Ltd., 18 Bedford Row, London W.C.1. Copyright 1959 by Henry S. Taylor. No performance to which the public is admitted may be lawfully given without permission of the author's agents, The League of Dramatists, 84 Drayton Gardens, London S.W. 10, who will be pleased to explain the terms under which a performing license is granted.

The Inspector General, by Nikolai Gogol, New version by Robert Saffron. Copyright 1962 by Robert Saffron. Reprinted by permission of the author. All rights to produce or perform this adaptation are fully protected by copyright. Application for any such use should be addressed to Robert Saffron, 48 West 12 Street, New York 11, N.Y.

Boy Meets Girl, by Bella and Samuel Spewack, reprinted by permission of the authors. Copyright 1936 by Bella and Samuel Spewack. Copyright 1946 (revised) by Bella and Samuel Spewack.

Caution: Professionals and amateurs are hereby warned that *Boy Meets Girl,* being fully protected under the copyright laws of the United States of America, the British Empire, including the Dominion of Canada and all other countries of the Copyright Union, is subject to a royalty. All rights, including professional, amateur, motion picture, recitation, public reading, radio broadcasting and the rights of translation into foreign languages, are strictly reserved. In its present form this play is dedicated to the reading public only.

The amateur acting rights of *Boy Meets Girl* are controlled exclusively by the Dramatists Play Service, Inc., 440 Park Ave. So., New York City, without whose permission in writing no production of the play may be made.

CONTENTS

INTRODUCTION

FARCE is not frivolous. Unfortunately, the label has been misused to designate frothy stage vehicles designed for the sole purpose of creating transient laughter in the theatre. The French manufactured, and at one time exported, hundreds of these bedroom kaleidoscopes in which the basic pattern was always adultery, or the appearance thereof. Doors slammed, lovers and husbands popped up at precisely the wrong moments, and ladies in filmy negligees were duly flustered. There were endless variations, but the theme was always the same. Action was of the essence, so that the audience would not have time to think; and comic business, broad and preferably vulgar, filled the vacuum created by the lack of characterization and serious purpose.

For true farce must have serious purpose. Witness the four classics presented here. What can be more solemn and, in fact, more timely than the terrifying theme of war and peace which is the substance of *Lysistrata*? *Le Bourgeois Gentilhomme* is social analysis; the pretensions of the *nouveau riche* social climber are as absurd today as they were in Molière's time.

Gogol's *The Inspector General* is concerned with corruption in government, a grave and omnipresent problem, shared by East and West alike. Only a brave and talented writer in czarist Russia would have dared attack this universal cancer with wit and venom. No such writer has appeared in modern Russia, unfortunately. The Russians will say, of course, that the problem does not exist, except at party congresses when they are busy downgrading past leaders for corruption, and shoveling their bones out of sacred tombs. There was a time when Soviet writers dealt with Soviet corruption. Perhaps new farce writers will emerge. Perhaps.

To ascribe serious purpose to Oscar Wilde may seem farfetched, but examine carefully the essence of *The Importance of Being Earnest*. It makes a mockery of the very foundation of British class society—the accident of birth. Although the welfare state is here to stay in Britain, and the accident of birth is no longer the sole determining factor in deciding what education you receive, the kind of work—if any—you do, whom you marry, where you live and how you are buried, enough of the tradition survives everywhere to make the theme understandable.

Which brings me to *Boy Meets Girl*, the play my wife,

Bella, and I wrote in the late Thirties. We were enormously flattered that Mr. Saffron chose it for this volume.

Our purpose in writing it was also serious—an exposé of manufactured entertainment. The specific locale is Hollywood, but the foibles we exploit exist in the theatre, in radio, in television and in publishing.

But it is not enough to approach farce with solemn theme and mien. Farce must entertain uproariously. And it must accomplish this with credible and recognizably real people who are, nevertheless, slightly larger than life. Farce must have an organic structure. Despite the popular myth, a farce does not consist of "funny lines." A first-rate writer of farce ruthlessly eliminates any scene, no matter how funny in itself, which does not serve the structure of his play.

Curiously, real farce does not become dated; not even when the reality it deals with has become history. Social organization has changed considerably over the centuries, but the human animal has not. The social climber and the snob will always be with us. So will the greedy bureaucrat. He may, under one form of society, be greedy for money; in another, for power; generally, for both. But he did not die with Gogol.

Boy Meets Girl is the youngest of the plays in this group— a mere twenty-seven, during which period it has managed to survive in professional and amateur productions at home and in some unlikely places abroad. The motion picture industry, as we wrote of it, no longer exists. Television has taken its place. But the infant has adopted the basic methods and mentality of its reluctant parent. If you add to these ingredients the idiocy of big business and its tremulous handmaiden, Madison Avenue, you find the modern manufacture of entertainment an even more ludicrous process than the one we present.

Now, it may be argued that, since the themes of farce are still valid, it is not an effective medium of reform. Granted. But neither is the grim social drama which, curiously enough, tends to rust far more quickly then the presumably ephemeral farce. Far too many "important" plays have taken their places in the history of the theatre, rather than in its life. In any case, writers delude themselves when they fancy that a novel or a play actually changes a fundamental social condition. *Uncle Tom's Cabin* did not abolish slavery in the South. At best, a writer serves a valuable social function in his moral support of those who already agree with him.

A note to students: Farce mechanics can be learned in

time, but not farce writing. Assuming that the student has the capacity for sketching real people in quick, broad strokes, that he himself enjoys the farcical essence of the world around him, that he has learned that the audience will forgive him almost anything except boredom (a hard lesson), then he should have no trouble learning to write a farce by writing one.

Sometimes the farce writer is carried away by the importance or urgency of his theme, and mixes polemics and pedestrian realism with his farce. The result, as I can testify, is almost inevitably failure. If he confuses his mediums, he confuses his audience.

The writer must bear in mind, too, that humor is the most fragile of commodities. If he, or his director or producer, does not cast the proper actors for his farce, he may discover to his tormented surprise that there is no farce. For, although good farces may be read with enjoyment, they spring to full life only on the stage—when the actors and director know what they are doing. The interpretation of farce is as difficult as its writing. And both look deceptively easy when they are expertly done, which is as it should be. Certainly there is nothing more rewarding for both the writer and the actor than the sound of laughter, intelligently achieved.

Perhaps these farces have survived because they are all intelligent. To make people think without pain is a formidable task. Most people rightly come to the theatre to be stirred, moved or amused. If attention wanders, the play is lost. A performance is not a book that can be put down and skimmed at some more appropriate moment.

Primarily, however, these farces survive because the characters in them live, on and off the stage—the Greeks, the French, the Russians, the English. Each generation of actors breathes new life into them.

Only the great poetic tragedies rival them in longevity. But that is not surprising, for, after all, man is a tragic as well as comic beast.

SAMUEL SPEWACK

Co-author with his wife of "Boy Meets Girl," which gave a phrase to the English language and ruined literary and dramatic criticism for all time, Bella and Samuel Spewack also made their bid for comedic posterity with other stage successes—among them, My Three Angels *and* Kiss Me, Kate.

LYSISTRATA

by Aristophanes

A new version by Dudley Fitts

Lysistrata was first performed in 411 B.C. The defeats suffered by Athens in the Peloponnesian War weighed heavily on everyone's mind, so that the actor chosen to play the leading role backed out for fear of public opposition. Aristophanes thereupon took over the role himself.

In this version, Mr. Fitts has used, as he describes it, a "low-comedy burlesque of Deep South talk" to differentiate the speech of the Spartans from the Athenians.

CHARACTERS

LYSISTRATA	COMMISSIONER
KALONIKE	KINESIAS
MYRRHINE	SPARTAN HERALD
LAMPITO	SPARTAN AMBASSADOR
CHORUS	A SENTRY

SCENE: *Athens. First, a public square; later, beneath the walls of the Akropolis; later, a courtyard within the Akropolis. Until the éxodos, the* CHORUS *is divided into two hemichori: the first, of Old Men; the second, of Old Women. Each of these has its* KORYPHAIOS. *In the éxodos, the hemichori return as Athenians and Spartans.*

The supernumeraries include the BABY SON *of* KINESIAS; STRATYLLIS, *a member of the hemichorus of Old Women; various individual speakers, both Spartan and Athenian.*

[9]

PROLOGUE

Athens; a public square; early morning; LYSISTRATA *sola*

LYSISTRATA.
If someone had invited them to a festival—
of Bacchos, say; or to Pan's shrine, or to Aphroditê's
over at Kôlias—, you couldn't get through the streets,
what with the drums and the dancing. But now,
not a woman in sight!

Except—oh, yes!

[*Enter* KALONIKE.]

Here's one of my neighbors, at last. Good
morning, Kalonikê.
KALONIKE.

Good morning, Lysistrata.

Darling,

don't frown so! You'll ruin your face!
LYSISTRATA.

Never mind my face.

Kalonikê,
the way we women behave! Really, I don't blame the men
for what they say about us.
KALONIKE.

No; I imagine they're right.

LYSISTRATA.
For example: I call a meeting
to think out a most important matter—and what hap-
pens?
The women all stay in bed!
KALONIKE.

Oh, they'll be along.
It's hard to get away, you know: a husband, a cook,
a child. . . . Home life can be *so* demanding!
LYSISTRATA.
What I have in mind is even more demanding.

[10]

KALONIKE.

Tell me: what is it?

LYSISTRATA.

It's big.

KALONIKE.

Goodness! *How* big?

LYSISTRATA.

Big enough for all of us.

KALONIKE.

But we're not all here!

LYSISTRATA.

We would be, if *that's* what was up!

No, Kalonikê,
this is something I've been turning over for nights,
long sleepless nights.

KALONIKE.

It must be getting worn down, then,
if you've spent so much time on it.

LYSISTRATA.

Worn down or not,
it comes to this: Only we women can save Greece!

KALONIKE.

Only we women? Poor Greece!

LYSISTRATA.

Just the same,
it's up to us. First, we must liquidate
the Peloponnesians—

KALONIKE.

Fun, fun!

LYSISTRATA.

—and then the Boiotians.

KALONIKE.

Oh! But not those heavenly eels!

LYSISTRATA.

You needn't worry.
I'm not talking about eels. —But here's the point:
If we can get the women from those places—
all those Boiotians and Peloponnesians—
to join us women here, why, we can save
all Greece!

KALONIKE.

But dearest Lysistrata!
How can women do a thing so austere, so
political? We belong at home. Our only armor's

our perfumes, our saffron dresses and
our pretty little shoes!

LYSISTRATA.

       Exactly. Those
transparent dresses, the saffron, the
perfume, those pretty shoes—

KALONIKE.

          Oh?

LYSISTRATA.

           Not a single man would lift
his spear—

KALONIKE.

     I'll send my dress to the dyer's tomorrow!

LYSISTRATA.

 —or grab a shield—

KALONIKE.

       The sweetest little negligée—

LYSISTRATA.

 —or haul out his sword.

KALONIKE.

       I know where I can buy
the dreamiest sandals!

LYSISTRATA.

       Well, so you see. Now, shouldn't
the women have come?

KALONIKE.

       Come? They should have *flown*!

LYSISTRATA.

 Athenians are always late.
      But imagine!
There's no one here from the South Shore, or from
   Sálamis.

KALONIKE.

 Things are hard over in Sálamis, I swear.
 They have to get going at dawn.

LYSISTRATA.

       And nobody from Acharnai.
 I thought they'd be here hours ago.

KALONIKE.

       Well, you'll get
that awful Theagenês woman: she'll be
a sheet or so in the wind.
      But look!
Someone at last! Can you see who they are?

[*Enter* MYRRHINE *and other women.*]

LYSISTRATA.

They're from Anagyros.

KALONIKE.

They certainly are.
You'd know them anywhere, by the scent.

MYRRHINE.

Sorry to be late, Lysistrata.

Oh come,
don't scowl so. Say something!

LYSISTRATA.

My dear Myrrhinê,
what is there to say? After all,
you've been pretty casual about the whole thing.

MYRRHINE.

Couldn't find
my girdle in the dark, that's all.

But what *is*
the whole thing?

KALONIKE.

No, we've got to wait
for those Boiotians and Peloponnesians.

LYSISTRATA.

That's more like it. —But, look!
Here's Lampitô!

[*Enter* LAMPITO *with women from Sparta.*]

LYSISTRATA.

Darling Lampitô,
how pretty you are today! What a nice color!
Goodness, you look as though you could strangle a bull!

LAMPITO.

Ah think Ah could! It's the workout
in the gym every day; and, of co'se that dance of ahs
where y' kick yo' own tail.

KALONIKE.

What an adorable figure!

LAMPITO.

Lawdy, when y' touch me lahk that,
Ah feels lahk a heifer at the altar!

LYSISTRATA.

And this young lady?
Where is she from?

LAMPITO.

Boiotia. Social-Register type.

LYSISTRATA.

Ah. "Boiotia of the fertile plain."

KALONIKE.

And if you look,
you'll find the fertile plain has just been mowed.

LYSISTRATA.

And this lady?

LAMPITO.

Hagh, wahd, handsome. She comes from
Korinth.

KALONIKE.

High and wide's the word for it.

LAMPITO.

Which one of you
called this heah meeting, and why?

LYSISTRATA.

I did.

LAMPITO.

Well, then, tell us:
What's up?

MYRRHINE.

Yes, darling, what *is* on your mind, after all?

LYSISTRATA.

I'll tell you. —But first, one little question.

MYRRHINE.

Well?

LYSISTRATA.

It's your husbands. Fathers of your children. Doesn't it
bother you
that they're always off with the army? I'll stake my life,
not one of you has a man in the house this minute!

KALONIKE.

Mine's been in Thrace the last five months, keeping an eye
on that general.

MYRRHINE.

Mine's been in Pylos for seven.

LAMPITO.

And mahn,
whenever he gets a *dis*charge, he goes raht back
with that li'l ole shield of his, and enlists again!

LYSISTRATA.

And not the ghost of a lover to be found!

From the very day the war began—

those Milesians!
I could skin them alive!

—I've not seen so much, even,
as one of those leather consolation prizes.—
But there! What's important is: If I've found a way
to end the war, are you with me?

MYRRHINE.

I should *say* so!
Even if I have to pawn my best dress and
drink up the proceeds.

KALONIKE.

Me too! Even if they split me
right up the middle, like a flounder.

LAMPITO.

Ah'm shorely with you.
Ah'd crawl up Taÿgetos on mah knees
if that'd bring peace.

LYSISTRATA.

All right, then; here it is:
Women! Sisters!
If we really want our men to make peace,
we must be ready to give up—

MYRRHINE.

Give up what?
Quick, tell us!

LYSISTRATA.

But *will* you?

MYRRHINE.

We will, even if it kills us.

LYSISTRATA.

Then we must give up going to bed with our men.

[*Long silence*]

Oh? So now you're sorry? Won't look at me?
Doubtful? Pale? All teary-eyed?

But come: be frank with me.
Will you do it, or not? Well? Will you do it?

MYRRHINE.

I couldn't. No.
Let the war go on.

KALONIKE.

Nor I. Let the war go on.

LYSISTRATA.
You, you little flounder,
ready to be split up the middle?

KALONIKE.
                         Lysistrata, no!
I'd walk through fire for you—you *know* I would!—, but
    don't
ask us to give up *that!* Why, there's nothing like it!

LYSISTRATA.
And you?

BOIOTIAN.
            No. I must say *I'd* rather walk through fire.

LYSISTRATA.
What an utterly perverted sex we women are!
No wonder poets write tragedies about us.
There's only one thing we can think of.
                              But you from Sparta:
if you stand by me, we may win yet! Will you?
It means so much!

LAMPITO.
            Ah sweah, it means *too* much!
By the Two Goddesses, it does! Asking a girl
to sleep—Heaven knows how long!—in a great big bed
with nobody there but herself! But Ah'll stay with you!
Peace comes first!

LYSISTRATA.
            Spoken like a true Spartan!

KALONIKE.
But if—
      oh dear!
            —if we give up what you tell us to,
will there *be* any peace?

LYSISTRATA.
                  Why, mercy, of course there will!
We'll just sit snug in our very thinnest gowns,
perfumed and powdered from top to bottom, and those
    men
simply won't stand still! And when we say No,
they'll go out of their minds! And there's your peace.
You can take my word for it.

LAMPITO.
                  Ah seem to remember
that Colonel Menelaos threw his sword away
when he saw Helen's breast all bare.

KALONIKE.

But, goodness me!
What if they just get up and leave us?

LYSISTRATA.

In that case
we'll have to fall back on ourselves, I suppose.
But they won't.

KALONIKE.

I must say that's not much help. But
what if they drag us into the bedroom?

LYSISTRATA.

Hang on to the door.

KALONIKE.

What if they slap us?

LYSISTRATA.

If they do, you'd better give in.
But be sulky about it. Do I have to teach you how?
You know there's no fun for men when they have to force
you.
There are millions of ways of getting them to see reason.
Don't you worry: a man
doesn't like it unless the girl co-operates.

KALONIKE.

I suppose so. Oh, all right. We'll go along.

LAMPITO.

Ah imagine us Spahtans can arrange a peace. But you
Athenians! Why, you're just war-mongerers!

LYSISTRATA.

Leave that to me.
I know how to make them listen.

LAMPITO.

Ah don't see how.
After all, they've got their boats; and there's lots of money
piled up in the Akropolis.

LYSISTRATA.

The Akropolis? Darling,
we're taking over the Akropolis today!
That's the older women's job. All the rest of us
are going to the Citadel to sacrifice—you understand me?
And once there, we're in for good!

LAMPITO.

Whee! Up the rebels!
Ah can see you're a good strat*ee*gist.

LYSISTRATA.

           Well, then, Lampitô,
what we have to do now is take a solemn oath.

LAMPITO.

     Say it. We'll sweah.

LYSISTRATA.

           This is it.
—But where's our Inner Guard?
             —Look, Guard: you see this shield?
Put it down here. Now bring me the victim's entrails.

KALONIKE.

     But the oath?

LYSISTRATA.

           You remember how in Aischylos' *Seven*
they killed a sheep and swore on a shield? Well, then?

KALONIKE.

     But I don't see how you can swear for peace on a shield.

LYSISTRATA.

     What else do you suggest?

KALONIKE.

           Why not a white horse?
We could swear by that.

LYSISTRATA.

           And where will you get a white horse?

KALONIKE.

     I never thought of that. *What* can we do?

LYSISTRATA.

           I have it!
Let's set this big black wine-bowl on the ground
and pour in a gallon or so of Thasian, and swear
not to add one drop of water.

LAMPITO.

           Ah lahk *that* oath!

LYSISTRATA.

     Bring the bowl and the wine-jug.

KALONIKE.

           Oh, what a simply *huge* one!

LYSISTRATA.

     Set it down. Girls, place your hands on the gift-offering.

O Goddess of Persuasion! And thou, O Loving-cup!
Look upon this our sacrifice, and
be gracious!

KALONIKE.

See the blood spill out. How red and pretty it is!

LAMPITO.

And Ah must say it smells good.

MYRRHINE.

Let me swear first!

KALONIKE.

No, by Aphroditê, we'll match for it!

LYSISTRATA.

Lampitô: all of you women: come, touch the bowl,
and repeat after me—remember, this is an oath—:
I WILL HAVE NOTHING TO DO WITH MY HUS-
BAND OR MY LOVER

KALONIKE.

I will have nothing to do with my husband or my lover

LYSISTRATA.

THOUGH HE COME TO ME IN PITIABLE CONDI-
TION

KALONIKE.

Though he come to me in pitiable condition
(Oh Lysistrata! This is killing me!)

LYSISTRATA.

IN MY HOUSE I WILL BE UNTOUCHABLE

KALONIKE.

In my house I will be untouchable

LYSISTRATA.

IN MY THINNEST SAFFRON SILK

KALONIKE.

In my thinnest saffron silk

LYSISTRATA.

AND MAKE HIM LONG FOR ME.

KALONIKE.

And make him long for me.

LYSISTRATA.

I WILL NOT GIVE MYSELF

KALONIKE.

I will not give myself

LYSISTRATA.

AND IF HE CONSTRAINS ME

KALONIKE.

And if he constrains me

LYSISTRATA.

I WILL BE AS COLD AS ICE AND NEVER MOVE

KALONIKE.
I will be as cold as ice and never move

LYSISTRATA.
I WILL NOT LIFT MY SLIPPERS TOWARD THE
   CEILING

KALONIKE.
I will not lift my slippers toward the ceiling

LYSISTRATA.
OR CROUCH ON ALL FOURS LIKE THE LIONESS
   IN THE CARVING

KALONIKE.
Or crouch on all fours like the lioness in the carving

LYSISTRATA.
AND IF I KEEP THIS OATH, LET ME DRINK FROM
   THIS BOWL

KALONIKE.
And if I keep this oath, let me drink from this bowl

LYSISTRATA.
IF NOT, LET MY OWN BOWL BE FILLED WITH
   WATER.

KALONIKE.
If not, let my own bowl be filled with water.

LYSISTRATA.
You have all sworn?

MYRRHINE.
                              We have.

LYSISTRATA.
                                        Then thus
I sacrifice the victim.

[*Drinks largely.*]

KALONIKE.
                              Save some for us!
Here's to you, darling, and to you, and to you!

[*Loud cries off-stage.*]

LAMPITO.
What's all *that* whoozy-goozy?

LYSISTRATA.
                              Just what I told you.
The older women have taken the Akropolis.
Now you, Lampitô,
rush back to Sparta. We'll take care of things here. Leave

these girls here for hostages.
                              The rest of you,
up to the Citadel: and mind you push in the bolts.
KALONIKE.

But the men? Won't they be after us?
LYSISTRATA.

                              Just you leave
the men to me. There's not fire enough in the world,
or threats either, to make me open these doors
except on my own terms.
KALONIKE.

                              I hope not, by Aphroditê!
After all,
we've got a reputation for bitchiness to live up to.

[*Exeunt.*]

PÁRODOS: CHORAL EPISODE

The hillside just under the Akropolis. Enter CHORUS OF OLD
MEN *with burning torches and braziers; much puffing and
coughing.*

LEADER OF MEN'S CHORUS.
    Forward march, Drakês, old friend: never you mind
    that damn big log banging hell down on your back.

MEN'S CHORUS.
    There's this to be said for longevity: [STROPHE I]
    You see things you thought that you'd never see.
        Look, Strymodôros, who would have thought it?
        We've caught it—
                    the New Femininity!
    The wives of our bosom, our board, our bed—
        Now, by the gods, they've gone ahead
        And taken the Citadel (Heaven knows why!),
        Profanèd the sacred statuar-y,

                              And barred the doors,
                              The subversive whores!

LEADER OF MEN'S CHORUS.
    Shake a leg there, Philûrgos, man: the Akropolis or
    bust!
    Put the kindling around here. We'll build one almighty
    big

bonfire for the whole bunch of bitches, every last one;
and the first we fry will be old Lykôn's woman.

MEN'S CHORUS.

[ANTISTROPHE 1]

They're not going to give me the old horse-laugh!
No, by Deméter, they won't pull this off!
   Think of Kleómenês: even he
   Didn't go free
              till he brought me his stuff.
A good man he was, all stinking and shaggy,
Bare as an eel except for the bag he
Covered his rear with. God, what a mess!
Never a bath in six years, I'd guess.
       Pure Sparta, man!
       He also ran.

LEADER OF MEN'S CHORUS.

That was a siege, friends! Seventeen ranks strong
we slept at the Gate. And shall we not do as much
against these women, whom God and Euripides hate?
If we don't, I'll turn in my medals from Marathon.

MEN'S CHORUS.

[STROPHE 2]

Onward and upward! A little push,
   And we're there.
Ouch, my shoulders! I could wish
   For a pair
Of good strong oxen. Keep your eye
   On the fire there, it mustn't die.
      Akh! Akh!
   The smoke would make a cadaver cough!

Holy Heraklês, a hot spark   [ANTISTROPHE 2]
   Bit my eye!
Damn this hellfire, damn this work!
   So say I.
Onward and upward just the same.
(Lachês, remember the Goddess: for shame!)
      Akh! Akh!
   The smoke would make a cadaver cough!

LEADER OF MEN'S CHORUS.

At last (and let us give suitable thanks to God
for his infinite mercies) I have managed to bring

my personal flame to the common goal. It breathes, it
  lives.
Now, gentlemen, let us consider. Shall we insert
the torch, say, into the brazier, and thus extract
a kindling brand? And shall we then, do you think,
push on to the gate like valiant sheep? On the whole, yes.
But I would have you consider this, too: if they—
I refer to the women—should refuse to open,
what then? Do we set the doors afire
and smoke them out? At ease, men. Meditate.
Akh, the smoke! Woof! What we really need
is the loan of a general or two from the Samos Command.
At least we've got this lumber off our backs.
That's something. And now let's look to our fire.

O Pot, brave Brazier, touch my torch with flame!
Victory, Goddess, I invoke thy name!
Strike down these paradigms of female pride,
And we shall hang our trophies up inside.

[*Enter* CHORUS OF OLD WOMEN *on the walls of the Akropolis,
carrying jars of water.*]

LEADER OF WOMEN'S CHORUS.
  Smoke, girls, smoke! There's smoke all over the place!
  Probably fire, too. Hurry, girls! Fire! Fire!
WOMEN'S CHORUS.
        Nikodikê, run!   [STROPHE I]
        Or Kalykê's done
        To a turn, and poor Kritylla's
        Smoked like a ham.
              Damn
        These old men! Are we too late?
        I nearly died down at the place
        Where we fill our jars:
           Slaves pushing and jostling—
           Such a hustling
        I never saw in all my days.

        But here's water at last.   [ANTISTROPHE I]
        Haste, sisters, haste!
        Slosh it on them, slosh it down,
        The silly old wrecks!
             Sex
        Almighty! What they want's
        A hot bath? Good. Send one down.

Athêna of Athens town,
    Trito-born! Helm of Gold!
    Cripple the old
Firemen! Help us help them drown!

[*The* OLD MEN *capture a woman,* STRATYLLIS.]

STRATYLLIS.
  Let me go! Let me go!
LEADER OF WOMEN'S CHORUS.
                    You walking corpses,
  have you no shame?
LEADER OF MEN'S CHORUS.
                    I wouldn't have believed it!
  An army of women in the Akropolis!
LEADER OF WOMEN'S CHORUS.
  So we scare you, do we? Grandpa, you've seen
  only our pickets yet!
LEADER OF MEN'S CHORUS.
                    Hey, Phaidrias!
  Help me with the necks of these jabbering hens!
LEADER OF WOMEN'S CHORUS.
  Down with your pots, girls! We'll need both hands
  if these antiques attack us.
LEADER OF MEN'S CHORUS.
                    Want your face kicked in?
LEADER OF WOMEN'S CHORUS.
  Want your balls chewed off?
LEADER OF MEN'S CHORUS.
                    Look out! I've got a stick!
LEADER OF WOMEN'S CHORUS.
  You lay a half-inch of your stick on Stratyllis,
  and you'll never stick again!
LEADER OF MEN'S CHORUS.
  Fall apart!
LEADER OF WOMEN'S CHORUS.
                    I'll spit up your guts!
LEADER OF MEN'S CHORUS.
                    Euripides! Master!
  How well you knew women!
LEADER OF WOMEN'S CHORUS.
                    Listen to him! Rhodippê,
  up with the pots!

LEADER OF MEN'S CHORUS.
> Demolition of God,
what good are your pots?
LEADER OF WOMEN'S CHORUS.
> > You refugee from the tomb,
what good is your fire?
LEADER OF MEN'S CHORUS.
> > Good enough to make a pyre
to barbecue you!
LEADER OF WOMEN'S CHORUS.
> We'll squizzle your kindling!
LEADER OF MEN'S CHORUS.
You think so?
LEADER OF WOMEN'S CHORUS.
> Yah! Just hang around a while!
LEADER OF MEN'S CHORUS.
Want a touch of my torch?
LEADER OF WOMEN'S CHORUS.
> > It needs a good soaping.
LEADER OF MEN'S CHORUS.
How about you?
LEADER OF WOMEN'S CHORUS.
> Soap for a senile bridegroom!
LEADER OF MEN'S CHORUS.
Senile? Hold your trap!
LEADER OF WOMEN'S CHORUS.
> > Just *you* try to hold it!
LEADER OF MEN'S CHORUS.
The yammer of women!
LEADER OF WOMEN'S CHORUS.
> Oh is that so?
You're not in the jury room now, you know.
LEADER OF MEN'S CHORUS.
Gentlemen, I beg you, burn off that woman's hair!
LEADER OF WOMEN'S CHORUS.
Let it come down!
[*They empty their pots on the men.*]
LEADER OF MEN'S CHORUS.
What a way to drown!
LEADER OF WOMEN'S CHORUS.
> Hot, hey?
LEADER OF MEN'S CHORUS.
> Say,
enough!

LEADER OF WOMEN'S CHORUS.
> Dandruff
needs watering. I'll make you
nice and fresh.

LEADER OF MEN'S CHORUS.
> For God's sake, you,
hold off!

Scene I

Enter a COMMISSIONER *accompanied by four constables.*

COMMISSIONER.
These degenerate women! What a racket of little drums,
what a yapping for Adonis on every house-top!
It's like the time in the Assembly when I was listening
to a speech—out of order, as usual—by that fool
Demostratos, all about troops for Sicily,
that kind of nonsense—
> and there was his wife
trotting around in circles howling
Alas for Adonis!—
> and Demostratos insisting
we must draft every last Zakynthian that can walk—
and his wife up there on the roof,
drunk as an owl, yowling
Oh weep for Adonis!—
> and that damned ox Demostratos
mooing away through the rumpus. That's what we get
for putting up with this wretched woman-business!

LEADER OF MEN'S CHORUS.
Sir, you haven't heard the half of it. They laughed at us!
Insulted us! They took pitchers of water
and nearly drowned us! We're still wringing out our clothes,
for all the world like unhousebroken brats.

COMMISSIONER.
Serves you right, by Poseidon!
Whose fault is it if these women-folk of ours
get out of hand? We coddle them,
we teach them to be wasteful and loose. You'll see a husband
go into a jeweler's. "Look," he'll say,
"jeweler," he'll say, "you remember that gold choker
you made for my wife? Well, she went to a dance last
night

and broke the clasp. Now, I've got to go to Sálamis,
and can't be bothered. Run over to my house tonight,
will you, and see if you can put it together for her."
Or another one
goes to a cobbler—a good strong workman, too,
with an awl that was never meant for child's play. "Here,"
he'll tell him, "one of my wife's shoes is pinching
her little toe. Could you come up about noon
and stretch it out for her?"

                 Well, what do you expect?
Look at me, for example. I'm a Public Officer,
and it's one of my duties to pay off the sailors.
And where's the money? Up there in the Akropolis!
And those blasted women slam the door in my face!
But what are we waiting for?

                —Look here, constable,
stop sniffing around for a tavern, and get us
some crowbars. We'll force their gates! As a matter of fact,
I'll do a little forcing myself.

[*Enter* LYSISTRATA, *above, with* MYRRHINE, KALONIKE, *and the*
BOIOTIAN.]

LYSISTRATA.

              No need of forcing.
Here I am, of my own accord. And all this talk
about locked doors—! We don't need locked doors,
but just the least bit of common sense.

COMMISSIONER.

Is that so, ma'am!

         —Where's my constable?

                 —Constable,
arrest that woman, and tie her hands behind her.

LYSISTRATA.

If he touches me, I swear by Artemis
there'll be one scamp dropped from the public payroll
    tomorrow!

COMMISSIONER.

Well, constable? You're not afraid, I suppose? Grab her,
two of you, around the middle!

KALONIKE.

             No, by Pándrosos!
Lay a hand on her, and I'll jump on you so hard
your guts will come out the back door!

COMMISSIONER.

That's what *you* think!
Where's the sergeant?—Here, you: tie up that trollop first,
the one with the pretty talk!

MYRRHINE.

By the Moon-Goddess,
just try! They'll have to scoop you up with a spoon!

COMMISSIONER.

Another one!
Officer, seize that woman!

I swear
I'll put an end to this riot!

BOIOTIAN.

By the Taurian,
one inch closer, you'll be one screaming bald-head!

COMMISSIONER.

Lord, what a mess! And my constables seem ineffective.
But—women get the best of us? By God, no!
—Skythians!

Close ranks and forward march!

LYSISTRATA.

"Forward," indeed!
By the Two Goddesses, what's the sense in *that?*
They're up against four companies of women
armed from top to bottom.

COMMISSIONER.

Forward, my Skythians!

LYSISTRATA.

Forward, yourselves, dear comrades!
You grainlettucebeanseedmarket girls!
You garlicandonionbreadbakery girls!
Give it to 'em! Knock 'em down! Scratch 'em!
Tell 'em what you think of 'em!

[*General mêlée; the Skythians yield.*]

—Ah, that's enough!
Sound a retreat: good soldiers don't rob the dead.

COMMISSIONER.

A nice day *this* has been for the police!

LYSISTRATA.

Well, there you are.—Did you really think we women
would be driven like slaves? Maybe now you'll admit
that a woman knows something about spirit.

COMMISSIONER.

                                            Spirit enough,
especially spirits in bottles! Dear Lord Apollo!

LEADER OF MEN'S CHORUS.

Your Honor, there's no use talking to them. Words
mean nothing whatever to wild animals like these.
Think of the sousing they gave us! and the water
was not, I believe, of the purest.

LEADER OF WOMEN'S CHORUS.

You shouldn't have come after us. And if you try it again,
you'll be one eye short!—Although, as a matter of fact,
what I like best is just to stay at home and read,
like a sweet little bride: never hurting a soul, no,
never going out. But if you *must* shake hornets' nests,
look out for the hornets.

LEADER OF MEN'S CHORUS.

    Of all the beasts that God hath wrought   [STROPHE I]
      What monster's worse than woman?
    Who shall encompass with his thought
      Their guile unending? No man.

    They've seized the Heights, the Rock, the Shrine—
      But to what end? I wot not.
    Sure there's some clue to their design!
      Have you the key? I thought not.

LEADER OF MEN'S CHORUS.

We might question them, I suppose. But I warn you, sir,
don't believe anything you hear! It would be un-Athenian
not to get to the bottom of this plot.

COMMISSIONER.

                                            Very well.
My first question is this: Why, so help you God,
did you bar the gates of the Akropolis?

LYSISTRATA.

                                            Why?
To keep the money, of course. No money, no war.

COMMISSIONER.

You think that money's the cause of war?

LYSISTRATA.

                                            I do.
Money brought about that Peisandros business
and all the other attacks on the state. Well and good!
They'll not get another cent here!

COMMISSIONER.

And what will you do?

LYSISTRATA.

What a question! From now on, we intend
to control the Treasury.

COMMISSIONER.

Control the Treasury!

LYSISTRATA.

Why not? Does that seem strange? After all,
we control our household budgets.

COMMISSIONER.

But that's different!

LYSISTRATA.

"Different?" What do you mean?

COMMISSIONER.

I mean simply this:
it's the Treasury that pays for national defense.

LYSISTRATA.

Unnecessary. We propose to abolish war.

COMMISSIONER.

Good God!—And national security?

LYSISTRATA.

Leave that to us.

COMMISSIONER.

You?

LYSISTRATA.

Us.

COMMISSIONER.

We're done for, then!

LYSISTRATA.

Never mind.
We women will save you in spite of yourselves.

COMMISSIONER.

What nonsense!

LYSISTRATA.

If you like. But you must accept it, like it or not.

COMMISSIONER.

Why, this is downright subversion!

LYSISTRATA.

Maybe it is.
But we're going to save you, Judge.

COMMISSIONER.

I don't *want* to be saved.

LYSISTRATA.
Tut. The death-wish. All the more reason.
COMMISSIONER.

But the idea
of women bothering themselves about peace and war!
LYSISTRATA.
Will you listen to me?
COMMISSIONER.

Yes. But be brief, or I'll—
LYSISTRATA.
This is no time for stupid threats.
COMMISSIONER.

By the gods,
I can't stand any more!
AN OLD WOMAN.

Can't stand? Well, well.
COMMISSIONER.
That's enough out of you, you old buzzard!
Now, Lysistrata: tell me what you're thinking.
LYSISTRATA.
Glad to.

Ever since this war began
We women have been watching you men, agreeing with
you,
keeping our thoughts to ourselves. That doesn't mean
we were happy: we weren't, for we saw how things were
going;
but we'd listen to you at dinner
arguing this way and that.

—Oh you, and your big
Top Secrets!—

And then we'd grin like little patriots
(though goodness knows we didn't feel like grinning) and
ask you:
"Dear, did the armistice come up in Assembly today?"
And you'd say, "None of your business! Pipe down!" you'd
say.
And so we would.
AN OLD WOMAN.

I wouldn't have, by God!
COMMISSIONER.
You'd have taken a beating, then!

—Go on.

LYSISTRATA.

Well, we'd be quiet. But then, you know, all at once
you men would think up something worse than ever.
Even *I* could see it was fatal. And, "Darling," I'd say,
"have you gone completely mad?" And my husband would
    look at me
and say, "Wife, you've got your weaving to attend to.
Mind your tongue, if you don't want a slap. War's
a man's affair!"

COMMISSIONER.

               Good words, and well pronounced.

LYSISTRATA.

You're a fool if you think so.

                        It was hard enough
to put up with all this banquet-hall strategy.
But then we'd hear you out in the public square:
"Nobody left for the draft-quota here in Athens?"
you'd say; and, "No," someone else would say, "not a man!"
And so we women decided to rescue Greece.
You might as well listen to us now: you'll have to, later.

COMMISSIONER.

You rescue Greece? Absurd.

LYSISTRATA.

                  You're the absurd one.

COMMISSIONER.

You expect me to take orders from a woman?

                              I'd die first!

LYSISTRATA.

Heavens, if that's what's bothering you, take my veil,
here, and wrap it around your poor head.

KALONIKE.

                           Yes,
and you can have my market-basket, too.
Go home, tighten your girdle, do the washing, mind
your beans! War's
a woman's affair!

LEADER OF WOMEN'S CHORUS.

               Ground pitchers! Close ranks!

WOMEN'S CHORUS.

        This is a dance that I know well,   [ANTISTROPHE]
           My knees shall never yield.
        Wobble and creak I may, but still
           I'll keep the well-fought field.

Valor and grace march on before,
  Love prods us from behind.
Our slogan is EXCELSIOR,
  Our watchword SAVE MANKIND.

LEADER OF WOMEN'S CHORUS.

Women, remember your grandmothers! Remember
that little old mother of yours, what a stinger she was!
On, on, never slacken. There's a strong wind astern!

LYSISTRATA.

O Erôs of delight! O Aphroditê! Kyprian!
If ever desire has drenched our breasts or dreamed
in our thighs, let it work so now on the men of Hellas
that they shall tail us through the land, slaves, slaves
to Woman, Breaker of Armies!

COMMISSIONER.

                            And if we do?

LYSISTRATA.

Well, for one thing, we shan't have to watch you
going to market, a spear in one hand, and heaven knows
what in the other.

KALONIKE.

                  Nicely said, by Aphroditê!

LYSISTRATA.

As things stand now, you're neither men nor women.
Armor clanking with kitchen pans and pots—
you sound like a pack of Korybantês!

COMMISSIONER.

A man must do what a man must do.

LYSISTRATA.

                                    So I'm told.
But to see a general, complete with Gorgon-shield,
jingling along the dock to buy a couple of herrings!

KALONIKE.

I saw a captain the other day—lovely fellow he was,
nice curly hair—sitting on his horse; and—can you believe
    it?—
he'd just bought some soup, and was pouring it into his
    helmet!
And there was a soldier from Thrace
swishing his lance like something out of Euripides,
and the poor fruit-store woman got so scared
that she ran away and let him have his figs free!

COMMISSIONER.

All this is beside the point.

                 Will you be so kind
as to tell me how you mean to save Greece?

LYSISTRATA.

                         Of course.

Nothing could be simpler.

COMMISSIONER.

                I assure you, I'm all ears.

LYSISTRATA.

Do you know anything about weaving?
Say the yarn gets tangled: we thread it
this way and that through the skein, up and down,
until it's free. And it's like that with war.
We'll send our envoys
up and down, this way and that, all over Greece,
until it's finished.

COMMISSIONER.

             Yarn? Thread? Skein?
Are you out of your mind? I tell you,
war is a serious business.

LYSISTRATA.

             So serious
that I'd like to go on talking about weaving.

COMMISSIONER.

All right. Go ahead.

LYSISTRATA.

             The first thing we have to do
is to wash our yarn, get the dirt out of it.
You see? Isn't there too much dirt here in Athens?
You must wash those men away.

                  Then our spoiled wool—
that's like your job-hunters, out for a life
of no work and big pay. Back to the basket,
citizens or not, allies or not,
or friendly immigrants.

             And your colonies?
Hanks of wool lost in various places. Pull them
together, weave them into one great whole,
and our voters are clothed for ever.

COMMISSIONER.

                It would take a woman
to reduce state questions to a matter of carding and
    weaving.

LYSISTRATA.

You fool! Who were the mothers whose sons sailed off
to fight for Athens in Sicily?

COMMISSIONER.

Enough!
I beg you, do not call back those memories.

LYSISTRATA.

And then,
instead of the love that every woman needs,
we have only our single beds, where we can dream
of our husbands off with the army.

Bad enough for wives!
But what about our girls, getting older every day,
and older, and no kisses?

COMMISSIONER.

Men get older, too.

LYSISTRATA.

Not in the same sense.

A soldier's discharged,
and he may be bald and toothless, yet he'll find
a pretty young thing to go to bed with.

But a woman!
Her beauty is gone with the first gray hair.
She can spend her time
consulting the oracles and the fortune-tellers,
but they'll never send her a husband.

COMMISSIONER.

Still, if a man can rise to the occasion—

LYSISTRATA.

Rise? Rise, yourself!

[*Furiously.*]

Go invest in a coffin!

You've money enough.

I'll bake you
a cake for the Underworld.

And here's your funeral
wealth!

[*She pours water upon him.*]

MYRRHINE.

And here's another!

[*More water.*]

KALONIKE.

And here's
my contribution!

[*More water.*]

LYSISTRATA.

What are you waiting for?
All aboard Styx Ferry!

Charôn's calling for you!
It's sailing-time: don't disrupt the schedule!

COMMISSIONER.
The insolence of women! And to me!
No, by God, I'll go back to town and show
the rest of the commission what might happen to them.

[*Exit* COMMISSIONER.]

LYSISTRATA.
Really, I suppose we should have laid out his corpse
on the doorstep, in the usual way.

But never mind.
We'll give him the rites of the dead tomorrow morning.

[*Exit* LYSISTRATA *with* MYRRHINE *and* KALONIKE.]

PARÁBASIS: CHORAL EPISODE

LEADER OF MEN'S CHORUS.

[ODE I]

Sons of Liberty, awake! The day of glory is at hand.

MEN'S CHORUS.
I smell tyranny afoot, I smell it rising from the land.
I scent a trace of Hippias, I sniff upon the breeze
A dismal Spartan hogo that suggests King Kleisthenês.
Strip, strip for action, brothers!
Our wives, aunts, sisters, mothers
Have sold us out: the streets are full of godless female
rages.
Shall we stand by and let our women confiscate our wages?

LEADER OF MEN'S CHORUS.

[EPIRRHEMA I]

Gentlemen, it's a disgrace to Athens, a disgrace
to all that Athens stands for, if we allow these grandmas
to jabber about spears and shields and making friends
with the Spartans. What's a Spartan? Give me a wild wolf
any day. No. They want the Tyranny back, I suppose.
Are we going to take that? No. Let us look like
the innocent serpent, but be the flower under it,
as the poet sings. And just to begin with,
I propose to poke a number of teeth
down the gullet of that harridan over there.

LEADER OF WOMEN'S CHORUS.

[ANTODE I]

Oh, is that so? When you get home, your own mammá
    won't know you!

WOMEN'S CHORUS.

Who do you think we are, you senile bravos? Well, I'll
    show you.
I bore the sacred vessels in my eighth year, and at ten
I was pounding out the barley for Athêna Goddess; then
    They made me Little Bear
    At the Braunonian Fair;
I'd held the Holy Basket by the time I was of age,
The Blessed Dry Figs had adorned my plump décolletage.

LEADER OF WOMEN'S CHORUS.

[ANTEPIRRHEMA I]

A "disgrace to Athens," am I, just at the moment
I'm giving Athens the best advice she ever had?
Don't I pay taxes to the state? Yes, I pay them
in baby boys. And what do you contribute,
you impotent horrors? Nothing but waste: all
our Treasury, dating back to the Persian Wars,
gone! rifled! And not a penny out of your pockets!
Well, then? Can you cough up an answer to that?
Look out for your own gullet, or you'll get a crack
from this old brogan that'll make your teeth see stars!

MEN'S CHORUS.

                Oh insolence!   [ODE 2]
                Am I unmanned?
                Incontinence!
                Shall my scarred hand

Strike never a blow
To curb this flow-
ing female curse?

Leipsydrion!
Shall I betray
The laurels won
On that great day?
Come, shake a leg,
Shed old age, beg
The years reverse!

LEADER OF MEN'S CHORUS.

[EPIRRHEMA 2]

Give them an inch, and we're done for! We'll have them
launching boats next and planning naval strategy,
sailing down on us like so many Artemisias.
Or maybe they have ideas about the cavalry.
That's fair enough, women are certainly good
in the saddle. Just look at Mikôn's paintings,
all those Amazons wrestling with all those men!
On the whole, a straitjacket's their best uniform.

WOMEN'S CHORUS.

Tangle with me,   [ANTODE 2]
And you'll get cramps.
Ferocity
's no use now, Gramps!
By the Two,
I'll get through
To you wrecks yet!

I'll scramble your eggs,
I'll burn your beans,
With my two legs.
You'll see such scenes
As never yet
Your two eyes met.
A curse? You bet!

LEADER OF WOMEN'S CHORUS.

[ANTEPIRRHEMA 2]

If Lampitô stands by me, and that delicious Theban girl,
Ismênia—what good are *you?* You and your seven
Resolutions! Resolutions? Rationing Boiotian eels

and making our girls go without them at Hekatê's Feast!
That was statesmanship! And we'll have to put up with it
and all the rest of your decrepit legislation
until some patriot—God give him strength!—
grabs you by the neck and kicks you off the Rock.

Scene II

Re-enter LYSISTRATA *and her lieutenants.*

LEADER OF WOMEN'S CHORUS [*tragic tone*].
    Great Queen, fair Architect of our empire,
    Why lookst thou on us with foreboding eyes?

LYSISTRATA.
  The behavior of these idiotic women!
  There's something about the female temperament
  that I can't bear!
LEADER OF WOMEN'S CHORUS.
          What in the world do you mean?
LYSISTRATA.
  Exactly what I say.
LEADER OF WOMEN'S CHORUS.
          What dreadful thing has happened?
  Come, tell us: we're all your friends.
LYSISTRATA.
               It isn't easy
  to say it; yet, God knows, we can't hush it up.
LEADER OF WOMEN'S CHORUS.
  Well, then? Out with it!
LYSISTRATA.
          To put it bluntly,
  we're dying to get laid.
LEADER OF WOMEN'S CHORUS.
          Almighty God!
LYSISTRATA.
  Why bring God into it?—No, it's just as I say.
  I can't manage them any longer: they've gone man-crazy,
  they're all trying to get out.
          Why, look:
  one of them was sneaking out the back door
  over there by Pan's cave; another
  was sliding down the walls with rope and tackle;
  another was climbing aboard a sparrow, ready to take off

for the nearest brothel—I dragged *her* back by the hair!
They're all finding some reason to leave.

                                          Look there!

There goes another one.

                        —Just a minute, you!

Where are you off to so fast?

FIRST WOMAN.

                              I've got to get home.

I've a lot of Milesian wool, and the worms are spoiling it.

LYSISTRATA.

Oh bother you and your worms! Get back inside!

FIRST WOMAN.

I'll be back right away, I swear I will.

I just want to get it stretched out on my bed.

LYSISTRATA.

You'll do no such thing. You'll stay right here.

FIRST WOMAN.

                                          And my wool?

You want it ruined?

LYSISTRATA.

                    Yes, for all I care.

SECOND WOMAN.

Oh dear! My lovely new flax from Amorgos—
I left it at home, all uncarded!

LYSISTRATA.

                    Another one!

And all she wants is someone to card her flax.
Get back in there!

SECOND WOMAN.

              But I swear by the Moon-Goddess,

the minute I get it done, I'll be back!

LYSISTRATA.

                              I say No.

If you, why not all the other women as well?

THIRD WOMAN.

O Lady Eileithyia! Radiant goddess! Thou
intercessor for women in childbirth! Stay, I pray thee,
oh stay this parturition. Shall I pollute
a sacred spot?

LYSISTRATA.

              And what's the matter with *you?*

THIRD WOMAN.

I'm having a baby—any minute now.

LYSISTRATA.

But you weren't pregnant yesterday.

THIRD WOMAN.

               Well, I am today.
Let me go home for a midwife, Lysistrata:
there's not much time.

LYSISTRATA.

             I never heard such nonsense.
What's that bulging under your cloak?

THIRD WOMAN.

                A little baby boy.

LYSISTRATA.

It certainly isn't. But it's something hollow,
like a basin or—Why, it's the helmet of Athêna!
And you said you were having a baby.

THIRD WOMAN.

                Well, I am! So there!

LYSISTRATA.

Then why the helmet?

THIRD WOMAN.

             I was afraid that my pains
might begin here in the Akropolis; and I wanted
to drop my chick into it, just as the dear doves do.

LYSISTRATA.

Lies! Evasions!—But at least one thing's clear:
you can't leave the place before your purification.

THIRD WOMAN.

But I can't stay here in the Akropolis! Last night I
    dreamed
of the Snake.

FIRST WOMAN.

          And those horrible owls, the noise they make!
I can't get a bit of sleep; I'm just about dead.

LYSISTRATA.

You useless girls, that's enough: Let's have no more lying.
Of course you want your men. But don't you imagine
that they want you just as much? I'll give you my word,
their nights must be pretty hard.

               Just stick it out!
A little patience, that's all, and our battle's won.
I have heard an Oracle. Should you like to hear it?

FIRST WOMAN.

An Oracle? Yes, tell us!

LYSISTRATA.

Here is what it says:
WHEN SWALLOWS SHALL THE HOOPOE SHUN
   AND SPURN HIS HOT DESIRE,
ZEUS WILL PERFECT WHAT THEY'VE BEGUN
   AND SET THE LOWER HIGHER.

FIRST WOMAN.
   Does that mean we'll be on top?

LYSISTRATA.
   BUT IF THE SWALLOWS SHALL FALL OUT
      AND TAKE THE HOOPOE'S BAIT,
   A CURSE MUST MARK THEIR HOUR OF DOUBT,
      INFAMY SEAL THEIR FATE.

THIRD WOMAN.
   I swear, *that* Oracle's all too clear.

FIRST WOMAN.
                              Oh the dear gods!

LYSISTRATA.
   Let's not be downhearted, girls. Back to our places!
   The god has spoken. How can we possibly fail him?

[*Exit* LYSISTRATA *with the dissident women.*]

CHORAL EPISODE

MEN'S CHORUS.

                                                [STROPHE]

   I know a little story that I learned way back in school
   Goes like this:
   Once upon a time there was a young man—and no fool—
   Named Melanion; and his
   One aversi-on was marriage. He loathed the very thought.
   So he ran off to the hills, and in a special grot
   Raised a dog, and spent his days
   Hunting rabbits. And it says
   That he never, never, never did come home.
   It might be called a refuge *from* the womb.
   All right,
            all right,
                     all right!
   We're as bright as young Melanion, and we hate the very
        sight
   Of you women!

A MAN.

 How about a kiss, old lady?

A WOMAN.

 Here's an onion for your eye!

A MAN.

 A kick in the guts, then?

A WOMAN.

 Try, old bristle-tail, just try!

A MAN.

 Yet they say Myronidês

 On hands and knees

 Looked just as shaggy fore and aft as I!

WOMEN'S CHORUS.

          [ANTISTROPHE]

 Well, *I* know a little story, and it's just as good as yours.

 Goes like this:

 Once there was a man named Timon—a rough diamond,
  of course,

 And that whiskery face of his

 Looked like murder in the shrubbery. By God, he was a
  son

 Of the Furies, let me tell you! And what did he do but run

 From the world and all its ways,

 Cursing mankind! And it says

 That his choicest execrations as of then

 Were leveled almost wholly at *old* men.

 All right,

    all right,

       all right!

 But there's one thing about Timon: he could always stand
  the sight

 Of us women.

A WOMAN.

 How about a crack in the jaw, Pop?

A MAN.

 I can take it, Ma—no fear!

A WOMAN.

 How about a kick in the face?

A MAN.

 You'd reveal your old caboose?

A WOMAN.

 What I'd show,

I'll have you know,
Is an instrument you're too far gone to use.

Scene III

Re-enter LYSISTRATA

LYSISTRATA.
Oh, quick, girls, quick! Come here!
A WOMAN.
                              What is it?
LYSISTRATA.
                                        A man.
A man simply bulging with love.
                              O Kyprian Queen,
O Paphian, O Kythereian! Hear us and aid us!
A WOMAN.
Where is this enemy?
LYSISTRATA.
                    Over there, by Demêter's shrine.
A WOMAN.
Damned if he isn't. But who *is* he?
MYRRHINE.
                                        My husband.
Kinêsias.
LYSISTRATA.
            Oh then, get busy! Tease him! Undermine him!
Wreck him! Give him everything—kissing, tickling, nudg-
    ing,
whatever you generally torture him with—: give him every-
    thing
except what we swore on the wine we would not give.
MYRRHINE.
Trust me.
LYSISTRATA.
            I do. But I'll help you get him started.
The rest of you women, stay back.

[*Enter* KINESIAS.]

KINESIAS.
                              Oh God! Oh my God!
I'm stiff from lack of exercise. All I can do to stand up.
LYSISTRATA.
Halt! Who are you, approaching our lines?

KINESIAS.

Me? I.

LYSISTRATA.
A man?

KINESIAS.
You have eyes, haven't you?

LYSISTRATA.
Go away.

KINESIAS.
Who says so?

LYSISTRATA.
Officer of the Day.

KINESIAS.
Officer, I beg you,
by all the gods at once, bring Myrrhinê out.

LYSISTRATA.
Myrrhinê? And who, my good sir, are you?

KINESIAS.
Kinêsias. Last name's Pennison. Her husband.

LYSISTRATA.
Oh, of course. I beg your pardon. We're glad to see you.
We've heard so much about you. Dearest Myrrhinê
is always talking about Kinêsias—never nibbles an egg
or an apple without saying
"Here's to Kinêsias!"

KINESIAS.
Do you really mean it?

LYSISTRATA.
I do.
When we're discussing men, she always says
"Well, after all, there's nobody like Kinêsias!"

KINESIAS.
Good God.—Well, then, please send her down here.

LYSISTRATA.
And what do *I* get out of it?

KINESIAS.
A standing promise.

LYSISTRATA.
I'll take it up with her.

[*Exit* LYSISTRATA.]

KINESIAS.
But be quick about it!
Lord, what's life without a wife? Can't eat. Can't sleep.

Every time I go home, the place is so empty, so
insufferably sad. Love's killing me. Oh,
hurry!

[*Enter* MANES, *a slave, with* KINESIAS' *baby; the voice of*
MYRRHINE *is heard off-stage*.]

MYRRHINE.

But of course I love him! Adore him!—But no,
he hates love. No. I won't go down.

[*Enter* MYRRHINE, *above*.]

KINESIAS.

Myrrhinê!
Darlingest Myrrhinette! Come down quick!

MYRRHINE.
Certainly not.

KINESIAS.

Not? But why, Myrrhinê?

MYRRHINE.
Why? You don't need me.

KINESIAS.

Need you? My God, *look* at me!

MYRRHINE.
So long!

[*Turns to go*.]

KINESIAS.

Myrrhinê, Myrrhinê, Myrrhinê!
If not for my sake, for our child!

[*Pinches* BABY.]

—All right, you: pipe up!

BABY.
Mummie! Mummie! Mummie!

KINESIAS.

You hear that?
Pitiful, I call it. Six days now
with never a bath; no food; enough to break your heart!

MYRRHINE.
My darlingest child! What a father *you* acquired!

KINESIAS.
At least come down for his sake.

MYRRHINE.

I suppose I must.

Oh, this mother business!

[*Exit.*]

KINESIAS.

How pretty she is! And younger!
The harder she treats me, the more bothered I get.

[MYRRHINE *enters, below.*]

MYRRHINE.

Dearest child,
you're as sweet as your father's horrid. Give me a kiss.

KINESIAS.

Now don't you see how wrong it was to get involved
in this scheming league of women? It's bad
for us both.

MYRRHINE.

Keep your hands to yourself!

KINESIAS.

But our house
going to rack and ruin?

MYRRHINE.

I don't care.

KINESIAS.

And your knitting
all torn to pieces by the chickens? Don't you care?

MYRRHINE.

Not at all.

KINESIAS.

And our debt to Aphroditê?
Oh, *won't* you come back?

MYRRHINE.

No.—At least, not until you men
make a treaty and stop this war.

KINESIAS.

Why, I suppose
that might be arranged.

MYRRHINE.

Oh? Well, I suppose
I might come down then. But meanwhile,
I've sworn not to.

KINESIAS.

Don't worry.—Now, let's have fun.

MYRRHINE.
No! Stop it! I said no!
                    —Although, of course,

I *do* love you.
KINESIAS.
                    I know you do. Darling Myrrhinê:
come, shall we?
MYRRHINE.
                    Are you out of your mind? In front of the child?

KINESIAS.
Take him home, Manês.

[*Exit* MANES *with* BABY.]

                    There. He's gone.
                                        Come on!

There's nothing to stop us now.
MYRRHINE.
                                        You devil! But where?

KINESIAS.
In Pan's cave. What could be snugger than that?
MYRRHINE.
But my purification before I go back to the Citadel?
KINESIAS.
Wash in the Klepsydra.
MYRRHINE.
                    And my oath?

KINESIAS.
                                        Leave the oath to me.

After all, I'm the man.
MYRRHINE.
                    Well . . . if you say so.
                                        I'll go find a bed.

KINESIAS.
Oh, bother a bed! The ground's good enough for me.
MYRRHINE.
No. You're a bad man, but you deserve something better
    than dirt.

[*Exit* MYRRHINE.]

KINESIAS.
What a love she is! And how thoughtful!

[*Re-enter* MYRRHINE.]

MYRRHINE.

Here's your bed.
Now let me get my clothes off.

But, good horrors!
We haven't a mattress.

KINESIAS.

Oh, forget the mattress!

MYRRHINE.

No.
Just lying on blankets? Too sordid.

KINESIAS.

Give me a kiss.

MYRRHINE.
Just a second.

[*Exit* MYRRHINE.]

KINESIAS.

I swear, I'll explode!

[*Re-enter* MYRRHINE.]

MYRRHINE.

Here's your mattress.
I'll just take my dress off.

But look—
where's our pillow?

KINESIAS.

I don't *need* a pillow!

MYRRHINE.

Well, *I* do.

[*Exit* MYRRHINE.]

KINESIAS.
I don't suppose even Heraklês
would stand for this!

[*Re-enter* MYRRHINE.]

MYRRHINE.

There we are. Ups-a-daisy!

KINESIAS.
So we are. Well, come to bed.

MYRRHINE.

But I wonder:
is everything ready now?

KINESIAS.

I can swear to that. Come darling!

MYRRHINE.
Just getting out of my girdle.

But remember, now,
what you promised about the treaty.

KINESIAS.
Yes, yes, yes!

MYRRHINE.
But no coverlet!

KINESIAS.
Damn it, I'll be
your coverlet!

MYRRHINE.
Be right back.

[*Exit* MYRRHINE.]

KINESIAS.
This girl and her coverlets
will be the death of me.

[*Re-enter* MYRRHINE.]

MYRRHINE.
Here we are. Up you go!

KINESIAS.
Up? I've been up for ages.

MYRRHINE.
Some perfume?

KINESIAS.
No, by Apollo!

MYRRHINE.
Yes, by Aphroditê!
I don't care whether you want it or not.

[*Exit* MYRRHINE.]

KINESIAS.
For love's sake, hurry!

[*Re-enter* MYRRHINE.]

MYRRHINE.
Here, in your hand. Rub it right in.

KINESIAS.
Never cared for perfume.
And this is particularly strong. Still, here goes.

MYRRHINE.
What a nitwit I am! I brought you the Rhodian bottle.

KINESIAS.

Forget it.

MYRRHINE.

No trouble at all. You just wait here.

[*Exit* MYRRHINE.]

KINESIAS.

God damn the man who invented perfume!

[*Re-enter* MYRRHINE.]

MYRRHINE.

At last! The right bottle!

KINESIAS.

I've got the rightest
bottle of all, and it's right here waiting for you.
Darling, forget everything else. Do come to bed.

MYRRHINE.

Just let me get my shoes off.

—And, by the way,
you'll vote for the treaty?

KINESIAS.

I'll think about it.

[MYRRHINE *runs away*.]

There! That's done it! The damned woman,
she gets me all bothered, she half kills me,
and off she runs! What'll I do? Where
can I get laid?

—and you, little prodding pal,
who's going to take care of *you*? No, you and I
had better get down to old Foxdog's Nursing Clinic.

MEN'S CHORUS.

Alas for the woes of man, alas
Specifically for you.
She's brought you to a pretty pass:
What are you going to do?
Split, heart! Sag, flesh! Proud spirit, crack!
Myrrhinê's got you on your back.

KINESIAS.

The agony, the protraction!

LEADER OF MEN'S CHORUS.

Friend,

What woman's worth a damn?
They bitch us all, world without end.

KINESIAS.
            Yet they're so damned sweet, man!

LEADER OF MEN'S CHORUS.
            Calamitous, that's what I say.
You should have learned that much today.

MEN'S CHORUS.
            O blessed Zeus, roll womankind
            Up into one great ball;
            Blast them aloft on a high wind,
            And once there, let them fall.
            Down, down they'll come, the pretty dears,
            And split themselves on our thick spears.

[*Exit* KINESIAS.]

Scene IV

Enter a SPARTAN HERALD.

HERALD.
    Gentlemen, Ah beg you will be so kind
    as to direct me to the Central Committee.
    Ah have a communication.

[*Re-enter* COMMISSIONER.]

COMMISSIONER.
                    Are you a man,
    or a fertility symbol?

HERALD.
                Ah refuse to answer that question!
    Ah'm a certified herald from Spahta, and Ah've come
    to talk about an ahmistice.

COMMISSIONER.
                    Then why
    that spear under your cloak?

HERALD.
                        Ah have no speah!

COMMISSIONER.
    You don't walk naturally, with your tunic
    poked out so. You have a tumor, maybe,
    or a hernia?

HERALD.
            You lost yo' mahnd, man?

COMMISSIONER.

                          Well,
something's up, I can see that. And I don't like it.

HERALD.

Colonel, Ah resent this.

COMMISSIONER.

                   So I see. But what *is* it?

HERALD.

                                    A staff
with a message from Spahta.

COMMISSIONER.

                        Oh. I know about those staffs.
Well, then, man, speak out: How are things in Sparta?

HERALD.

Hahd, Colonel, hahd! We're at a standstill.
Cain't seem to think of anything but women.

COMMISSIONER.

How curious! Tell me, do you Spartans think
that maybe Pan's to blame?

HERALD.

Pan? No. Lampitô and her little naked friends.
They won't let a man come nigh them.

COMMISSIONER.

How are you handling it?

HERALD.

                      Losing our mahnds,
if y' want to know, and walking around hunched over
lahk men carrying candles in a gale.
The women have swohn they'll have nothing to do with
    us
until we get a treaty.

COMMISSIONER.

                   Yes. I know.
It's a general uprising, sir, in all parts of Greece.
But as for the answer—
                  Sir: go back to Sparta
and have them send us your Armistice Commission.
I'll arrange things in Athens.
                  And I may say
that my standing is good enough to make them listen.

HERALD.

A man after mah own haht! Seh, Ah thank you.

[*Exit* HERALD.]

CHORAL EPISODE

MEN'S CHORUS.

      Oh these women! Where will you find   [STROPHE]
      A slavering beast that's more unkind?
        Where a hotter fire?
      Give me a panther, any day.
      He's not so merciless as they,
        And panthers don't conspire.

WOMEN'S CHORUS.

      We may be hard, you silly old ass,   [ANTISTROPHE]
      But who brought you to this stupid pass?
        You're the ones to blame.
      Fighting with us, your oldest friends,
      Simply to serve your selfish ends—
        Really, you have no shame!

LEADER OF MEN'S CHORUS.

  No, I'm through with women for ever.

LEADER OF WOMEN'S CHORUS.

                          If you say so.

  Still, you might put some clothes on. You look too absurd
  standing around naked. Come, get into this cloak.

LEADER OF MEN'S CHORUS.

  Thank you; you're right. I merely took it off
  because I was in such a temper.

LEADER OF WOMEN'S CHORUS.

                    That's much better.

  Now you resemble a man again.

                    Why have you been so horrid?

  And look: there's some sort of insect in your eye.
  Shall I take it out?

LEADER OF MEN'S CHORUS.

             An insect, is it? So that's

  what's been bothering me. Lord, yes: take it out!

LEADER OF WOMEN'S CHORUS.

  You might be more polite.

                  —But, heavens!

  What an enormous mosquito!

LEADER OF MEN'S CHORUS.

              You've saved my life.

  That mosquito was drilling an artesian well
  in my left eye.

LEADER OF WOMEN'S CHORUS.
                    Let me wipe
those tears away.—And now: one little kiss?

LEADER OF MEN'S CHORUS.
    No, no kisses.

LEADER OF WOMEN'S CHORUS.
                    You're so difficult.

LEADER OF MEN'S CHORUS.
    You impossible women! How you do get around us!
    The poet was right: Can't live with you, or without you.
    But let's be friends.
    And to celebrate, you might join us in an ode.

MEN'S AND WOMEN'S CHORUSES.
                    Let it never be said   [STROPHE 1]
                    That my tongue is malicious:
                    Both by word and by deed
        I would set an example that's noble and gracious.
                    We've had sorrow and care
                    Till we're sick of the tune.
                    Is there anyone here
                    Who would like a small loan?
                        My purse is crammed,
                        As you'll soon find;
        And you needn't pay me back if the Peace gets signed.

                    I've invited to lunch   [STROPHE 2]
                    Some Karystian rips—
                    An esurient bunch,
        But I've ordered a menu to water their lips.
                    I can still make soup
                    And slaughter a pig.
                    You're all coming, I hope?
                    But a bath first, I beg!
                        Walk right up
                        As though you owned the place,
        And you'll get the front door slammed to in your face.

Scene V

Enter SPARTAN AMBASSADOR, *with entourage.*

LEADER OF MEN'S CHORUS.
    The commission has arrived from Sparta.
                                        How oddly

they're walking!

               Gentlemen, welcome to Athens!

How is life in Lakonia?

AMBASSADOR.

                        Need we discuss that?

Simply use your eyes.

MEN'S CHORUS.

                  The poor man's right:
                  What a sight!

AMBASSADOR.

                       Words fail me.

But come, gentlemen, call in your commissioners,
and let's get down to a Peace.

LEADER OF MEN'S CHORUS.

                  The state we're in! Can't bear
a stitch below the waist. It's a kind of pelvic
paralysis.

COMMISSIONER.

              Won't somebody call Lysistrata? —Gentlemen,
we're no better off than you.

AMBASSADOR.

                 So I see.

A SPARTAN.

Seh, do y'all feel a certain strain
early in the morning?

AN ATHENIAN.

              I do, sir. It's worse than a strain.
A few more days, and there's nothing for us but Kleisthenês,
that broken blossom.

LEADER OF MEN'S CHORUS.

              But you'd better get dressed again.
You know these people going around Athens with chisels,
looking for statues of Hermês.

ATHENIAN.

                Sir, you are right.

SPARTAN.

He certainly is! Ah'll put mah own clothes back on.

[*Enter* ATHENIAN COMMISSIONERS.]

COMMISSIONER.

Gentlemen from Sparta, welcome. This
    is a sorry business.

SPARTAN [*To one of his own group*].

Colonel, we got dressed just in time. Ah sweah,

if they'd seen us the way we were, there'd have been a
    new wah
between the states.

COMMISSIONER.

Shall we call the meeting to order?

                                    Now, Lakonians,
    what's your proposal?

AMBASSADOR.

                            We propose to consider peace.

COMMISSIONER.

Good. That's on our minds, too.

                                    —Summon Lysistrata.
We'll never get anywhere without her.

AMBASSADOR.

                                            Lysistrata?
Summon Lysis-*any*body! Only, summon!

LEADER OF MEN'S CHORUS.

                                    No need to summon:
here she is, herself.

[*Enter* LYSISTRATA.]

COMMISSIONER.

                    Lysistrata! Lion of women!
This is your hour to be
hard and yielding, outspoken and shy, austere and
gentle. You see here
the best brains of Hellas (confused, I admit,
by your devious charming) met as one man
to turn the future over to you.

LYSISTRATA.

                            That's fair enough,
unless you men take it into your heads
to turn to each other instead of to us. But I'd know
soon enough if you did.

                    —Where is Reconciliation?
Go, some of you: bring her here.

[*Exeunt two women.*]

                            And now, women,
lead the Spartan delegates to me: not roughly
or insultingly, as our men handle them, but gently,
politely, as ladies should. Take them by the hand,
or by anything else if they won't give you their hands.

[The SPARTANS *are escorted over.]*

There. —The Athenians next, by any convenient handle.

[The ATHENIANS *are escorted.]*

Stand there, please. —Now, all of you, listen to me.

[During the following speech the two women re-enter, carrying an enormous statue of a naked girl; this is RECONCILIATION.*]*

I'm only a woman, I know; but I've got a mind,
and, I think, not a bad one: I owe it to my father
and to listening to the local politicians.
So much for that.
     Now, gentlemen,
since I have you here, I intend to give you a scolding.
We are all Greeks.
Must I remind you of Thermopylai, of Olympia,
of Delphoi? names deep in all our hearts?
Are they not a common heritage?
       Yet you men
go raiding through the country from both sides,
Greek killing Greek, storming down Greek cities—
and all the time the barbarian across the sea
is waiting for his chance!
     —That's my first point.

AN ATHENIAN.
Lord! I can hardly contain myself.

LYSISTRATA.
      As for you Spartans:
Was it so long ago that Perikleidês
came here to beg our help? I can see him still,
his gray face, his sombre gown. And what did he want?
An army from Athens. All Messênê
was hot at your heels, and the sea-god splitting your land.
Well, Kimôn and his men,
four thousand strong, marched out and saved all Sparta.
And what thanks do we get? You come back to murder
  us.

AN ATHENIAN.
They're aggressors, Lysistrata!

A SPARTAN.
     Ah admit it.
When Ah look at those laigs, Ah sweah Ah'll aggress
 mahself!

LYSISTRATA.

    And you, Athenians: do you think you're blameless?
Remember that bad time when we were helpless,
and an army came from Sparta,
and that was the end of the Thessalian menace,
the end of Hippias and his allies.

                       And that was Sparta,
and only Sparta; but for Sparta, we'd be
cringing slaves today, not free Athenians.

[*From this point, the male responses are less to*
LYSISTRATA *than to the statue.*]

A SPARTAN.
    A well shaped speech.
AN ATHENIAN.

               Certainly it has its points.
LYSISTRATA.

    Why are we fighting each other? With all this history
of favors given and taken, what stands in the way
of making peace?
AMBASSADOR.

             Spahta is ready, ma'am,
so long as we get that place back.
LYSISTRATA.

                   What place, man?

AMBASSADOR.
    Ah refer to Pylos.
COMMISSIONER.

             Not a chance, by God!
LYSISTRATA.

    Give it to them, friend.
COMMISSIONER.

           But—what shall we have to bargain with?
LYSISTRATA.

    Demand something in exchange.
COMMISSIONER.

              Good idea. —Well, then:
Cockeville first, and the Happy Hills, and the country
between the Legs of Mégara.
AMBASSADOR.

             Mah government objects.
LYSISTRATA.

    Overruled. Why fuss about a pair of legs?

[*General assent. The statue is removed.*]

AN ATHENIAN.

I want to get out of these clothes and start my plowing.

A SPARTAN.

Ah'll fertilize mahn first, by the Heavenly Twins!

LYSISTRATA.

And so you shall,
once you've made peace. If you are serious,
go, both of you, and talk with your allies.

COMMISSIONER.

Too much talk already. No, we'll stand together.
We've only one end in view. All that we want
is our women; and I speak for our allies.

AMBASSADOR.

Mah government concurs.

AN ATHENIAN.

So does Karystos.

LYSISTRATA.

Good. —But before you come inside
to join your wives at supper, you must perform
the usual lustration. Then we'll open
our baskets for you, and all that we have is yours.
But you must promise upright good behavior
from this day on. Then each man home with his woman!

AN ATHENIAN.

Let's get it over with.

A SPARTAN.

Lead on. Ah follow.

AN ATHENIAN.

Quick as a cat can wink!

[*Exeunt all but the* CHORUSES.]

WOMEN'S CHORUS.

Embroideries ánd   [ANTISTROPHE I]
Twinkling ornaments ánd
Pretty dresses—I hand
Them all over to you, and with never a qualm.
They'll be nice for your daughters
On festival days
When the girls bring the Goddess
The ritual prize.
Come in, one and all:
Take what you will.
I've nothing here so tightly corked that you can't make
it spill.

You may search my house,   [ANTISTROPHE 2]
But you'll not find
The least thing of use,
Unless your two eyes are keener than mine.
Your numberless brats
Are half starved? and your slaves?
Courage, grandpa! I've lots
Of grain left, and big loaves.
I'll fill your guts,
I'll go the whole hog;
But if you come too close to me, remember: 'ware the
dog!

[*Exeunt* CHORUSES.]

ÉXODOS

[*A* DRUNKEN CITIZEN *enters, approaches the gate, and is halted by a sentry.*]

CITIZEN.

Open. The. Door.

SENTRY.

Now, friend, just shove along!
—So you want to sit down. If it weren't such an old joke,
I'd tickle your tail with this torch. Just the sort of gag
this audience appreciates.

CITIZEN.

I. Stay. Right. Here.

SENTRY.

Get away from there, or I'll scalp you! The gentlemen
from Sparta
are just coming back from dinner.

[*Exit* CITIZEN; *the general company re-enters; the two* CHORUSES *now represent* SPARTANS *and* ATHENIANS.]

A SPARTAN.

Ah must say,
Ah never tasted better grub.

AN ATHENIAN.

And those Lakonians!
They're gentlemen, by the Lord! Just goes to show,
a drink to the wise is sufficient.

COMMISSIONER.
>   And why not?

A sober man's an ass.
Men of Athens, mark my words: the only efficient
ambassador's a drunk ambassador. Is that clear?
Look: we go to Sparta,
and when we get there we're dead sober. The result?
Everyone cackling at everyone else. They make speeches;
and even if we understand, we get it all wrong
when we file our reports in Athens. But today—!
Everybody's happy. Couldn't tell the difference
between *Drink to Me Only* and
The Star-Spangled Athens.
>   What's a few lies,
washed down in good strong drink?

[*Re-enter the* DRUNKEN CITIZEN.]

SENTRY.
>   God almighty,

he's back again!

CITIZEN.
>   I. Resume. My. Place.

A SPARTAN [*to an* ATHENIAN].
Ah beg yo', seh,
take yo' instrument in yo' hand and play for us.
Ah'm told
yo' understand the in*tri*cacies of the floot?
Ah'd lahk to execute a song and dance
in honor of Athens,
>   and, of cohse, of Spahta.

CITIZEN.
Toot. On. Your. Flute.

[*The following song is a solo—an aria—accompanied by the
flute. The* CHORUS OF SPARTANS *begins a slow dance.*]

A SPARTAN.
>   O Memory,
>   Let the muse speak once more
>   In my young voice. Sing glory.
>   Sing Artemision's shore,
>   Where Athens fluttered the Persians. *Alalai,*
>   Sing glory, that great
>   Victory! Sing also
>   Our Leonidas and his men,

Those wild boars, sweat and blood
Down in a red drench. Then, then
The barbarians broke, though they had stood
Numberless as the sands before!

O Artemis,
Virgin goddess, whose darts
Flash in our forests: approve
This pact of peace and join our hearts,
From this day on, in love.
Huntress, descend!

LYSISTRATA.

All that will come in time.

                    But now, Lakonians,
take home your wives. Athenians, take yours.
Each man be kind to his woman; and you, women,
be equally kind. Never again, pray God,
shall we lose our way in such madness.

LEADER OF ATHENIAN'S CHORUS.

                        And now
let's dance our joy.

[*From this point the dance becomes general.*]

ATHENIANS' CHORUS.

Dance, you Graces

                Artemis, dance

Dance, Phoibos, Lord of dancing

                    Dance,

In a scurry of Maenads, Lord Dionysos

                  Dance, Zeus Thunderer

          Dance, Lady Hêra

Queen of the Sky

                Dance, dance, all you gods

Dance witness everlasting of our pact

Evohí Evohé

Dance for the dearest

                the Bringer of Peace

Deathless Aphroditê!

COMMISSIONER.

Now let us have another song from Sparta.

SPARTANS' CHORUS.

>From Taÿgetos, from Taÿgetos,
> Lakonian Muse, come down.
>Sing to the Lord Apollo
> Who rules Amyklai Town.

>*Sing Athêna of the House of Brass!*
>Sing Lêda's Twins, that chivalry
> Resplendent on the shore
>Of our Eurôtas; sing the girls
> That dance along before:

>Sparkling in dust their gleaming feet,
> Their hair a Bacchant fire,
>And Lêda's daughter, thyrsos raised,
> Leads their triumphant choir.

ATHENIANS' *and* SPARTANS' CHORUSES.

>Evoché!
>   Evohaí!
>   Evohé!
>   We pass
>   Dancing
>   dancing
>   to greet
>Athêna of the House of Brass.

LE BOURGEOIS GENTILHOMME

by Molière

Translated and adapted by Henry S. Taylor

Le Bourgeois Gentilhomme, a comedy of five acts in prose, was acted at Chambord in October, 1670, and in Paris at the theatre of the Palais-Royal on November 29.

THE CAST

MR. JOURDAIN, *retired merchant, of Paris*
MRS. JOURDAIN
LUCILE, *their daughter*
NICOLE, *their maidservant*
CLÉONTE, *a young man, in love with Lucile*
COVIELLE, *his valet, in love with Nicole*
DORANTE, *a count, in love with Dorimène*
DORIMÈNE, *a countess*
MASTERS OF MUSIC, DANCING, FENCING *and* PHILOSOPHY
A STUDENT OF MUSIC
FIRST *and* SECOND LACKEYS
A MASTER TAILOR *and his* BOY, *a* TURKISH MUFTI, DERVISHES, MUSICIANS, TAILOR'S BOYS *and* TURKS.

The action takes place at the home of Mr. Jourdain in Paris, in the second half of the seventeenth century.

ACT ONE

[MUSIC, DANCING, FENCING AND PHILOSOPHY MASTERS, STUDENT, JOURDAIN, FIRST AND SECOND LACKEYS, TAILOR, TAILOR'S BOY]

A hall in MR. JOURDAIN'S *house in Paris. A bunch of musicians, with their instruments, shuffle into the room, directed by the* MUSIC MASTER. *After him comes the* DANCING MASTER, *followed by various dancers. At a small table a young man is composing a song, waving a quill from time to time.*

MUSIC MASTER. This way: we'll wait for Mr. Jourdain in here.

DANCING MASTER. And you over there: make a group on that rug.

MUSIC MASTER [*looking over pupil's shoulder*]. Is it finished?

STUDENT. Yes, sir.

MUSIC MASTER [*taking manuscript and humming with self-satisfied air*]. Let's have a look . . . [*Nodding as he hums.*] Mmmmmmmm . . . mmmmmmmm . . . Yes, not at all bad!

DANCING MASTER. Is that from your new oratorio?

MUSIC MASTER. No, no, just a simple tune he's working on while we wait for Mr. Jourdain to get up.

DANCING MASTER. May one have a look?

MUSIC MASTER. You'll hear it when he comes. He won't be long now.

DANCING MASTER [*confidentially*]. Plenty of work on our hands these days, haven't we?

MUSIC MASTER [*heartily*]. Rather. We've found here just the man we need. These fantastic ideas of improving himself that dear Mr. Jourdain has got into his head make a nice little thing for us—I only wish there were a few more like him. . . .

DANCING MASTER [*dubious*]. Yes, but I do wish he'd show a little real understanding for the work we do for him.

MUSIC MASTER [*chuckling and rubbing hands*]. His understanding of much of those noble arts which we two represent is certainly very . . . well, let's be frank . . . limited: I'm with you there. But there's no limit to his cash, and that's something we artists can't afford to overlook, these days.

DANCING MASTER [*quite excited as he warms to his theme*]. I confess, I enjoy a little appreciation. Real applause. There's no greater torture for an artist than showing his work before a crowd of silly barbarians. There's a satisfaction in working for people who understand the finer points of one's art. To be repaid by enlightened appreciation is a pleasure I find . . . exquisite . . . ravishing . . .

MUSIC MASTER [*unimpressed*]. I agree, I agree . . . there's nothing like this enlightened appreciation, as you call it— but you can't eat compliments. [*He nudges the* DANCING MASTER.] If you ask me, the most enlightened appreciation comes from the pocket, eh? Now this Jourdain fellow, for instance: not much intelligence, I grant you, talking nonsense and always getting hold of the wrong idea, saying a thing's good when it's confoundedly bad, and so forth . . . but his money makes up for his muddle-headedness: he has *financial* understanding! His praises are banknotes, and he's worth a good deal more to us, as you know, than this cultured high-brow Lord What's-his-name who introduced us here.

DANCING MASTER [*shrugging*]. There's something in what you say, but you make too much of the mercenary side—such an utterly unworthy consideration. No true gentleman ever shows the slightest concern for *money*. [*A pause:* MUSIC MASTER *looks rather surprised*.] Anything wrong?

MUSIC MASTER. I'm trying to remember when I last saw you refuse any.

DANCING MASTER. I still wish he had a bit more taste.

MUSIC MASTER [*jovially*]. And so do I, so do I: isn't that exactly what we're both working for? Let *him* pay while the others praise!

DANCING MASTER. Sh! Here he is!

[MR. JOURDAIN *enters, in a nightcap and a gaudy dressing gown quite unsuited to someone of his years. He is followed by two lackeys in magnificent livery. His eyes brighten when he sees the two masters, and he shakes their hands with a vigour which makes them recoil.*]

JOURDAIN. Good morning, good morning: very glad to see you. [*Speaking to* MUSIC MASTER *and jerking head in direction of musicians*.] Are you going to do your little bit of fiddle-dee-dee for me now?

DANCING MASTER [*astonished*]. I beg your pardon? Fiddle-dee-dee?

JOURDAIN. Well, er, the er . . . what-d'you-call-it. The pro-
logue or what-you-call-it thing about music and dancing.

DANCING MASTER. ! ! ! ! !

MUSIC MASTER [*indicating musicians*]. We're all ready.

JOURDAIN. Afraid I kept you waiting, but you see I'm having
myself dressed like a real gentleman today, and my tailor
sent me round such a tight pair of stockings . . . I thought
I'd never get into them!

MUSIC MASTER [*bowing*]. We are entirely at your service.

JOURDAIN. I hope you'll both stay with me until the suit arrives, so that you can see me in it.

DANCING MASTER [*swallowing a grimace*]. Anything you
please.

JOURDAIN [*proudly*]. You'll see me dressed from top to toe,
every inch a gentleman!

MUSIC MASTER. But of course!

JOURDAIN [*turning clumsily to display gown*]. I had this thing
made up myself.

DANCING MASTER. Magnificent!

JOURDAIN. My tailor tells me that real gentlemen always wear
these in the morning.

MUSIC MASTER. It fits you beautifully.

JOURDAIN [*smirks, then, sharply*]. Hoy! Lackeys there, both
of you!

[*The* LACKEYS *move up and bow on either side of* JOUR-
DAIN.]

FIRST LACKEY. What does monsieur wish?

JOURDAIN [*abruptly*]. Nothing. Just want to see if you're
attending me properly. [LACKEYS *bow and retire.* JOURDAIN
turns to the DANCING MASTER, *indicating the* LACKEYS.]
What do you think of my livery?

DANCING MASTER. Magnificent!

JOURDAIN [*opening dressing-gown to show what is underneath,
tight velvet breeches and a loose white blouse*]. Now here's
a little outfit for my morning exercises.

MUSIC MASTER. Splendid!

JOURDAIN [*abruptly*]. Lackey!

FIRST LACKEY [*doubling forward and bowing*]. Monsieur?

JOURDAIN. T'other lackey!

SECOND LACKEY [*doubling forward and bowing*]. Monsieur?

JOURDAIN [*taking off his gown, and posturing*]. Hold my dressing gown. . . . Now, how do you think I look?

DANCING MASTER. Splendid, splendid, you couldn't do better!

JOURDAIN [*nodding complacently*]. Now let's get on with the what-d'you-call-it.

MUSIC MASTER [*clapping hands to call attention of musicians, and introducing his pupil to* JOURDAIN]. First of all I take the liberty of asking you to listen to a song this young man has just written as part of the serenade you commissioned. He's one of my students who has an excellent ear for these things.

JOURDAIN [*dubious*]. Yes, yes, but I don't think you should have got a student to do it for you. You shouldn't be above doing things like that yourself.

MUSIC MASTER [*reassuringly*]. Ah, good sir, don't let the term student deceive you. These students know very nearly as much about their art as the master musicians—[*With glance at* STUDENT.]—very nearly. Listen.

[STUDENT *comes forward, clears his throat and is about to sing when . . .*]

JOURDAIN [*gruffly, to lackey*]. Give me my dressing-gown, so that I can hear properly.

[LACKEY *steps forward and puts gown on* JOURDAIN. STUDENT *is just about to sing when . . .*]

JOURDAIN. Wait: I think I'll hear better without it.

[LACKEY *removes gown with great fuss. All again settle down to hear the song when . . .*]

JOURDAIN. No, I'd better have it on. Give it back to me. . . .

STUDENT [*sings in exaggerated operatic style.*].
> At night I lie in bed and my head
> Is aflame with your name,
> Is aflame with your name,
> With your name all aflame;
> And your eyes like a dart making smart
> Every part of my heart,
> Of my heart every part,
> Every heart of my part . . .
> From your lips, where love sips,
> Nectar drips——

JOURDAIN [*interrupting with a loud groan*]. Bit mournful, isn't it? Sends me to sleep, that does: can't you liven it up a little here and there?

MUSIC MASTER. But the music, sir, has to go with the words.

JOURDAIN [*scratching his head*]. I used to know a lovely one, once . . . Let's see . . . wait: tra la la lo . . . is that it?

DANCING MASTER. I haven't the faintest idea.

JOURDAIN [*hopefully*]. There were some sheep in it.

DANCING MASTER. Some sheep?

JOURDAIN. Yes. Ah!

> *I used to think my Janey girl*
> *As gentle as a little lamb;*
> *I used to think my Janey girl*
> *As sweet as mother's apple jam.*
> *But now I know it is not so:*
> *For since my heart's in jeopardy*
> *She's fiercer than a leopardy!*

[*Wiping his brow.*] Isn't that lovely?

MUSIC MASTER. I never heard anything more moving!

DANCING MASTER. And you have such a voice!

JOURDAIN [*delighted*]. Mind you, I never learned any music.

MUSIC MASTER. You *should* learn music, my dear sir, just as you are learning to dance. The two arts are closely allied.

DANCING MASTER [*striking attitude*]. And open to man's spirit a world of aesthetic pleasures!

JOURDAIN. What about the posh people? Do they learn music?

MUSIC MASTER. Certainly, monsieur.

JOURDAIN. Then I will, too. But I don't know how I'm going to find the time. There's my fencing lesson already this morning, and I've just taken on a teacher of philosophy as well.

MUSIC MASTER [*critically*]. Well, philosophy is, of course, quite important, but music, my dear sir, music——

DANCING MASTER. Music *and* dancing . . . Music *and* dancing: that's everything you need.

MUSIC MASTER. There's nothing more useful in life than music. . . .

DANCING MASTER. There's nothing so essential to mankind as dancing. . . .

MUSIC MASTER. Without music, life couldn't go on. . . .

DANCING MASTER. Without dancing, a man wouldn't know what to do with himself. . . .

MUSIC MASTER [*crescendo*]. All political disorders, all wars all over the world, are caused by people who have never learned music. . . .

DANCING MASTER. All mankind's misfortunes, all the devastating setbacks of history, the follies of statesmen and the shortcomings of great leaders, all these things quite obviously proceed from not knowing how to dance. . . .

JOURDAIN [*puzzled*]. How's this?

MUSIC MASTER. Doesn't war arise from a lack of harmony among men?

JOURDAIN. Yes, that's true.

MUSIC MASTER. And if all men learned music, wouldn't that be a way of establishing harmony among them, resulting in universal peace?

JOURDAIN [*delighted*]. You're quite right!

DANCING MASTER. When a man makes a serious mistake, at home or in affairs of state, or at the head of an army, don't we say he's taken a *false step*?

JOURDAIN [*puzzled*]. Yes, we do.

DANCING MASTER. And doesn't taking a false step arise purely and simply from not knowing how to dance?

JOURDAIN [*even more delighted*]. Yes, yes, yes, you're right, both of you!

DANCING MASTER. I hope that monsieur now understands the full importance of dancing . . . and music.

JOURDAIN [*smiling*]. Oh, yes, it's all clear now . . . how wonderful!

MUSIC MASTER. Now, would you like to see our two little entertainments?

JOURDAIN. Yes, please.

MUSIC MASTER. As I told you before, it's a little piece which tries to show the different emotions that can be expressed by music.

JOURDAIN [*smiling*]. Good, good.

MUSIC MASTER [*beckoning to musicians*]. Right: are you ready? [*To* JOURDAIN.] Remember that they're all supposed to be dressed up as shepherds.

JOURDAIN [*dropping his smile*]. Why always shepherds? They seem to be all over the place!

DANCING MASTER [*as if explaining to child*]. When you want to make people talk to each other in music, you have to dress them up as shepherds—to make it lifelike.

JOURDAIN. Oh, all right. All right. Come on, then.

[*The* STUDENT *and two other singers come forward.* MUSIC MASTER *conducts.*]

FEMALE.

> A heart that lives within love's bond
>   From fretful care is never free;
> They say that Love can look beyond
>   The care, and live in liberty—
>   But not for me, but not for me!

1 MALE [*serious*].
>   There's nothing in this life more sweet,
>   More certain to bring lasting pleasure,
>   Than happy lovers' hearts that beat
>   Contentedly to Cupid's measure—
>   To me, life's treasure, to me life's treasure!

2 MALE [*comic*].
>   I could resign myself to Love's dominion,
>   And live content forever in his sway,
>   Had experience not taught me this opinion,
>   That a woman's fancy barely lasts a day—
>   And therefore Love away, I say, away!

1 MALE.	Bliss complete!
FEMALE.	But, freedom's sweet!
2 MALE.	O fair deceit!
1 MALE.	O sweet, make haste!
FEMALE.	Shall I love taste?
2 MALE.	And prove two-faced?
FEMALE [*to 1*].	To prove him wrong, I offer you my heart!
1 MALE [*to 2*].	Desist your scorn, and bow to Cupid's dart!
2 MALE.	No, for too long I've known the female heart!
1 MALE.	Cease this furore!
FEMALE.	Accept Love's law!
2 MALE.	Well, just once more.
TRIO.	Ah, the joy's of Love's sweet raptures
	Evermore the heart recaptures,
	Life no joy can hold to this
	Of true enduring married bliss.

JOURDAIN. Is that the end?

MUSIC MASTER. Yes.

JOURDAIN. Well, it was nicely served up: there was some good stuff in that. Thank you.

DANCING MASTER [*hastily*]. My part of the entertainment is a little ballet sketch showing all the most beautiful and important movements.

JOURDAIN [*suspiciously*]. Not more shepherds?

DANCING MASTER [*clapping hands and beginning to dance himself as the orchestra plays the ballet music*]. Anything you like!

[*The ballet advance and go through various steps, with occasional interjections from the* DANCING MASTER. *JOURDAIN's expression shows that he really enjoys the ballet, though occasionally registers surprise when a leg shoots out suddenly more or less under his nose. When it is over, he claps loudly.*]

JOURDAIN. Now that was something like it!—those girls certainly know how to stir their stumps.

DANCING MASTER. When we've had a few more rehearsals it will be even better!

JOURDAIN. Yes, a little later on, when the grand lady for whom I'm taking all this trouble does me the honor of dining here.

DANCING MASTER [*bowing*]. Everything will be ready. [*He signals to dancers to go off.*]

MUSIC MASTER. But that's not enough, sir. A grand gentleman like yourself, who aspires to be a patron of the arts, must certainly have a musical soirée once a week on Wednesdays or Thursdays.

JOURDAIN. Is that what the swells do?

MUSIC MASTER. Most certainly.

JOURDAIN. I'll do it, then. [*Pause.*] Will it be nice?

MUSIC MASTER. Of course. You will need three singers, soprano, contralto and bass, with cello, two violins and harpsichord accompaniment.

JOURDAIN [*emphatically*]. *And* a marine trumpet. That's a fine instrument. Yes, I'm very fond of the marine trumpet.

MUSIC MASTER [*patiently*]. Just leave it to us. . . . You shall have everything you could possibly require.

JOURDAIN. And the ballet must be really splendid.

MUSIC MASTER. You'll like it, I'm sure, especially some minuets I'm arranging for you.

JOURDAIN [*delighted*]. Oh! Oh! The minuet's my favourite— just watch me dance one. Come along, Mr. Dancing Master.

DANCING MASTER. You'll need a hat then, sir.

[JOURDAIN *grabs his lackey's hat and puts it on top of his nightcap. The* DANCING MASTER *takes one hand and leads* JOURDAIN *through the minuet, humming it with strong emphasis on time. At a signal from the* MUSIC MASTER, *the orchestra joins in.*]

La, la, la, lull lull lull lull lull la le la le la . . . don't jiggle the shoulders . . . la, la, la, la, lull, lull, lull, lull . . . more give in the arms . . . la la la la tiddle om pom pom pom . . . keep the head up . . . pom pom om pom pom . . . point the foot outwards . . . OUTWARDS . . . lull lull lull lull . . . keep the body upright. . . .

JOURDAIN [*exhausted*]. Phew . . .

DANCING MASTER [*finishing with an elaborate curtsey*]. Excellent, excellent . . . just a little more grace. . . .

JOURDAIN. That reminds me: can you show me the right way to bow to a countess? I'll need to know that before long.

[MUSIC MASTER *signals to dismiss orchestra.*]

DANCING MASTER [*drawing himself up with a smirk*]. To bow to a countess?

JOURDAIN [*simply*]. Yes, a countess. Called Dorimène.

DANCING MASTER. Give me your hand.

JOURDAIN. No. Just do one yourself. I'll remember.

DANCING MASTER. If you wish to show the greatest possible respect you must make your first bow stepping backwards—so—then three more while you step forwards—so—so—going down, on the last one, to the level of her knee—so. [*He swiftly performs the movements with great precision and completely baffles* JOURDAIN.]

JOURDAIN. Just do a few more, will you. [DANCING MASTER *repeats three times.*] Good.

FIRST LACKEY [*coming forward from door*]. Sir, your fencing master is outside.

JOURDAIN. Tell him to come up and give me my lesson in here. [*To* MUSIC *and* DANCING MASTERS, *who are taking this opportunity to depart.*] No, don't go. I'd like you to stay and watch me.

[FENCING MASTER *enters, rather fierce, bristly man, in fencing kit. He takes the foils from the* LACKEY, *giving one to* JOURDAIN. *His instructions are barked out like a Sergeant-Major's, very rapidly, so that* JOURDAIN *is always a move behind.*]

FENCING MASTER. Now, sir, the salute! Body erect. Weight a little on the left foot. Legs not too far apart, feet in line. Hilt in line with the hips. Point opposite the shoulders. Don't stretch out your arm so far. Right hand up to the eye. Left shoulder round a little more . . . other way! Head up! Look straight ahead . . . more confidence! Advance. Don't rock about like that. . . . Engage in quart and lunge . . . one TWO. Recover. . . . Once more, one TWO, balance, balance! Step backwards. When you make a thrust, sir, it is important to withdraw the blade like this—so—keeping the body well covered. One, two—so. Now, attack in tierce and lunge. Forward. Body steady. Balance, balance. Now begin. One, TWO. Recover. [JOURDAIN, *exhausted, begins to relax, but in vain.*] Once again. One, TWO! One step backwards. Now I attack. [*He does, making two or three startling thrusts.*] Parry, sir, parry! Parry!

JOURDAIN [*collapses into chair*]. Phew!

MUSIC MASTER. You did very well, very well . . . just a little more poise. . . .

FENCING MASTER [*continuing remorselessly in Sergeant-Major voice*]. As I have already told you, the whole secret of fencing lies in two simple rules: one, to hit; two, not to be hit back. As I showed you the other day in a logical demonstration, it is impossible to be hit if you can deflect the blade of your opponent from the line of your body, depending entirely on a very slight movement of the wrist, outwards or inwards, so, so!

JOURDAIN [*innocently*]. So if he does what you say, then, even a not very fierce man can kill his opponent and not be killed himself?

FENCING MASTER. Certainly. Didn't I give you a logical demonstration?

JOURDAIN. Yes.

FENCING MASTER. And that's exactly why we people deserve more consideration in the country, and why the science of combat is so much more important than these other useless branches of knowledge like dancing, music or—

DANCING MASTER. Just a minute, Mr. Sword-swasher: a little more respect for dancing!

MUSIC MASTER. To say nothing of the noble art of music!

FENCING MASTER. Are you trying to be funny, comparing your professions with mine?

MUSIC MASTER. Oh yes, look at his highness, there's a man for you!

DANCING MASTER. A dummy, you mean, with a stuffed shirt, too!

FENCING MASTER. Another remark like that and I'll really make you dance, my friend! As for you, my chorister, I'll make you sing out as you never sang before!

DANCING MASTER. Ironmonger!

JOURDAIN [*alarmed, to* DANCING MASTER]. You must be mad, quarreling with a man who knows all about tierce and quart, who can kill a man by logical demonstration!

DANCING MASTER [*snapping his fingers*]. I don't give a rap for his logical demonstration or his tierce and quart!

JOURDAIN. Sh! Quietly, please.

FENCING MASTER. What! Little whipper-snapper!

JOURDAIN. Sh!

DANCING MASTER. Clumsy carthorse!

JOURDAIN. Sh!

FENCING MASTER. If I lift my sword at you . . .

JOURDAIN. Gentlemen, gentlemen!

DANCING MASTER. If I lay hands on you. . . .

JOURDAIN. Gentlemen, please!

FENCING MASTER. . . . I'll slash you to ribbons!

[JOURDAIN *continues to try to pacify them, alternatively*.]

DANCING MASTER. . . . I'll grind you to mincemeat!

MUSIC MASTER [*to* JOURDAIN]. Just leave it to us to teach this ape a few manners!

JOURDAIN. For heaven's sake, control yourselves!

[MR. JOURDAIN'S PHILOSOPHER *enters, a shrivelled little man, all in black, with a pile of books which he places on a table.* JOURDAIN *greets him with relief.*]

Ah, just in time my dear sir, just in time. We need a little of your philosophy this very minute. Come and be a peacemaker between these three here.

PHILOSOPHER. T,t,t,t, tut! What's wrong? What is the matter, gentlemen?

JOURDAIN. They're all in a terrible rage about whose profession is the most important—just about to start tearing each other to pieces!

PHILOSOPHER [*scandalized*]. Good gracious! Gentlemen, do you really have to behave in this childish manner? Have you never read Seneca's little treatise on anger? Is there anything more ridiculous and shameful than this passion, which reduces mankind to the animals? Is not reason the mistress of all conduct?

DANCING MASTER. Now then, now then, sir. He's just been insulting us both!

PHILOSOPHER [*smoothly*]. A wise man is quite above all such trifling considerations: the most effective reply one can make to such vituperation is patient forbearance.

FENCING MASTER [*enraged*]. They actually had the impertinence to compare their professions with mine!

PHILOSOPHER [*taking snuff with great deliberation*]. My dear good sir, there is no cause for excitement. Intelligent men do not waste time arguing about the mere vanity of external circumstances. Wisdom and virtue alone have significance.

DANCING MASTER. I still maintain that dancing is an art to which no one can do too much honour!

MUSIC MASTER. And I, that music is an art that has been praised and revered through the centuries!

FENCING MASTER. And I tell the pair of them that the art of swordplay is the most splendid, and the most necessary, of them all!

PHILOSOPHER [*snapping snuff-box shut, crossly*]. And where, pray, does philosophy come in all this? I find a certain impertinence in all three of you, talking in this way in front of me, and indeed in applying the name of science to subjects hardly worthy of being classed among the arts at all! Subjects, I might say, whose true professional status might well be comprehended in the names of gladiator, balladmonger and—gigolo!

FENCING MASTER. What! Get out, you dog of a philosopher!

MUSIC MASTER. Get out, you rotten hair-splitter!

DANCING MASTER. Get out, you muddle-headed ape of a schoolmaster!

PHILOSOPHER [*throwing himself upon them in fury*]. What, you bunch of ignorant nincompoops! . . .

JOURDAIN [*scandalized*]. Mr. Philosopher!

PHILOSOPHER [*lashing out with a dictionary*]. Jack-a-napes! Buffoons! Ragamuffins! Quacks!

[*In between each of the following speakers, JOURDAIN interjects a vain attempt to keep the peace.*]

FENCING MASTER. Milksop!

PHILOSOPHER. Overweening jackasses!

DANCING MASTER. To the devil with him and his Seneca!

PHILOSOPHER. Bunch of crooks!

MUSIC MASTER. Damned impudent idiot!

PHILOSOPHER. Cheats! Quacks! Pack of thieving mountebanks!

JOURDAIN [*as all four go out in a furious brawling mass*]. Mr. Philosopher! Gentlemen! Mr. Philosopher! Gentlemen! Please, please, please. . . .

JOURDAIN. Oh well, fight away, then! I'm hanged if I'll ruin my new dressing-gown trying to separate you. I'd be a fine fool meddling with that lot and getting a black eye for nothing!

[PHILOSOPHER *returns, dusting himself off and straightening his collar. In spite of a black eye, he seems to have acquitted himself well.*]

PHILOSOPHER. Let's get on with our lesson.

JOURDAIN. Mr. Philosopher, I'm very sorry for what happened.

PHILOSOPHER. Oh, nothing at all. A philosopher knows how to deal with such trifles. Now, what is it you wish to learn?

JOURDAIN. Everything. [*Pause.*] There's nothing I want more than to be properly educated. I'm very angry that my mother and father didn't make me learn all that Greek and stuff when I was a kid.

PHILOSOPHER. A very noble sentiment: *nam, sine doctrina, vita est quasi mortis imago.* You understand Latin, I suppose?

JOURDAIN. Er . . . yes. But go on just as if I didn't. Explain what that means.

PHILOSOPHER. It means that without knowledge, life is no better than a picture of death.

JOURDAIN. This Latin stuff's all right, isn't it?

PHILOSOPHER. Tell me, have you no education at all, no first principles?

JOURDAIN. Oh yes, I can read and write.

PHILOSOPHER. Well, how would you like to begin? Shall I teach you logic?

JOURDAIN. What's all that about?

PHILOSOPHER. Logic teaches us the three processes of reasoning.

JOURDAIN. And what are the three processes of reasoning?

PHILOSOPHER [*very swiftly*]. Firstly, to apprehend rightly from universal principles; secondly, to distinguish adequately, by means of categorical differentiations; thirdly, to draw the appropriate inferences by means of syllogisms.

JOURDAIN. What horrible hard words! No, I don't think I've time for logic. Let's do something nicer.

PHILOSOPHER. What about moral philosophy?

JOURDAIN [*puzzled and a little suspicious*]. Moral philosophy?

PHILOSOPHER. Yes.

JOURDAIN. Well, what's it all about?

PHILOSOPHER [*entering upon a high-flown discourse*]. Moral philosophy deals with contentment, teaching men to moderate their passions and to——

JOURDAIN. No. I've the devil of a temper myself and I'll be as angry as I blooming well like whenever I feel like it.

PHILOSOPHER. Hm. [*Pause.*] Well, would you like to learn some physics?

JOURDAIN. Physics? What does that do?

PHILOSOPHER. Nothing. [*Pause.*] Physics teaches the principles of natural phenomena, including the nature of the elements, metals, minerals, rocks, plants and animals, and explains what causes meteors, rainbows, St. Elmo's fire, comets, lightning [sheet and forked], thunder, rain, snow, hails, winds and hurricanes.

JOURDAIN. Bit noisy, isn't it?

PHILOSOPHER. Well, what *do* you want, then?

JOURDAIN. Teach me how to spell.

PHILOSOPHER. Certainly.

JOURDAIN. Then you can show me how to use an almanac so that I can tell whether there's a moon or not.

PHILOSOPHER. By all means. But to deal with the question philosophically, it is essential, in the logical order of approach, to begin with an exact understanding of the nature of the letters of the alphabet and their different pronunciations. In this connection I must first explain that the letters of the alphabet are divided into vowels, from the Latin *vox, vocis,* a voice, and consonants, from the late Latin *con,* with, *sonare,* to sound, because they are used in conjunction with the vowels to mark the different articulations of the voice. There are five vowels: A E I O U.

JOURDAIN. Yes, I know all that.

PHILOSOPHER. The vowel A is formed by opening the mouth thus: A.

JOURDAIN. A . . . A . . . A. Yes.

PHILOSOPHER. The sound E is produced by a raising of the lower jaw and a lowering of the upper jaw, at the same time stretching the corners of the mouth towards the ears, thus: E.

JOURDAIN [*experimenting*]. A . . . E . . . A . . . E . . . Good heaven's, it's true! Wonderful!

PHILOSOPHER. The sound I is produced by shaping the mouth as for A, raising the upper jaw slightly while allowing the tongue to relax, thus: I.

JOURDAIN. A . . . E . . . I,I,I,I, yes, yes, that's quite right! Hurrah for science!

PHILOSOPHER. The O is formed by opening the mouth and rounding the lips: O.

JOURDAIN. O . . . O . . . O. It's absolutely true! A E I O I O. Oh, this is splendid: I O I O I O !

PHILOSOPHER. The opening of the mouth is really a circle resembling the letter O.

JOURDAIN. O . . . O . . . O . . . ! You're right! you're right, you're right! Isn't education wonderful!

PHILOSOPHER. We make the sound U by not quite closing the teeth and keeping the lips also slightly apart, like this: U.

JOURDAIN. U . . . U . . . Yes, right again! U . . . Oh, why didn't I start my studies earlier: just think, I might have known this all my life!

PHILOSOPHER. Tomorrow we will consider the consonants.

JOURDAIN [*clapping his hands*]. Are they as good as the vowels?

PHILOSOPHER. Certainly. The consonant D, for instance, is formed by placing the tip of the tongue against the upper teeth: D.

JOURDAIN. D . . . D . . . Such discoveries! Such discoveries! How I hate my mother and father for keeping this from me!

PHILOSOPHER. And the sounds R, rrrrr, by pushing the tip of the tongue against the palate so that the air from the throat causes a vibration: R, rrrrr.

JOURDAIN. R, rrrrr . . . rrrrr . . . rrrrr . . . rrrrrrrrrrrrrrrr! Of course! What a genius you are! Oh, all that time wasted . . . rrrrrrrrrrrrrrrrrrrrrrrrrr!

PHILOSOPHER. I can explain all these little details.

JOURDAIN. Yes, do, do! How delightful . . . But first, I must make a confession. I have lost my heart to a very high and mighty young lady, and I want you to help me write a little letter I'm going to throw with a kiss before her feet.

PHILOSOPHER. Very well.

JOURDAIN [*anxiously*]. That is the thing to do, isn't it?

PHILOSOPHER. Undoubtedly. Do you want me to write it in verse?

JOURDAIN [*hastily*]. No, no: not in verse.

PHILOSOPHER. Just a straightforward effort in prose, then?

JOURDAIN. No, I don't want any prose either.

PHILOSOPHER. It must be one or the other.

JOURDAIN. Why?

PHILOSOPHER. For the simple reason, good sir, that there are only two ways of expressing oneself: prose . . . or verse!

JOURDAIN [*puzzled*]. Only prose or verse?

PHILOSOPHER. Exactly. Everything not in prose is in verse, and everything not in verse is in prose.

JOURDAIN [*suspiciously*]. And when I'm talking, what's that?

PHILOSOPHER. That's prose.

JOURDAIN. What! When I tell Nicole to find my nightcap or bring my bedroom slippers, you mean to say that's prose?

PHILOSOPHER. Yes.

JOURDAIN [*astonished*]. So I've been talking prose for forty years without knowing it! [*Clapping his hands with delight.*] Oh, I can't thank you enough for teaching me that! Well then, about this letter. I want to say something like this: Sweet countess, your beautiful eyes are making me die for love . . . but I want you to polish it up a bit, improve it; make it sound dignified and gentleman-like.

PHILOSOPHER [*after thinking*]. Say something like this: that the fire in her eyes is reducing your heart to ashes, that you suffer, day and night, the tortures of a——

JOURDAIN. No, no, no, I don't want anything like that. I only want something like what I said: Sweet countess, your beautiful eyes are making me die for love.

PHILOSOPHER. But it has to be expanded a little!

JOURDAIN. No. I mean, I only want those words of mine in the letter, but I want them arranged more elegantly—as if a real gentleman had written them.

PHILOSOPHER [*judiciously*]. Well, one can, of course, express it just as you did: *Sweet countess, your beautiful eyes are making me die for love.* Or, *your beautiful eyes, sweet countess, are making me die for love.* Again, *For love, sweet countess, your beautiful eyes are making me die.* [*Thinks.*] *Your beautiful sweet countess eyes are making me for love die.* . . . Or, perhaps, *Countess sweet, me for love are making die your eyes . . . beautiful.*

JOURDAIN. Which is the smartest of the whole lot?

PHILOSOPHER [*after much thought*]. The one you said first: *Sweet countess, your beautiful eyes are making me die for love.* . . .

JOURDAIN [*very pleased*]. Without any education, I hit the nail on the head first go! I'm most grateful to you, dear Mr. Philosopher, and I hope you'll come again tomorrow—early.

[*The* PHILOSOPHER *goes out.* JOURDAIN *turns to a* LACKEY.]

Well, hasn't my outfit arrived yet?

FIRST LACKEY. No, sir.

JOURDAIN [*working himself into a passion*]. This blasted tailor making me wait a whole day when I've so much to do! Enough to make a man mad! Confounded nuisance! Devil take the man! If I had him here now, the old idiot, I'd——

[*Enter* TAILOR, *with boy carrying a gorgeous costume.*]

——Ah! There you are! I was just saying to myself that I hoped you were all right. . . .

TAILOR [*severely*]. Mr. Jourdain, I've had twenty cutters working on these clothes: quite impossible to get them ready any sooner.

JOURDAIN [*feeling his calves*]. Those stockings you sent me this morning were so tight I had the devil of a job getting into them. They already have runs in two places.

TAILOR [*absently, as he takes clothes from boy*]. They'll stretch, sir, they'll stretch in time.

JOURDAIN [*loudly*]. Yes, by the time they've run to ribbons. And another thing, Mr. Tailor, those shoes you made pinch like blazes!

TAILOR [*as before*]. Impossible!

JOURDAIN. What d'you mean, impossible?

TAILOR. They don't pinch you.

JOURDAIN. I tell you they do pinch me!

TAILOR. You're just imagining it.

JOURDAIN [*very cross*]. I imagine it because I feel them pinching. Isn't that a good enough reason?

TAILOR [*spreading out coat*]. Now, sir, this'll be the finest coat in the whole court; what cloth, sir, just feel it, what cloth. A touch of genius it was to produce a formal coat that wasn't too dark.

JOURDAIN [*examining coat*]. Hey, what's this? The pattern's upside down!

TAILOR [*swiftly*]. You never told me you wanted it the other way up!

JOURDAIN. Was I supposed to tell you?

TAILOR. Of course. All the best people have it that way these days.

JOURDAIN. All the best people have the pattern upside down?

TAILOR. Certainly.

JOURDAIN. Oh, that's all right then.

TAILOR. If you want it changed, you only have to say. . . .

JOURDAIN [*holding coat against himself and swaggering about*]. No, no, no, no, no: it's all right. D'you think it suits me?

TAILOR [*taking periwig from boy and stroking out curls*]. My dear sir, what a question! I defy any painter in the world to do you justice in that suit!

JOURDAIN [*taking hat with huge feathers from boy and examining from all angles*]. Is this wig all right? And the hat?

TAILOR. Very handsome! Quite overwhelming, in fact.

JOURDAIN [*looking closely at TAILOR's own coat*]. I say, Mr. Tailor, that's the very same material I gave you to make my last jacket! I'm certain I recognize it.

TAILOR [*smoothly*]. Yes, I liked the pattern so much I thought I'd have a coat cut for myself.

JOURDAIN. Yes, but you shouldn't have had it cut from my cloth!

TAILOR. Ahem. Will you kindly try it on, sir?

JOURDAIN. Yes, give it to me.

TAILOR. A moment, please. These things are not done just like that. I've brought some of my boys along to dress you properly. A costume like this should be put on with a certain amount of ceremony. [*Clapping his hands sharply, to bring the assistants in.*] Now then, you, just fit these robes on Mr. Jourdain here in the usual way expected by a gentleman of quality.

[*The dressing of* MR. JOURDAIN *can be performed as a ballet, as in the original, with stylized movements by the four dressers in perfect rhythm, or performed straight with ad lib. buffoonery. In any case the result is the same. The gorgeous coat and breeches, the peruke with long hanging curls, the flamboyant hat all look quite incongruous on* JOURDAIN, *who struts about showing them off.*]

TAILOR'S BOY. Please, kind gentleman, spare a tip for the tailor's lads.

JOURDAIN [*turning suddenly*]. What did you call me?

TAILOR'S BOY. Kind gentleman.

JOURDAIN [*delighted*]. Kind gentleman! That's what comes of dressing like a man of quality! If you stay dressed like a shopkeeper all your life, no one calls you kind gentleman! [*Giving a tip.*] There you are, for your *kind gentleman.*

TAILOR'S BOY. Thank you, my lord.

JOURDAIN [*more delighted, taking out purse again*]. My lord! Ho, ho! My lord! Just a moment, my friend: *My lord's* worth a little more, it's no common phrase, that isn't. There, there, that's what *my lord* gives you.

TAILOR'S BOY. My lord, we'll all go out and drink to Your Grace's health.

JOURDAIN. Your Grace! Oh, oh, oh! Wait a minute, don't go. Come here. Your Grace's health! [*Aside.*] If he goes as far as Your Highness, I'll give him everything in my purse! [*To* TAILOR'S BOY.] There you are, for *Your Grace.*

TAILOR'S BOY. Sire, we humbly thank his lordship for Your Grace's liberality.

[JOURDAIN, *overjoyed, throws his purse to the boy as he, and his fellows, all make a formal bow before withdrawing, followed by the* TAILOR.]

ACT TWO

[MR. AND MRS. JOURDAIN, FIRST LACKEY, NICOLE, DORANTE, COVIELLE, CLÉONTE]

[The action is continued directly from the end of Act 1.]

JOURDAIN *[to* LACKEYS*]*. Follow me. I'm off into town to let people see my new clothes, and just make sure you keep close behind so that everyone can see you belong to me!

FIRST LACKEY. Yes, sir.

JOURDAIN. But first of all call for Nicole: I've one or two things to tell her. No, never mind: here she is. Nicole!

NICOLE. Yes, sir.

JOURDAIN. Listen a moment.

*[*NICOLE *catches sight of* JOURDAIN'*s new clothes. In the following scene, she has to laugh her head off every time she opens her mouth; loud, deep and irrepressible laughter.]*

NICOLE. Te he, he, he, he, he, he!

JOURDAIN *[puzzled]*. What's up with this fathead?

NICOLE *[walking round* JOURDAIN *and inspecting him]*. Te, he, he, he! Where'd you pick that lot up? Oh, te, he, he, he!

JOURDAIN. What?

NICOLE. Oh, heavens! He, he, he, he, he!

JOURDAIN. Saucy baggage! Are you laughing at me?

NICOLE. Oh no, master, I'd never do that. . . . *[Pause.]* He, he, he, he, he.

JOURDAIN. I'll box your ears, if you laugh again.

NICOLE. But sir, I can't help it! *[Pause.]* He, he, he, he, he!

JOURDAIN *[advancing to her]*. So you won't stop?

NICOLE. I beg your pardon, sir . . . but you're so funny, I can't stop laughing! Te, he, he, he, he, he! Oh, I'm sorry, sir, really . . . he, he, he!

JOURDAIN. Look here, if there's another laugh from you, I'll give you such a bang on the head that you won't know what hit you!

NICOLE *[trying to control herself]*. I'm all right now, sir, look: no more laughing.

JOURDAIN. Well, just be careful. Now, this morning, I want you to clean——

*[*NICOLE *again bursts out laughing, for a second, and stops.]*

JOURDAIN. I say, I want you to clean the big room, and
    then——

[NICOLE *same as before*.]

JOURDAIN. What, again?

NICOLE [*amid a real explosion of laughter*]. Look, sir, bang
    me one afterwards, but let me have a good laugh first—
    that'll be much better for me. Te, he, he, he, he, he, he he,
    he.

JOURDAIN [*advancing on* NICOLE, *who dodges*]. If I get hold
    of you, you——

NICOLE. But sir, I'll burst if I try to keep it in. He, he, he,
    he, he.

JOURDAIN [*shrugging*]. I never knew anything like it. Shriek-
    ing like a hussy in the streets when she ought to be listening
    to my instructions!

NICOLE. What instructions, sir?

JOURDAIN. Instructions, miss, that you pull yourself together
    and start getting the house ready for company. I'm expect-
    ing some important friends today.

NICOLE [*crossly*]. Huh, that's the end of the joke, all right.
    Your wonderful friends always leave the place in such a
    mess. Just to know they're coming, puts me in a bad temper
    for the rest of the day.

JOURDAIN. And am I to slam the door on my friends simply
    because of your tantrums?

NICOLE. Not a bad idea if you did, to some of them, if you
    ask me!

[MRS. JOURDAIN *enters, and sees her husband's dress*.]

MRS JOURDAIN [*shrieking when she sees* JOURDAIN, *and cover-
    ing her eyes for a moment*]. Heavens, why d'you let them
    dress you up like a doll? Have you any idea what you look
    like? Of course, if you want the whole town to have a good
    laugh. . . .

JOURDAIN. And I tell you, woman, that only fools and idiots
    laugh at me.

MRS. JOURDAIN. Not that it would be anything new. These
    latest fads of yours have made you a laughingstock to
    plenty of people already.

JOURDAIN. And which people, may I ask?

MRS. JOURDAIN. People with a lot more sense than you have!
    I really don't know what's going on in the house these days:
    it isn't like our house any more. More like a fancy dress

ball all the time: squeaking fiddles and squawling voices all
hours of the day and night; the whole street's in an uproar.

NICOLE [*folding her arms righteously*]. Madam is right. I can't
even keep the place clean for all these people trailing in
and out after you with their filthy feet. Poor old Francoise
is nearly worn out trying to scrub the muck off the floors.

JOURDAIN. Yes, that's right, Miss Impertinence: the sort of
vulgar cackle anyone would expect from the daughter of a
peasant!

MRS. JOURDAIN. Nicole's quite right: she has more sense than
you. I ask you: a dancing master at your age!

NICOLE. Or that great oaf of a fencing master, thumping about
and bringing the ceilings down!

JOURDAIN. Shut up both of you!

MRS. JOURDAIN [*scornful*]. You'd better get a move on if
you're hoping to teach yourself dancing before you're too
old to walk without crutches!

NICOLE. And all this fencing! Madam, I think he's planning
to murder someone!

JOURDAIN. Be quiet, I tell you. You're both far too ignorant
to understand what's behind all that.

MRS. JOURDAIN. You'd do far better to spend a bit of time
thinking about finding a husband for your daughter, before
it's too late.

JOURDAIN. I'll think about marrying my daughter when someone comes to ask for her; in the meantime I want to learn
something about art and science and suchlike.

NICOLE [*giggling*]. They say philosophy's his latest, madam.

JOURDAIN. And why not? Why shouldn't a man try to sharpen
his wits a bit? No harm in that, is there?

MRS. JOURDAIN. It's a bit late to go to school and sit in the
corner at your age, isn't it?

MR. JOURDAIN. I wouldn't mind sitting in the corner, or even
being whacked, either, if I only knew everything they learn
at school nowadays!

NICOLE. A lot of good it would do you, too!

MRS. JOURDAIN. I simply don't see what's the use of all this
education.

JOURDAIN. No, no, of course you don't! Both of you stand
there arguing like ignorant savages. I'm ashamed of the
pair of you. For instance, [*addressing* MRS. JOURDAIN *with
triumph*] do you know what it is you were saying just then?

MRS. JOURDAIN. Yes, I know that it's good common sense,
and I wish you did, too.

JOURDAIN. I don't mean that. I mean, what were those words which you have just been using?

MRS. JOURDAIN. Very sensible ones, I'm sure—more sensible than your behaviour.

JOURDAIN [getting impatient]. I tell you, I don't mean that. I want to know what it is when I'm talking to you: what I'm saying now.

MRS. JOURDAIN. A lot of rubbish!

JOURDAIN. Oh, you can't even understand! The language we use when we talk, what is it called?

MRS. JOURDAIN. Well, then, what is it called?

JOURDAIN. The correct name for this language is—Prose.

MRS. JOURDAIN. Prose!

JOURDAIN. Yes, prose! Yes, everything not in prose is in verse, and everything not in verse is in prose. That's what education does for you. . . . And you, Nicole, do you know how to say U?

NICOLE. Eh?

JOURDAIN [patiently]. Do you know how to say U?

NICOLE. Who?

JOURDAIN. Look, just say U, and we'll see.

NICOLE. All right. U.

JOURDAIN. What did you do?

NICOLE. I said U.

JOURDAIN. Yes, but when you say U, what are you doing?

NICOLE. I'm doing what you tell me.

JOURDAIN [shrugging fiercely]. Oh, what it is to have to reason with idiots! When you say U, if you were a little better than an ignorant peasant, you would realize that you were raising the lower jaw and lowering the upper jaw, at the same time stretching the corners of the mouth towards the ears. U, U, U, U, U!

[NICOLE giggles. MRS. JOURDAIN shrugs. JOURDAIN continues, eagerly.]

Of course, it's quite different if you want to say O, or D, Da, D, Da, Da, Da, Da, Da!

MRS. JOURDAIN. Silly twaddle!

NICOLE. What I want to know is, what's he going to do with it all?

JOURDAIN [shrugging]. Can anything annoy a man more than the stupidity of woman?

MRS. JOURDAIN. Seriously, now, you ought to get rid of those tutors and such like, putting all this nonsense and tarriddidle into your head.

NICOLE. Especially that ape of a fencing-master—ugh!

JOURDAIN. Hey! Now I'll just show you right away how wrong you are about him. [*Seizing the foils on the table, he gives one to* NICOLE.] Now then. A logical demonstration of the basic principles. To a thrust in quart, you parry thus, or if he comes at you in tierce, like this: it's all quite simple, once you understand the basic principles. That's the way to avoid being killed—now isn't it splendid to be able to feel that you can defend yourself in a tight corner, eh? Look, just try to hit me, and I'll show you.

NICOLE. What, me? . . . All right, come on, then!

[NICOLE *starts slashing around with foil in an utterly wild and unrestrained way, taking* JOURDAIN *completely by surprise. He is driven back and pursued round the room by the delighted* NICOLE.]

JOURDAIN [*breathless*]. Hey, gently, gently! Ow! Confound you!

NICOLE. Well, you told me to hit you!

JOURDAIN [*anxious to explain*]. Yes, but you came at me in tierce before you tried quart, and didn't wait for me to parry!

MRS. JOURDAIN. You've gone quite off your head, dear, with all these notions—and it all started when you began to try to mix in with the well-to-do.

JOURDAIN. It's this mixing with the well-to-do, as you call it, that shows my good taste.

MRS. JOURDAIN. Personally, I don't think this fine Count What's-his-name you're so thick with nowadays shows your good taste up very well!

JOURDAIN. Quiet, woman! Do you really have any idea who it is you're talking about? This count is a man of far more importance than you think: a man with a position at court, who speaks to the King himself just as I'm speaking to you now. If a man like this comes to my house from time to time, so much the more honour to me! He's really too kind and considerate sometimes: when he puts his arms round my shoulders, it nearly makes me blush.

MRS. JOURDAIN. Oh, he's kind and considerate all right, especially when you're lending him money!

JOURDAIN. Well, isn't it an honour to lend money to such a

distinguished nobleman? Could I do any less for a count who calls me his dear friend?

MRS. JOURDAIN. Yes, but what does this fine friend do for *you?*

JOURDAIN. You'd be surprised if you knew.

MRS. JOURDAIN. Well, what, then?

JOURDAIN. Oh, shut up! You wouldn't understand. As far as you're concerned, all you need know is that even if he has borrowed money from me, he's going to pay it back all right, and fairly soon, too.

MRS. JOURDAIN. Of course! I'll believe you when he does!

JOURDAIN. I assure you that he has promised on his honour as a gentleman. . . .

MRS. JOURDAIN. Fiddlesticks!

JOURDAIN. Pah! You're as stubborn as a mule. I tell you that he'll keep his word—I'm absolutely certain!

MRS. JOURDAIN. And I'm absolutely certain that he won't, and that all his fine friendship is a way of cadging money out of you!

JOURDAIN. Shh! Here he comes!

MRS. JOURDAIN. Yes, for another little loan, no doubt. Ugh, I'm sick of the sight of him!

JOURDAIN. Be quiet, I tell you!

[DORANTE *enters, making an elaborate salute to* MRS. JOURDAIN, *which is ignored, and greeting* JOURDAIN *with an air of familiarity.* JOURDAIN *removes his hat, and holds it awkwardly.*]

DORANTE. My dear Jourdain, I hope you're well today?

JOURDAIN. Very well, and at your service, count.

DORANTE. And dear Mrs. Jourdain: she is also well?

MRS. JOURDAIN. Mrs. Jourdain is quite well enough, thank you.

DORANTE. I say, Jourdain, how splendid you look in that costume! Just the thing!

JOURDAIN [*to* MRS. JOURDAIN, *who turns aside with a toss of the head*]. There you are!

DORANTE. A coat like that really does give you an air—there aren't many people around the court these days in an outfit like that.

[JOURDAIN *makes bashful grimace and noises.*]

MRS. JOURDAIN [*half aside*]. Disgusting flattery!

DORANTE. Turn around, dear fellow! Oh yes, really most gallant.

MRS. JOURDAIN [*as before*]. As daft behind as in front!

DORANTE. By Jove, Jourdain, I'm glad to see you! I've a very high opinion of you, you know—as a matter of fact, I was just talking to the King about you this morning.

JOURDAIN. You do me too much honour, good sir. [*To* MRS. JOURDAIN.] To the King!

DORANTE. Please put your hat on, dear fellow.

JOURDAIN. Sir, please! I know the respect due to our ancient and distinguished aristocracy.

DORANTE. No, do put it on. No ceremony between us, I implore you.

JOURDAIN. But——

DORANTE. No, my dear Jourdain, I insist. You are my friend.

JOURDAIN. Your humble servant, sir.

DORANTE. Well, I shall not put mine on, if you won't.

JOURDAIN [*putting on his hat*]. Well, I don't want to be a nuisance. . . .

DORANTE. Don't forget, dear Jourdain, that I owe you something, too.

MRS. JOURDAIN. No, we'll remember that all right!

DORANTE. You have, on one or two occasions in the past, very generously obliged me. . . .

JOURDAIN. Please don't mention it.

DORANTE. But I am one who knows how to repay what is lent, and to give due recognition for any other little favours, too.

JOURDAIN. Assuredly, sir.

DORANTE. Now I want to get things straight with you, and I've come especially to settle our accounts.

JOURDAIN [*aside, to* MRS. JOURDAIN]. What did I tell you?

DORANTE. There's nothing in this world I hate more than owing money!

JOURDAIN [*aside to* MRS. JOURDAIN]. Just as I said!

DORANTE. Now let's tally up how much it comes to.

JOURDAIN [*as before*]. Your nasty suspicious mind!

DORANTE. Have you kept an account of what I've had?

JOURDAIN. Yes. I believe so. Ah, here it is. Let's see. August 1st, two hundred guineas.

DORANTE [*nodding*]. Yes.

JOURDAIN. August 15th, one hundred and twenty.

DORANTE. That's correct.

JOURDAIN. September 3rd, a hundred and forty.

DORANTE. Quite right.

JOURDAIN. That comes to . . . er . . . four hundred and sixty guineas—say four hundred and eighty pounds.

DORANTE [*nodding as he reckons to himself*]. No. no, my dear Jourdain, let's keep it quite exact: four hundred and eighty-*three* pounds.

JOURDAIN. Now then, let's see . . . er, yes: ninety pounds, sixteen shillings and sixpence to your hatter.

DORANTE. Mmmmmm.

JOURDAIN. Tailor: three hundred and thirty-nine pounds, ten and fourpence.

DORANTE. Go on.

JOURDAIN. Grocer: two hundred and twenty pounds, four shillings and twopence three-farthings.

DORANTE. Four shillings and twopence three-farthings. Yes, I can see you know how to look after figures.

JOURDAIN. Eighty-seven pounds eight shillings and sixpence for your saddler.

DORANTE. Yes, quite right. Now what does all that come to?

JOURDAIN. Total: One thousand two hundred pounds, nineteen shillings and sixpence.

DORANTE [*pretending to add up meanwhile*]. Exactly! Now put down another three hundred that I need today, and that'll make the round fifteen hundred which I'll pay you at the end of the month.

MRS. JOURDAIN [*aside, to* JOURDAIN]. How about that, eh?

JOURDAIN [*to* MRS. JOURDAIN]. Quiet, I say!

DORANTE. Of course, my dear fellow, if that little sum I've just mentioned isn't convenient. . . .

JOURDAIN. Not at all. . . .

MRS. JOURDAIN [*aside to* JOURDAIN]. He twists you round his little finger!

JOURDAIN [*aside, to* MRS. JOURDAIN]. Be quiet!

DORANTE. I can easily ask someone else. . . .

JOURDAIN. Oh, please don't do that. . . .

MRS. JOURDAIN. He won't stop this game until we're ruined.

JOURDAIN. Shut up, I tell you!

DORANTE. You know you have only to say the word and I'll not . . .

JOURDAIN. Please, please don't think of such a thing.

MRS. JOURDAIN. Humbug! He'll squeeze you to the last farthing!

DORANTE. Naturally, I've half a dozen friends who are only too willing to oblige, but I think too much of you, my dear Jourdain, not to give you the first chance.

JOURDAIN. You're really too kind, sir. I'll just go and see what I can do.

MRS. JOURDAIN [*aside, to* JOURDAIN]. You don't mean to say that you're going to let him have it?

JOURDAIN [*aside, to* MRS. JOURDAIN]. Well, what else can I do? How can I possibly refuse a man who mentioned my name in the Royal Presence this morning?

MRS. JOURDAIN [*as* JOURDAIN *goes off*]. A perfect fool!

DORANTE [*to* MRS. JOURDAIN]. You don't seem very cheerful. Is anything the matter, Mrs. Jourdain?

MRS. JOURDAIN. I've got a head on my shoulders, sir, that's what's the matter.

DORANTE. And your charming daughter, Mrs. Jourdain, I don't see her about. Where may she be?

MRS. JOURDAIN. My charming daughter is quite happy where she is, thank you.

DORANTE. And how is she keeping?

MRS. DORANTE. She's keeping herself to herself.

JOURDAIN [*coming in with purse*]. There's three hundred pounds for you.

DORANTE [*tossing purse up and down before pocketing*]. I assure you, dear Jourdain, that there's no one I have more affection for than you. My one aim is to be of some service to you at the Palace.

JOURDAIN. You're too kind.

DORANTE. If Mrs. Jourdain would like to see any of the royal command shows, I should be delighted to get you the very best seats.

MRS. JOURDAIN. Mrs. Jourdain says you can keep your very best seats.

DORANTE [*aside, to* JOURDAIN]. Did you get my note saying that a certain young lady would be accepting your invitation to dine here?

JOURDAIN [*aside, to* DORANTE]. Yes, but let's move away a little.

DORANTE [*as they go aside*]. I also managed to persuade her, after a good deal of talk, to accept the jewelry that you wanted to give her. She feels so delicately about accepting such things, it wasn't easy to get her to accept it. Only when I assured her that it was a stone of the very finest water would she consent.

JOURDAIN. Did she like it?

DORANTE. Very much: and unless I'm mistaken this little

present will have a certain influence on her feeling toward
you. . . .

JOURDAIN. Oh, I do hope it does!

MRS. JOURDAIN [*to* NICOLE]. As thick as thieves, once they get
together.

DORANTE. I took care, I assure you, to drop a hint or two
about the price of that diamond. Then I said that, coming
from a man like you, it was a mere nothing.

JOURDAIN [*rather surprised*]. Oh, did you?

DORANTE. Nothing, that is, in comparison with gifts that will
follow it—or, indeed, with the warmth of your admiration
for her.

JOURDAIN [*relieved*]. Yes, yes, that's right. How clever you
are! Really, it's embarrassing to have a man of your distinction doing all this for me, you know.

DORANTE. My dear fellow, you're joking. Nothing should be
too much trouble between friends, close friends as we are,
Jourdain. Wouldn't you do the same for me if the need
ever arose?

JOURDAIN. Oh, yes, yes, of course I would!

MRS. JOURDAIN [*aside, to* NICOLE]. He gives me a headache!

DORANTE [*still apart, with* JOURDAIN]. As far as I'm concerned,
when it's a question of helping a friend, all other considerations are put aside: yes, my dear fellow, all. Now,
since you've told me of your little weakness for the dear
countess, which whom I have a certain, a certain—as you
might say—relationship—well, you saw for yourself that I
didn't hesitate to give you what help I could?

MRS. JOURDAIN. Is he never going?

DORANTE. Confidentially, my dear Jourdain, you've hit upon
the right approach, you know. There's nothing a woman
likes more than to have a bit of money showered on her.
These serenades of yours, the flowers you're always sending, that surprise fireworks display on the lake, and now
your diamonds—these are the voices that please a woman
more than any words. Keep it up, of course, dear fellow,
keep it up: you mustn't stop running before the race is
won, eh?

JOURDAIN. I don't care how much I spend, if I can find the
key to her heart. Such a distinguished lady! I can't resist
her! I'll pay anything for the honour that the love of such
a lady would bring me!

MRS. JOURDAIN. What on earth are they blathering about? Slip
over quietly and see if you can hear anything.

DORANTE. It won't be long before you'll have the pleasure of meeting her, then your eyes can feast themselves at leisure.

JOURDAIN [*chuckling*]. I've arranged that my wife will spend the evening at my sister's!

DORANTE. Splendid. A wife is *de trop* on these occasions. I've drawn up the menu with the chef on your behalf, and made arrangements about the ballet. If it comes off as I hope it will, I'm sure you'll find——

JOURDAIN [*discovering* NICOLE *eavesdropping, boxes her ears*]. That's for your impertinence! Come, sir, let's be on our way.

[DORANTE *and* JOURDAIN *go off.* NICOLE *returns to* MRS. JOURDAIN, *rubbing her ear.*]

NICOLE. That's what comes of being too curious! Still, although I didn't hear much, I'm sure there's something up, and they're trying to keep you out of it.

MRS. JOURDAIN. It's not the first time, Nicole, that I've had suspicions about the master. He's a wily bird when there's some love-affair in the offing; I'd give a lot to know who the woman is. But we'll not bother our heads about that now, because I want to talk to you about Lucile. You know Cléonte's in love with her; a very suitable match, I think, and I want to do what I can to help him bring it off.

NICOLE. I'm delighted to hear you say so, madam! You see, since Mr. Cléonte meets with madam's approval, Mr. Cléonte's valet meets with mine, so if one wedding comes off, perhaps another will, too!

MRS. JOURDAIN [*going off*]. Run along and tell him to come here at once. Say that I'm quite ready to stand by him if he wants to ask for my daughter's hand, and that I think we should see Mr. Jourdain about it at once.

NICOLE [*running off the other way*]. Very good, madam. . . . Well, I know two people who're going to be made very happy by this bit of news. . . .

[*She crashes right into* CLÉONTE *and* COVIELLE *who enter as she reaches the door. She is too excited at first to notice that they are behaving very stiffly.*]

NICOLE. Oh, here you are, just at the right moment. Listen, I've some splendid——

CLÉONTE [*sternly*]. Out of my way, traitress, and deceive me no more with your lying words!

NICOLE. What's this? I tell you I've got some——

CLÉONTE [*as before*]. Away, I say, and tell your two-faced mistress that she has deceived the simple, honest Cléonte for the last time!

NICOLE. Are you feeling all right? Dear Covielle, just explain to me, sweetheart, what all this is about.

COVIELLE [*same tone as* CLÉONTE]. Dear Covielle—you little wretch! Get out of my sight!

NICOLE. Here, you're not going to tell me you're in the same——

COVIELLE. Out of my sight, I say. I never want to hear a word from you again!

NICOLE [*going off, puzzled and angry*]. Both bitten by the same bug! I'd better let the mistress know about this.

CLÉONTE. Oh, to betray one's lover in this way! And what a faithful, passionate lover, too!

COVIELLE. What these two have done to us two is just—well, there aren't any words bad enough for it!

CLÉONTE [*theatrically*]. The girl receives all the tender devotion that a man can give her; she is the sole aim in my life, the object of my every waking thought, my joy, my happiness, my inspiration! I speak only of her, my thoughts are of her alone, my very heart beats only for her sake! And this is the reward for such devotion! I miss seeing her for two days—and it's more like two centuries, such is my agony when she's not there—then I see her coming towards me in the street. My eyes light up, my whole face shows uncontrollable joy, I fly towards her on wings of desire—and she cuts me dead as mutton!

COVIELLE. Sir, all that I can say is, ditto, ditto.

CLÉONTE. Did you ever see anything to equal the treachery of that wicked renegade of a Lucile?

COVIELLE. Or the deceit, sir, of that rotten little slut Nicole?

CLÉONTE. After all the eager sacrifices, the sighs and vows I have made to her charms!

COVIELLE. After all the little jobs I've done for her in the kitchen!

CLÉONTE. The tears I have poured out before her feet!

COVIELLE. The buckets I've carted around for her!

CLÉONTE. The warmth I've expressed in showing my affections!

COVIELLE. The heat I've had to put up with, turning the spit for her!

CLÉONTE. She turns from me with scorn!

COVIELLE. She drops me like a hot potato!

CLÉONTE. Such treachery's beyond the reach of any mortal punishment!

COVIELLE. Such two-faced tricks deserve a blooming good box on the ears!

CLÉONTE. Please don't ever mention her name to me again: never!

COVIELLE. What, me, sir? Certainly not!

CLÉONTE [*sternly*]. Don't attempt to make the slightest excuse for her behaviour.

COVIELLE. Of course not!

CLÉONTE. No, I tell you it's not the slightest use trying to defend her. . . .

COVIELLE. Wouldn't dream of it, sir!

CLÉONTE. I must make an absolutely complete break with her!

COVIELLE. That's right, sir.

CLÉONTE. Perhaps that count fellow who's always hanging around the house these days has stepped into my shoes: there's a certain type of woman who just can't resist a title. . . . All the same, I'm not going to give her the chance to throw me off just like that, I'll certainly show her that it isn't all one-sided!

COVIELLE. You're absolutely right, sir, and I'm with you all the way!

CLÉONTE [*taking* COVIELLE'S *hand*]. Let's shake hands on it. There. [*Pause.*] Never again.

COVIELLE. Never again.

CLÉONTE. Look, just to make quite sure, suppose you tell me what you think of her, and be sure to make it uncomplimentary. Describe all her faults to me.

COVIELLE [*after a pause while he considers*]. To be frank with you, sir, I never could understand how you fell in love with such an affected, stuck-up piece of goods. At the best, I'd say she was nothing more than ordinary, and now that you're free again, there's no doubt at all that you'll find hundreds of prettier girls far more worth your while. To begin with, her eyes are too small.

CLÉONTE. Yes, she has small eyes, that's true . . . but what fire in them, what sparkle. When she fixes you with a——

COVIELLE [*with a warning cough*]. And her mouth's too large.

CLÉONTE. Yes, I must say her mouth is rather large . . . on the other hand, I find it has qualities one doesn't often find in mouths. . . . It's a mouth you just can't look at without longing to——

COVIELLE [*another cough*]. And she's not very tall.

CLÉONTE. No, but she's graceful. When she walks it's as if an angel were——

COVIELLE. As for her intelligence——

CLÉONTE. Ah, now you must admit, she has a most delicate, a most subtle, wit!

COVIELLE. Well, her conversation——

CLÉONTE. Is quite charming.

COVIELLE. And she's always so serious.

CLÉONTE. Yes, but who wants one of these extrovert types, ghastly girls always bubbling over with high spirits? Is there anything worse than these girls who let out a giggle every time they open their lips?

COVIELLE. And yet, at the same time, she's as flighty as any of the others!

CLÉONTE [*judiciously*]. Well, she is a little capricious, perhaps, yes, I admit that: but when a girl's beautiful, you have to put up with her failings. You know: suffer in the cause of beauty.

COVIELLE [*shrugging*]. Well, it looks as though you're going to go on loving her just like you used to.

CLÉONTE [*indignant*]. Me! I'd rather die! I'm going to hate her just as much as ever I loved her!

COVIELLE. How d'you work that out?

CLÉONTE. Ah, that's just how my revenge is going to work! I'm going to show just how savagely I can hate her in spite of all her attractions. . . .

[*LUCILE and NICOLE enter, NICOLE explaining excitedly to her mistress*]

NICOLE [*excitedly, to LUCILE*]. I just couldn't believe my ears!

LUCILE. Yes, but there must have been a mistake. You'll see.

CLÉONTE. I shan't even say a word to her.

COVIELLE. Me neither.

[*They strike an attitude with their arms folded. The girls shoot questions at them.*]

LUCILE. What's all this about, Cléonte? Is something the matter?

NICOLE. Are you feeling all right, Coville?

LUCILE. Why are you looking so cross?

NICOLE. What are you scowling at me like that for?

LUCILE. Cléonte, why don't you answer me?

NICOLE. Have you lost your tongue?

CLÉONTE [*to COVIELLE*]. Look at the traitress!

COVIELLE. A Judas if ever there was one!

LUCILE. Ah, I know what it is. You've been upset because we cut you in the street this morning.

CLÉONTE [to COVIELLE]. There you are, you see! She must have done it deliberately!

LUCILE. That's it, isn't it, Cléonte? You're hurt because we didn't speak to you this morning?

CLÉONTE [majestically]. Yes, faithless wretch, that's exactly what the trouble is about. But don't you think for a moment that you're going to leave me in the lurch like that, because I'm telling you here and now that it's all over between us — finished. And I hope you appreciate that I'm telling you before you tell me . . . you won't have the pleasure of getting yours in first. [LUCILE about to reply: he cuts in.] Oh, yes, I know it's going to cost me agonies of heartache, but I'd rather kill myself than be so feeble as to make it up with you.

COVIELLE [to NICOLE]. And the same to you, so there!

LUCILE [laughing and approaching CLÉONTE to take his hand] Well, what a lot of fuss about nothing! I came here specially to tell you why I had to avoid you this morning, Cléonte.

CLÉONTE [stepping aside to avoid her]. I don't want to hear.

NICOLE [approaching COVIELLE]. Look, I'll tell you why we had to rush past you like that.

COVIELLE [side-stepping]. Keep your mouth shut!

LUCILE [following CLÉONTE]. Listen. This morning we——

CLÉONTE [always escaping from LUCILE]. Not a word!

NICOLE [following COVIELLE]. I tell you we didn't——

COVIELLE [always escaping from NICOLE]. Quiet, Judas!

LUCILE. Listen.

CLÉONTE. Quite pointless to talk.

NICOLE. Just let me tell you. . . .

COVIELLE [putting hands over ears]. I'm deaf.

LUCILE. Cléonte!

CLÉONTE. No!

NICOLE. Covielle!

COVIELLE. No.

LUCILE. Oh, stay still for a moment!

CLÉONTE. Rubbish!

NICOLE. Listen.

COVIELLE. Twaddle!

LUCILE. Just for a moment.

CLÉONTE. No. No. NO!

NICOLE. Just a little patience.

COVIELLE [*putting out his tongue*]. Yah!

LUCILE. In two words . . .

CLÉONTE. All over and done with.

NICOLE. *One* word.

[COVIELLE *again puts out his tongue.*]

LUCILE [*coming to a halt*]. All right, if you just won't listen to me, you can think whatever you like, and do exactly as you please. [*She stands with her arms folded, furious. For the first time,* CLÉONTE *looks her in the face.*]

CLÉONTE [*moving towards* LUCILE]. Well, since you're determined to tell me, I might as well know what it's all about.

NICOLE [*standing like her mistress, with* COVIELLE *interested at last*]. If that's how you feel, you can take it how you like!

LUCILE [*coldly, moving away from* CLÉONTE]. I am no longer interested in explaining.

COVIELLE [*moving toward* NICOLE]. Well, let's have it, then.

NICOLE [*coldly, moving away from* COVIELLE]. No. I don't think I want to tell you any more.

CLÉONTE [*following* LUCILE]. Please tell me.

LUCILE [*always avoiding* CLÉONTE]. I'll tell you nothing!

COVIELLE [*following* NICOLE]. Now come on!

NICOLE [*always avoiding* COVIELLE]. Leave me alone!

CLÉONTE. Please!

LUCILE. I tell you, no!

COVIELLE. Be a sport!

NICOLE. Nothing doing!

CLÉONTE. Come on: don't be unkind.

LUCILE. Leave me alone.

COVIELLE. Please. Please, Please . . .

NICOLE. Get out of here!

CLÉONTE. Lucile!

LUCILE. No!

COVIELLE. Nicole!

[NICOLE *stamps furiously and makes a rude face.*]

CLÉONTE. For heaven's sake!

LUCILE. No, I don't feel like it!

COVIELLE. At least speak to me!

NICOLE. No!

CLÉONTE. At least clear up my suspicions.

LUCILE. I don't give a hang for your suspicions.

COVIELLE. You're making me miserable.

NICOLE. Good.

CLÉONTE [*tragically*]. All right. Since you can't be bothered to save me from the agony of my doubts, or excuse your own cold-heartedness, I'll go. You see me for the last time: I shall get as far away from you as possible and die in solitude—of a broken heart.

COVIELLE [*following*]. And I'll come with you.

LUCILE ⎱ [*calling him back*]. Cléonte!
NICOLE ⎰ Covielle!

CLÉONTE [*stopping suddenly*]. What's that?

COVIELLE [*ditto*]. Eh?

LUCILE. Where are you going?

CLÉONTE. Where I told you.

COVIELLE [*parrot-wise*]. We're going off to die in solitude of a broken heart.

LUCILE. Are you really going to die, Cléonte?

CLÉONTE. Since you ask me, yes. That's what you wanted, isn't it?

LUCILE. Me, want you to die! Who said that?

CLÉONTE. Isn't that just the same thing as refusing to explain your behaviour this morning?

LUCILE. It wasn't my fault. If you'd only listened to me, I'd have told you that I had to cut you this morning because of my aunt. She's so strait-laced that she thinks a man dishonours a girl when he takes off his hat to her. If she knew we were meeting, it would get back home in no time.

NICOLE. The whole thing in a nutshell!

CLÉONTE. Do you mean to say that's all there was to it?

LUCILE. Just that and no more.

NICOLE. The truth, the whole truth and nothing but the truth!

COVIELLE [*to* CLÉONTE]. Shall we call it a day?

CLÉONTE. Just a word from your lips and all's well! How easily we allow ourselves to be persuaded by someone we're in love with!

COVIELLE [*embracing* NICOLE]. How easily we let these pests pull the wool over our eyes!

[MRS. JOURDAIN *enters*.]

MRS. JOURDAIN. Ah, here you are, Cléonte! I was hoping to have a word with you. Mr. Jourdain's just coming along. This would be a good moment for you to ask him for his consent.

CLÉONTE. Madam, there's nothing I could do more willingly.

[JOURDAIN *enters.*]

Sir, I have a request to make which I have been hesitating to put to you for a long time. The time has come, and I must put it off no longer. It is none other than to have the honour and great privilege of becoming your son-in-law!

JOURDAIN. Before I give you the answer, sir, I want to know one thing: Do you call yourself a gentleman?

CLÉONTE. [*looking cordially at* MR. JOURDAIN]. Well, sir, most people nowadays wouldn't hesitate to answer yes. The word is easily used. But it's a point about which I feel strongly: myself, I've no desire to borrow titles due to others. I've served six years in the army and made a position of some standing for myself, but, all the same, whatever others might say in my place, I'm going to tell you quite frankly . . .

JOURDAIN. Yes?

CLÉONTE. That my parentage doesn't entitle me to claim the rank of gentleman.

JOURDAIN. In which case, sir, you can't possibly marry my daughter!

CLÉONTE. I beg your pardon?

MRS. JOURDAIN. Oh, you and your gentleman! We're not exactly descended from St. Louis ourselves!

JOURDAIN. No need for you to butt in!

MRS. JOURDAIN. And who are we descended from, pray, but honest tradefolk on both sides?

JOURDAIN. How dare you mention such an idea!

MRS. JOURDAIN. Wasn't your father a shopkeeper just like mine?

JOURDAIN. Confound the woman, she's never done! If your father was a shopkeeper, so much the worse for him; as for mine, anyone who says that, doesn't know what he's talking about. Anyway, all I say is, that I insist on a gentleman son-in-law!

MRS. JOURDAIN [*with scorn*]. Your daughter needs a husband who'll match her properly. A good looking fellow with a decent position is far better than one of your down-at-heel, weak-kneed gentlemen friends!

NICOLE. Yes, that's quite right. The squire's son in our village at home is the biggest booby I've ever set eyes on!

JOURDAIN. Quiet, you! Always sticking your nose into other people's business. I've quite enough money to make my

daughter comfortable when she marries: all I need now is a
title. I'm going to make her a countess.

MRS. JOURDAIN. A countess?

JOURDAIN. Yes, a countess!

MRS. JOURDAIN. Heaven help us. He's quite mad!

JOURDAIN. I say, a countess!

MRS. JOURDAIN. And I say, fiddlesticks! I don't want a son-in-
law who's going to make my own daughter laugh at me.
Do you think I want my own daughter's children to be
ashamed of speaking to their grandmother? Can't you hear
people's tongues wagging when Lucile drives up in her
carriage to pay us a visit! I can just imagine what would
happen if she forgot to say good afternoon to one of our
friends—quite by accident, mind you. *Oh yes, that's Mr.
Jourdain's daughter,* they'd say, *she didn't always use to be
so stuck up, you know, used to be glad enough to play with
our Barbara, once upon a time. You'd never think her
father used to sell cheap cloth in the market, would you?
Of course, it isn't always the most honest that gets rich
quickest, is it?* Well, I tell you flat I don't want any of that
sort of tittle-tattle. I want a son-in-law I can talk to like
anyone else, and say 'Sit down, lad, and have a bit of
supper with us.'

JOURDAIN. There's that low side of you coming out again!
Fancy wanting to stay in the lower-classes all your life! I
won't listen to another word, anyway; she's going to be a
countess, that's certain, and if there's any more nonsense
from you, I'll make her a duchess! [*He storms off.*]

MRS. JOURDAIN [*aside*]. Don't let this put you off, Cléonte.
[*Going off another way, with* LUCILE.] Come with me,
Lucile, and later on you can tell Papa that if you can't
marry Cléonte you won't get married at all.

COVIELLE. You've certainly made a hash of things with all
those fine upright ideas of yours!

CLÉONTE. Oh, I don't expect you to understand the behaviour
of a man of principle!

COVIELLE. Can't you see that the old man's mad? Why d'you
take him seriously? It wouldn't be so difficult just to humour
him a little.

CLÉONTE. Perhaps you're right. I certainly didn't think I'd
have to produce a pedigree in order to have the honour of
becoming son-in-law to Mr. Jourdain! . . . Now what the
deuce are you laughing about, Coville?

COVIELLE [*chuckling*]. I've just had an idea. We can have a little game with Mr. Jourdain and at the same time you can get yourself hooked up with the young lady.

CLÉONTE. How do you work that out?

COVIELLE [*bursting with laughter*]. Oh, it's a good one, this is.

CLÉONTE. Come on then, let's have it.

COVIELLE. Remember that masquerade we saw the other week at the carnival? All those Turks and such-like, dancing about like madmen? Well, I've an idea to do something on those lines that'll properly take in our dear Mr. Jourdain. I think I could get the costumes and some of the folk that were in it. Oh, we won't half have him on, good and proper!

CLÉONTE. I don't understand the——

COVIELLE [*whispering and leading* CLÉONTE *off*]. I'll tell you all about it later.

ACT THREE

[MR. AND MRS. JOURDAIN, FIRST LACKEY, DORIMÈNE, DORANTE, COVIELLE, CLÉONTE, MUFTI, DERVISHES, LUCILE]

JOURDAIN [*grumbling to himself as he enters*]. Can't understand some people! Getting all upset because I want to bring off a high-class marriage for Lucile! There's nothing I want more, myself, than to be able to mix with the quality—so polite and well-mannered! Oh, I'd give my right hand to have been born a Your Lordship!

FIRST LACKEY [*entering*]. Sir, here's the count to see you. There's a lady with him, too.

JOURDAIN. Oh, heavens, and I've just remembered I've forgotten something! Bring them in here and say I'll be down in a second!

[*He rushes off. The* LACKEY *goes off and returns with* DORANTE *and* DORIMÈNE. DORANTE *has tricked* DORIMÈNE *into thinking that* MR. JOURDAIN's *presents actually come from himself, also that the banquet she is about to attend has been arranged by himself in her honour, merely by courtesy of* MR. JOURDAIN. *She is quite unaware that* JOURDAIN *is an admirer.*]

FIRST LACKEY. The master says he won't keep you a minute.

[*He goes off.*]

DORIMÈNE. I'm still not too happy about all this, Dorante, letting you bring me here to this strange house where I don't know a soul.

DORANTE. And just where do you propose that I should bring you, my love, since you won't have me at your house or let me entertain you at mine?

DORIMÈNE. Nor am I at all sure that I was wise to accept your presents: anyone who knew whom those magnificent jewels came from would consider it highly compromising. And the idea of sending those musicians to serenade me, that was really too bold of you—yet I could not very well send them away. . . . Really, you are so persevering in your attentions, I can see only one way out: marriage!

DORANTE. And why not, my dear lady? A widow may chose as she pleases, surely, and I'm my own master: what's to prevent us from getting married this very day?

DORIMÈNE. But, Dorante, people who want to share their lives
have to have all sorts of things in common. Even the most
agreeable people don't always find it easy to make a good
match together.

DORANTE. You're joking, to make it sound so difficult! Because
your first marriage wasn't a success it doesn't follow that
your second would be a failure!

DORIMÈNE. And again, I can't help worrying about all this
money you must be spending for my sake. Not only because
it makes me feel, as I say, obliged to you, but because I
am not at all sure that you are in a position to afford it.

DORANTE. Oh, mere trifles, nothing at all to it. I assure you
that——

DORIMÈNE. Yes, but I know what I'm talking about. That
diamond that you sent yesterday—now that really was
extravagant.

DORANTE. If you feel like that, my dear, about a mere knick-
knack that utterly fails to do you justice, I protest that I . . .
[*as* JOURDAIN *enters unexpectedly*] Ah, here you are, my
dear fellow!

[JOURDAIN *repeats the triple bow he has learned, but finds
there is not room for the third one.*]

JOURDAIN. A little further, madam, please.
DORIMÈNE [*surprised*]. I beg your pardon?
JOURDAIN. Just one step, if you don't mind.
DORIMÈNE. I'm afraid I don't quite—
JOURDAIN. To make room for the third one, you know.

[*She takes a step back, and* JOURDAIN *completes his bow with
a flourish.*]

DORANTE. Mr. Jourdain, madam, is a great one for formalities.
JOURDAIN [*making a prepared statement*]. Madam, it is a great
honour to find myself blessed with the good fortune that you
have been kind enough to honour me with in granting me
the honour of your company; if I also had the merit to merit
a merit like your merit, and that fortune—envious of my
felic—felicity—granted me—the advantage of being able to
—consider myself worthy—of—

DORANTE. That's all right, Jourdain. The countess doesn't
want all these compliments—and she knows already what
a witty fellow you are. [*Over his shoulder to* DORIMÈNE.] A
real clown—you'll see!

DORIMÈNE [*aside*]. I have, already!

DORANTE [*heartily*]. This, madam, is one of my greatest friends.

JOURDAIN. Oh, you're too kind to me, sir!

DORANTE. And a gentleman with a thousand good qualities.

DORIMÈNE. I am delighted to meet him.

JOURDAIN. Madam, I confess—so far—nothing worthy er—such merit.

DORANTE [*hisses aside, to* JOURDAIN]. Whatever you do, be careful not to mention the diamond!

JOURDAIN [*to* DORANTE]. Can't I even ask her if she liked it?

DORANTE [*horrified*]. Good gracious, the worst thing you could possibly do! You must simply behave as if it wasn't you at all who sent it to her! [*Aloud, to* DORIMÈNE.] Mr. Jourdain is telling me, madam, how enchanted he is to be able to entertain you here.

DORIMÈNE. He does me great honour.

JOURDAIN [*squeezing* DORANTE'S *hand in excitement*]. Oh, you don't know how grateful I am to you for speaking of me like that!

DORANTE [*aside to* JOURDAIN]. I had a terrible time persuading her to come!

JOURDAIN. I can't think how I can ever make it up to you.

DORANTE. Now he says he finds you the most exquisite beauty he has ever set eyes on!

DORIMÈNE. He does me too much honour!

JOURDAIN [*hopping nervously from one foot to the other*]. Madam, no doubt ... honour ... too much ... you ...

LACKEY [*interrupting just in time*]. Sir, dinner is served.

DORANTE. Splendid. Let's sit down at once.

[*Musicians enter and play discreetly while servants bring in a table and serve a banquet.*]

DORIMÈNE [*as they eat*]. What a splendid feast!

JOURDAIN [*a little recovered from his shyness*]. Madam, I only wish it could be more worthy of the honour of your countess's presence.

DORANTE [*bowing*]. Mr. Jourdain is right, madam, and I can only say that I agree with what he says.

DORIMÈNE [*helping herself*]. I will repay all these compliments by doing justice to what you have provided.

JOURDAIN [*half aside, enraptured*]. Ah, what delightful hands!

DORIMÈNE [*smiling, and showing hands to display ring*]. Oh, I don't think my hands are anything out of the ordinary.

Now, if you were to say something about that diamond: that really is beautiful!

JOURDAIN [*nervously*]. What, me? No, no, heaven forbid I should mention a word about your—er—diamond. That would not be correct, and in any case, it's a very simple little—er—diamond.

DORIMÈNE [*surprised*]. Well, you must be extremely hard to please.

JOURDAIN [*in difficulties*]. Your honour does me too much—er—honour—

DORANTE. Come drink up, Mr. Jourdain, and while we have the next course, let's have some more music.

[*He nods to the musicians, who play, while the others eat and drink.* MR. JOURDAIN *makes several attempts to catch* DORIMÈNE's *eye, and each time he succeeds, lacks the nerve to open a conversation. When the music finishes . . .*]

DORIMÈNE. Beautiful! Really beautiful!

JOURDAIN [*taking the plunge*]. I can see something, madam, even more beautiful!

DORIMÈNE. Oooh? Mr. Jourdain is more of a gallant than I thought he was!

DORANTE. And what did you take Mr. Jourdain for, madam?

JOURDAIN. I wish madam would take Mr. Jourdain for something I could name!

DORIMÈNE [*giggles*].

DORANTE. Mr. Jourdain has hidden qualities, madam.

JOURDAIN. The countess has only to ask, to see them.

DORIMÈNE [*more giggles*]. I fear Mr. Jourdain would be too much for me!

DORANTE. Mr. Jourdain is a real wit, I warn you. But what passion beneath it all: don't you notice, madam, that he is eating all the things you have put aside?

DORIMÈNE [*presenting her hand to be kissed*]. Mr. Jourdain is perfectly adorable!

JOURDAIN [*taking her hand*]. M-Madam, if the honour . . . adoring *you* . . . would give me the greatest—

[MRS. JOURDAIN *enters, and stands in astonishment, taking the scene in.*]

MRS. JOURDAIN. Well, well, well! I see you're entertaining—and that *I* wasn't to be invited! Now I see why you were so kind in suggesting that a visit to Marie would cheer me up! I see there's a theatre downstairs, and here we have a spread fit for a wedding! This is where all the money goes—entertaining your lady friends behind my back in my own house: and sending me out for the evening, indeed!

DORANTE [*standing*]. You should be more careful of what you say, Mrs. Jourdain. Where did you get all these ridiculous ideas that it's your husband who's doing the entertaining? Kindly realize that *I* am doing the entertaining, he's only lending me his house to do it in. You really must try not to make these wild statements!

JOURDAIN [*much relieved*]. Yes, it's the count himself who's doing all this for the countess—a lady of quality, as you see. If he should do me the honour to use my house to do madam the honour—

MRS. JOURDAIN. You don't think I believe all that rubbish? I can see what's going on.

DORANTE. Then I don't think you see very straight, madam.

MRS. JOURDAIN. I see straight enough, without spectacles, either, and perhaps I've been seeing straight longer than you think. What I can't see is how any so-called gentleman could stoop to take advantage of my husband's stupidities! Nor, madam, countess though you may be, can I see anything honourable in encouraging this feeble-witted husband of mine as an admirer!

DORIMÈNE [*rising and going off in anger*]. I can't begin to understand what all this is about! Dorante, I find it insufferable of you to let me in for the suspicions of this extraordinary female!

DORANTE. Dorimène, please wait a moment! [*He rushes off after* DORIMÈNE.]

JOURDAIN. Oh, please, your lady, my lordship . . . tell her we'll explain everything! [*Turning to his wife.*] You're a fine one: insulting me in front of my guests, and driving people of breeding out of the house!

MRS. JOURDAIN. I don't care twopence for their so-called breeding! If there's any insulting been done, you know who to blame! A wife has to stick up for her rights. Just let me catch the pair of them in this house again. . . . [*She goes off muttering, and indicating to* MUSICIANS *to depart, which they do.*]

JOURDAIN. Just as well you've cleared out! I might have done something violent! Fancy turning up just at that moment! I had all sorts of clever things on the tip of my tongue: never felt so witty in my life before! Now who the deuce is this?

[COVIELLE, *disguised in Turkish costume, with a beard, enters and makes a deep bow to* JOURDAIN.]

COVIELLE. Sir, I don't know if I have the honour to be known to you?

JOURDAIN. No.

COVIELLE. And yet, sir, I once saw you when you were no bigger than that! [*Putting out hand to height of knee.*]

JOURDAIN. Me?

COVIELLE. Yes. Oh, you were a lovely child. Women used to fight each other to hold you in their arms and kiss you.

JOURDAIN. Kiss me?

COVIELLE. Yes. As a matter of fact, I used to be a great friend of that very respected gentleman, your father, now, alas, no longer with us.

JOURDAIN. That very respected gentleman my father?

COVIELLE. Certainly. A most highly respected gentleman.

JOURDAIN. Say that again.

COVIELLE. I said, A most highly respected gentleman.

JOURDAIN. My father?

COVIELLE. Yes.

JOURDAIN. And you knew him well?

COVIELLE. Certainly.

JOURDAIN. And you considered him a highly respected gentleman?

COVIELLE. Most definitely.

JOURDAIN. I don't know what to make of it!

COVIELLE. Make of what?

JOURDAIN. Well, certain evil-minded people say he was a shop-keeper.

COVIELLE. A shopkeeper! Good heavens! Pure jealousy. All he did was put his knowledge of fabrics at the service of his friends. Being an obliging sort of fellow, he used to go around collecting samples, and have the goods delivered to his house, where he would give them to his friends in exchange for money.

JOURDAIN [*shaking* COVIELLE's *hand vigorously*]. I'm really delighted to have met you, especially since you tell me that my father really was a gentleman.

COVIELLE. I'd like to meet the man who could say otherwise to my face!

JOURDAIN. You're very kind. Now what brings you here just at present?

COVIELLE. Well, since I used to know that extremely highly

respected and honourable gentleman your father, now, alas, no longer with us, I have travelled all over the world.

JOURDAIN. All over the world?

COVIELLE. That's right.

JOURDAIN. Sounds a long way.

COVIELLE. Well, I've been back only four days actually, and, always having in mind the interests of that respected gentleman, the son of the late Mr. Jourdain, I had to come straight here to tell you the great news.

JOURDAIN. The great news?

COVIELLE. You know, of course, that His Highness the Grand Turk's son is in Paris?

JOURDAIN. His Highness the Grand Turk's son? Who's he?

COVIELLE. Good gracious! Everybody's talking about the magnificence of his retinue. His visit is regarded as a state occasion.

JOURDAIN. I'm sorry to say I've never heard of His Grand Turkish Highness. . . . I've been busy.

COVIELLE. But the amazing thing, which can, of course, be tremendously to your benefit, is that he has taken a fancy to your daughter!

JOURDAIN. Eh?

COVIELLE. He wants to be your son-in-law.

JOURDAIN [*delighted*]. His Grand High Turkishness's son my son-in-law!

COVIELLE. Exactly. I had met him on my travels, you see, and so when I heard he was in Paris, I went to one of the audiences. As I speak Turkish perfectly, he has always been rather fond of me, you know. After chatting of this and that for some time, he suddenly whispers to me: *Acciam croc soler onch alla moustapha skeedadelum varahini oussere carbulath,* that is to say, Do you know anything about a certain young lady who's the daughter of Mr. Jourdain, a gentleman living in this city?

JOURDAIN. He said that about me?

COVIELLE. Yes. Then when I told him that I happened to know you quite well, and that I had seen your daughter on several occasions, he said, *Ah, marababa sahem!* That is, Heavens, how I'm in love with her!

JOURDAIN. *Ah Marababa sahem* means Heavens, how I'm in love with her?

COVIELLE. Yes.

JOURDAIN. I'm very pleased you've told me. If you hadn't, I don't think I'd ever have realized that *Ah marababa sahem* meant Heavens, how I'm in love with her. What a language!

COVIELLE. Yes, it has some fine expressions. Do you know what *cacaracamouchem* means?

JOURDAIN. *Cacaracamouchem?* No.

COVIELLE. It means sweetheart.

JOURDAIN. *Cacaracamouchem* means sweetheart?

COVIELLE. Yes.

JOURDAIN. Wonderful! *Cacaracamouchem*: sweetheart. Now whoever would have thought that! Astonishing!

COVIELLE. Anyway, he sent me on to warn you that His Highness will pay a call this evening in order to make a formal request for the hand of your daughter. Now His Highness the Grand Turk's son is naturally the last person to look down on the rank of such a noble gentleman as Mr. Jourdain of Paris; nevertheless, it is felt, in official circles, that it would be more seemly if the father-in-law of the son of His Highness the Sultan were elevated to the Turkish peerage. It is therefore proposed by His Highness that Mr. Jourdain should be honoured with the title of *mamamouchi*.

JOURDAIN. *Mamamouchi?*

COVIELLE. Yes, *mamamouchi*. That means, in Turkish, paladin. Paladin, of course, is the title of the ancient . . . of the illustrious, of the . . . of the paladins, in fact. It is the supreme title of dignity in the Turkish aristocracy, and will enable you to be on equal terms with the bluest blood in Europe.

JOURDAIN. His Highness does me too much honour: I hope you will take me straight to his apartments so that I can thank him in person.

COVIELLE. Don't you understand? He's coming here himself.

JOURDAIN. Coming here himself?

COVIELLE. Just so, and he'll be bringing everything needed for the ceremony of mamamouchination.

JOURDAIN. He doesn't waste much time!

COVIELLE. My dear sir, these eastern monarchs are not accustomed to allow any obstacle to interfere with their pleasures.

JOURDAIN. The only thing that worries me is that my girl is so obstinate. As long as she's got the other fellow in mind, nothing's going to persuade her to marry anyone else.

COVIELLE. Don't worry, she'll soon change her mind when she sees the Sultan's son—and here's the most astonishing part of the story. Believe it or not, the Sultan's son is the living image of Mr. Cléonte. . . . [JOURDAIN *is about to protest.*] Oh, yes, dear sir, don't imagine that I don't know all about this other gentleman: we who act on behalf of His Royal Highness are not in the habit of rushing into such delicate matters without making careful inquiries before-hand. Ahem. Ah, I think I can hear him coming.

[*Enter a Turkish retinue, with drums, cymbals, and scimitars, leaping wildly, shouting and clashing swords. After a hectic dance they meekly kneel in silence, facing the door through which* CLÉONTE, *bearded and in Turkish dress, enters.*]

CLÉONTE. *Amboushaim oqui boraf, Jourdina, alamalequi.*

COVIELLE. That means, Mr. Jourdain, *may your heart ever flourish like a rose in bloom.* A pretty little phrase they use in Turkish.

JOURDAIN [*bowing deeply*]. I am His Turkish Highness's humble servant!

COVIELLE. *Carigar camboto oustin moraf.*

CLÉONTE. *Oustin voc catamalequie basum basee alla moran.*

COVIELLE. He says: *May heaven grant you the strength of the lion and the wisdom of the serpent.*

JOURDAIN. His Turkish Highness is too kind. I wish him every prosperity.

COVIELLE. *Ossa bina mina bally bally caff caff.*

CLÉONTE. *Bella mena.*

COVIELLE. He says that you are to go with him at once to make yourself ready for the ceremony, so that he may after-ward meet your daughter and make all necessary formal arrangements for the wedding.

JOURDAIN [*amazed*]. All that in two words?

COVIELLE. Yes. A concise language. Now hurry along with him, he doesn't like to be kept waiting.

[CLÉONTE *and* COVIELLE *go off, with the retinue, who this time move with mysterious silence.*]

COVIELLE [*laughing loudly*]. Oh, oh, what a farce! What a fool! He couldn't have done it better if he'd learned the lines by heart! [*More laughter.* DORANTE *enters, at first rather mystified.*] Excuse me, sir, but I hope we can count on your help in a little business we have in hand? [*Pulling down his beard, held on by elastic, for a moment*]

DORANTE. Good heavens: Covielle! I'd never have known you! What a rig!

COVIELLE. Suits me, doesn't it? [*He laughs again.*]

DORANTE. What's the joke?

COVIELLE. Something to laugh about, I can tell you. You'd

never guess the game we're up to, all in order to make old
Jourdain allow the master to marry his daughter.

DORANTE. I certainly don't know what the game is, but I know
that it'll come off all right, if you've anything to do with it!

COVIELLE. Yes, you know me, don't you, sir? Anyway, if
you'll just stand behind here [*Indicating screen.*] you can
see part of it yourself, and I'll tell you the rest later.

[*Eastern music.* SIX TURKS *make a formal entry in pairs, each
pair holding aloft a mat. They dance several figures, then
assume a tableau position for entry of* MUFTI *and* DERVISHES,
*who pass under the prayer-mats, chanting loudly under leader-
ship of* MUFTI. *After a short but very vigorous dance in which
the* DERVISHES *lash out wildly with their scimitars, the mats
are laid down. The* MUFTI *makes an invocation, with much
gesticulation and chanting, while the others kneel round him
in a circle on the mats, alternatively prostrating themselves to
cries of* Allih! *and raising hands towards sky to* Allah!

At the end of the invocation, all stand and shout Alla
eckbar! *three times. This is the signal for* JOURDAIN's *entry,
chaired by more* TURKS. *He is dressed in Turkish costume,
but without wig, hat, or scimitar.*]

MUFTI [*chanting very loudly to* JOURDAIN].

> If you compree
> You must speakee;
> If no compree,
> Shuttee mouthee!

[*Last two lines repeated by chorus* con spirito; JOURDAIN *is
about to reply, when* MUFTI *continues.*]

> Me am Mufti,
> What am you be?
> Him no compree,
> Him no compree!

[*Last two lines repeated as before; this time the* DERVISHES
brandish scimitars at JOURDAIN.]

> How him callee?
> How him callee?

DERVISHES.	Giourdina, Giourdina!
MUFTI.	Giourdina, Giourdina!
DERVISHES.	Ya, ya, ya! Ya, ya, ya!
MUFTI.	Him defendee Palestina?
DERVISHES.	Ya, ya, ya! Ya, ya, ya!
MUFTI.	Giourdina,

Palestina,
Sonnent les matines!

DERVISHES. Ya, ya, ya!
MUFTI. Alli, Baba, ya, ya, ya!
DERVISHES. Alli, Baba, ya, ya, ya!

[MUFTI *goes off, and remainder perform dance around* JOUR-
DAIN. *When the* MUFTI *returns, he is wearing a grand ceremonial turban, decorated with several rows of lighted candles.
Two* DERVISHES *follow, wearing pointed hats with single
candles, and carry an enormous book between them.*

The other DERVISHES *push* JOURDAIN *onto hands and knees
in such a way that his back forms desk for the book, which
the* MUFTI, *making a second invocation, beats frantically from
time to time, also turning pages rapidly. As before, the rest
kneel and prostrate themselves, etc. At the end of the invocation,* MUFTI *says* Hou! ALL *stand, and repeat three times. The
book is removed from* JOURDAIN'S *back. He stands up, wiping
his forehead.*]

JOURDAIN. Phew!
MUFTI [*taking a turban from assistant*].

Him no bad man,
Him no stealee?
Him give Sultan
Squaree dealee?

DERVISHES [*circling* JOURDAIN *once*].

Ya, ya, Sultan
Squaree dealee!

[MUFTI *places turban on* JOURDAIN'S *head, then takes scimitar
from assistant.*]

MUFTI. Him no coward,
Him be bravee?
Him go fight for
Prophet's gravee?

DERVISHES [*circling* JOURDAIN *once*].

Ya, him fight for
Prophet's gravee!

[MUFTI *hangs scimitar at* JOURDAIN'S *side.*]

MUFTI. Give him, hard-o.
Bastinado!

DERVISHES [*circling* JOURDAIN *once, slapping him with scimitars as they pass*].

Give him, hard-o,
Bastinado!

> Bastinado,
> Ya, ya, ya!
> Give him hard-o,
> Bastinado!
> Bastinado,
> Ya, ya, ya!

MUFTI [*making obeisance to* JOURDAIN].

> Ouchy, pouchy,
> Mamamouchi!

DERVISHES.   Mamamouchi,
> Ya, ya, ya!

MUFTI and DERVISHES. Ma . . . ma . . . MOUCHI [*They seize him and rush off the stage.*]

[JOURDAIN *presently returns, mopping his brow.* MRS. JOURDAIN *enters and stands amazed.*]

MRS. JOURDAIN. Merciful heavens, what's going on now? Who on earth has dolled you up like that?

JOURDAIN. What cheek, addressing a *mamamouchi* in that sort of language!

MRS. JOURDAIN. Eh?

JOURDAIN. Yes, you'll have to treat me with more respect now that I've been made a *mamamouchi*.

MRS. JOURDAIN. What's all this *mamamouchi* nonsense about?

JOURDAIN. I tell you *I'm* a *mamamouchi!*

MRS. JOURDAIN. What sort of animal's that?

JOURDAIN. *Mamamouchi* is a very high rank of Turkish nobleman. I've just been made one. That's what the ceremony was for.

MRS. JOURDAIN. Ceremony?

JOURDAIN. Giourdina Palestina.

MRS. JOURDAIN. What?

JOURDAIN. Giourdina, that means Jourdain.

MRS. JOURDAIN. Well, what about it?

JOURDAIN.   Giourdina, Giourdina,
> Him defendee Palestina!

MRS. JOURDAIN. What's wrong with the man!

JOURDAIN.   Smackee hard-o
> Bastinado!
> Bastinado,
> Ya, ya, ya!

[*He repeats the chant, dancing round* MRS. JOURDAIN *and giving her imaginary bastinado treatment. In the end, he trips himself up over scimitar and collapses.*]

MRS. JOURDAIN [*worried*]. He's mad! He is really is mad! Oh!

JOURDAIN [*getting up and walking out with dignity*]. Silence, you impertinent woman! Show some respect for Mr. Mamamouchi!

MRS. JOURDAIN. We must keep him in the house! He mustn't be allowed out by himself!

[*She rushes after him.* DORANTE *and* DORIMÈNE *enter.*]

DORANTE. You couldn't believe it until you'd seen it with your own eyes. It's incredible. Anyway, we can amuse ourselves and do the young lad a good turn: why not?

DORIMÈNE. All right. And I must confess, that if you help to bring this marriage off, I'll be strongly tempted to add a second. [*She embraces* DORANTE.] I can't bear to think of you wasting all this money which we'll need later on, and that seems to be the only way to stop it!

DORANTE. Your beauty, my dear, is only matched by your brains! Things will be very different after we are married, I promise you. But do you really consent?

DORIMÈNE [*kissing him*]. I do. And now that—

[JOURDAIN *enters.* DORANTE *draws away from* DORIMÈNE *just in time, and greets* JOURDAIN *in a loud hearty voice.*]

DORANTE. Well, well, well, my dear sir! This young lady and I have come to congratulate you on your new dignity, added to the good fortune of the marriage which I understand is about to take place.

JOURDAIN [*after making several Turkish obeisances*]. Sir, I wish you the strength of the serpent and the cunning of the lion!

DORIMÈNE. I'm very glad, sir, to be one of the first to congratulate you on your new position in society.

JOURDAIN. Madam, may your rose-bushes bloom all winter! I'm delighted to find you here again, madam, and perhaps you'll allow me the honour to ask you to forgive me for Mrs. Jourdain. The way she lost her head.

DORIMÈNE. Of course. I can quite understand her excitement. Any woman's passions might be driven to extremes by a husband like Mr. Jourdain!

JOURDAIN. Very kind of you, madam, very kind.

DORANTE. You see, madam, Mr. Jourdain is not one of those people whose heads are turned by good fortune, who won't have anything to do with their old friends.

DORIMÈNE. Of course not: the sign of a truly noble nature!

DORANTE. But where is his Turkish majesty? We want to pay our respects to him as well.

JOURDAIN. Here he is now, and my daughter ought to be along any minute.

[CLÉONTE *enters, with attendants.*]

DORANTE [*bowing*]. Sire, as friends of your Highness' honoured and respected father-in-law-to-be we wish to pay our respects and offer our humble allegiance.

[CLÉONTE *deliberately looks vacant and shakes his head.*]

JOURDAIN. Where's that interpreter got to? He can explain everything to his Highness. Where the devil has he got to? [*to* CLÉONTE] Hello! *Striff, striff, stroff.* This gentleman *grande signore—grand signore—grande—grande signore—* and madam also *granda dama—granda granda dama.* [CLÉONTE *shows no reaction.*] T,t,t, tut! Sire, him French *mamamouchi,* and her French *mamamouchina!* Ah! [COVIELLE *enters.*] Come on, come on, we can't speak a word without you! Tell his Highness that these are people of the greatest consequence in France, who have come as friends of Mr. Jourdain, to pay their respects to his Highness [*to* DORIMÈNE *and* DORANTE] Now just listen to how they talk!

COVIELLE [*after making obeisance*]. *Alabala boram alabama.*

CLÉONTE [*inclining his head slightly*]. *Cataleeki tubal ourin amalouchi.*

JOURDAIN [*to* DORIMÈNE *and* DORANTE]. See?

COVIELLE. His Highness says, may the waters of prosperity forever rain upon the garden of your ancestors!

JOURDAIN. I told you! He understands every word! [LUCILE *enters.*] Ah, here you are! Now then, Lucile, come along and give your hand to His Highness, who has done us the honour of requesting to marry you.

LUCILE [*unable to take eyes off father*]. Father, what on earth's the matter with you? Are you going on the stage? You're joking!

JOURDAIN. I certainly am not. This is a very serious business indeed. Honours like this don't come into the family every day. [*Taking her over to* CLÉONTE.] Here, young lady, is your future husband.

LUCILE. *My* future husband!

JOURDAIN. Yes, your future husband. Go on, hold his hand.

LUCILE [*refusing* CLÉONTE's *offered hand and turning away*].
No! I don't want to get married.

JOURDAIN. And I say you're going to get married!

LUCILE. I tell you I won't!

JOURDAIN. Stubborn as a mule! Take his hand, I tell you!

LUCILE [*very emphatically. During the speech, however, while*
JOURDAIN *isn't looking,* CLÉONTE *pulls down his beard sev-*
eral times, and at last LUCILE *recognizes him*]. No, father,
my mind's made up, and there's nothing on this earth will
make me accept anyone but Cléonte, and I promise you I'll
resist any of your stupid . . . it is, of course, true that a
daughter should submit to her father's better judgment, and
it is your right to decide these things as you please.

JOURDAIN. Ah, that's better! I'm pleased to find you so full of
respect for your father's wishes. I knew you'd be a good
girl.

[MRS. JOURDAIN *enters, to find the "Turkish Prince" and*
LUCILE *holding hands.*]

MRS. JOURDAIN. Here, what's all this about? They say you're
going to let your daughter marry a colored minstrel!

JOURDAIN. I wish you'd keep your mouth shut! You always
come along with your fat-headed ideas at the wrong moment, and it's hopeless trying to make you understand!

MRS. JOURDAIN. I like that. You're the one with the fat-headed
ideas, and now you're going from bad to worse! What do
you want to mix yourself up with this circus for?

JOURDAIN [*with, he hopes, simple dignity*]. I wish to marry my
daughter to the son of the Sultan of Turkey.

MRS. JOURDAIN. The Sultan's son?

JOURDAIN. Exactly. Pay your respects through the interpreter
here.

MRS. JOURDAIN. [*During this part of the scene all the con-*
spirators are trying to let her into the secret by making
signs, snapping their beards on and off, etc., but she doesn't
see them.] I don't need any interpreter, thank you, and I
tell His Highness here and now that he's not having
my daughter!

JOURDAIN. Shhh!

DORANTE. Madam, you're surely not going to refuse to have
His Highness as your son-in-law?

MRS. JOURDAIN. You mind your own business!

DORIMÈNE. It's too great an honour to be refused.

MRS. JOURDAIN. Madam, I'll thank you as well to keep your nose out of other people's affairs!

DORANTE. It's only our great affection for you which makes us try to help.

MRS. JOURDAIN. I'll manage without your affection!

DORANTE. You only have to look at your daughter. She has nothing against it.

MRS. JOURDAIN [*amazed*]. Lucile has nothing against marrying a Turk?

DORANTE. Just so.

MRS. JOURDAIN. But what about Cléonte?

DORANTE. Who wouldn't jump at such a chance of marrying into royalty?

MRS. JOURDAIN. If she does, I'll strangle her with my own hands!

JOURDAIN. Interfering old dragon! I tell you it's all arranged and that's that!

MRS. JOURDAIN. And I tell you it's going to be unarranged, here and now!

JOURDAIN. Quiet!

LUCILE [*taking* MRS. JOURDAIN's *arm.*] Mother!

MRS. JOURDAIN [*roughly*]. Let go! You're just a little fool!

JOURDAIN. What, you tell her that just because she obeys her father?

MRS. JOURDAIN. She's as much mine as yours!

COVIELLE [*quietly, to* MRS. JOURDAIN]. Madam!

MRS. JOURDAIN. What do *you* want?

COVIELLE. Just a quiet word with you.

MRS. JOURDAIN. Don't waste my time!

COVIELLE [*to* JOURDAIN]. Sir, if only madam would have a word with me in private, I'm sure I could persuade her to do as you wish.

MRS. JOURDAIN. And I'm sure you couldn't!

COVIELLE. Just listen for a single moment.

MRS. JOURDAIN. No!

JOURDAIN. Oh . . . [*Tearing his hair.*] Why not listen to him?

MRS. JOURDAIN. Because I don't want to, that's why.

JOURDAIN. He'll explain all—

MRS. JOURDAIN. He'll explain nothing!

JOURDAIN. Just like a woman! Sheer obstinacy! Will it hurt you to listen to him for a moment?

COVIELLE [*desperately*]. Just listen, then do what you like.

MRS. JOURDAIN. All right, then. What is it?

COVIELLE [*aside, to* MRS. JOURDAIN]. I've been trying to catch your eye for ten minutes! Don't you see that it's all a trick to take advantage of Mr. Jourdain's fads? We're all disguised. Look, the sultan's son is Cléonte! [CLÉONTE *obligingly removes his beard for a second, and* MRS. JOURDAIN *catches on.*] And Mr. Interpreter is none other than Covielle, at your service, madam!

MRS. JOURDAIN. Ah! That's different! All right, I'm with you. [*Aloud, to* JOURDAIN.] Well, I confess that this gentleman has made out a better case than you could have done! Perhaps I was hasty. Yes, I suppose I must give my consent.

JOURDAIN. Ah, now that's more reasonable. Splendid, splendid. You see, you didn't want to listen. I knew he'd tell you just what sort of a man the son of His Highness the Sultan is.

MRS. JOURDAIN. He did. And I admit he surprised me. Well, let's not waste any time. What about sending for a solicitor?

DORANTE [*after a look from* DORIMÈNE]. A very sound idea. And another thing, Mrs. Jourdain: in order to put you quite at ease, and so that you won't have any more absurd suspicions of your husband's loyalty, [*Winking at* JOURDAIN.] with your permission, this lady and myself will get the same lawyer to prepare *our* wedding contract!

MRS. JOURDAIN. Yes, I agree to that, too.

JOURDAIN [*aside, to* DORANTE]. To pull the wool over her eyes, eh? Oh, you are a cunning one!

DORANTE [*aside, to* JOURDAIN]. Yes, just to keep her happy in the meantime!

JOURDAIN. Splendid. [*Aloud.*] Well, send someone to fetch the solicitor.

DORANTE. While we're waiting, why not have the little entertainment we prepared? No doubt His Turkish Majesty would be amused.

JOURDAIN. Good idea. Let's all make ourselves comfortable.

MRS. JOURDAIN. What about Nicole?

JOURDAIN. I give her to the interpreter—and my wife to anyone who'll have her!

COVIELLE [*bowing*]. Sir, I thank you. May the waters of prosperity forever rain upon the garden of your ancestors. [*Aside.*] And if there's a bigger idiot than this anywhere in the world, I'll eat my blooming turban!

The comedy concludes with a Turkish ballet.

THE INSPECTOR GENERAL

by Nikolai Gogol

A new version by Robert Saffron

The Inspector General was first produced at St. Petersburg in April, 1836, during the reign of Czar Nicholas I. Despite the play's criticism of the regime's corruption, the Czar never ordered it to be censored or banned.

THE CAST

ANTON ANTONOVICH, *Mayor of a provincial town*
ANNA ANDREYEVNA, *his wife*
MARYA ANTONOVNA, *his daughter*
LUKA LUKICH HLOPOV, *Commissioner of Schools*
HIS WIFE
AMMOS FYODOROVICH LYAPKIN-TYAPKIN, *a Judge*
ARTEMI PHILIPOVICH ZEMLYANIKA, *Commissioner of Charities*
IVAN KUZMICH SHPYOKIN, *Postmaster*
IVAN ALEXANDROVICH HLESTAKOV, *a government clerk from St. Petersburg*
OSIP, *his servant*
DOBCHINSKI, *a landowner*
BOBCHINSKI, *a landowner*
HUBNER, *a doctor*
LYULYUKOV
RASTAKOVSKI } *Former officials*
KAROBKIN
UKHAVYORTOV, *Police superintendent*
SVISTUNOV
PUGOVKIN } *Policemen*
DERZHIMORDA
ABDULIN, *a merchant*
LOCKSMITH'S WIFE
SERGEANT'S WIFE
MISHKA, *Mayor's servant*
WAITER *at the inn*
Other merchants, citizens, ladies and gentlemen of the town

The action of the play takes place in a provincial town in Russia, in the 1830's.

GOGOL'S NOTES ON THE CHARACTERS

THE MAYOR: An old-timer in government service who knows all the tricks. He has an air of dignified respectability but is not adverse to taking a gift. His coarse features and frequently uneducated language betray the lower-class man who has worked his way up; he shifts quickly from fear to joy and from servility to arrogance.

ANNA ANDREYEVNA: His wife, still tolerably young, is a small-town coquette, raised on romantic novels and the trivia of the household. She is most inquisitive and vain, and henpecks her husband whenever she can get away with it. She changes her costume four times during the play.

HLESTAKOV: A young man, about 23, rather insignificant in appearance; dresses in the latest fashion. He would be considered frivolous in the government offices. He speaks and acts abruptly, without thinking, and cannot concentrate on one subject for long. . . . He is not a professional liar or imposter; he forgets he is telling lies and almost believes what he is saying. As he realizes he is believed, he becomes expansive, poetic, inspired.

OSIP: His servant, middle-aged, keeps his head down in mock servility but lectures his master bluntly, even rudely. He is the cleverer of the two, a real rogue.

BOBCHINSKI AND DOBCHINSKI: Both are short, fat and inquisitive and look like twins. Both wear short waistcoats, and talk fast with constant gestures. DOBCHINSKI is taller and more practical; BOBCHINSKI is somewhat lightheaded.

LYAPKIN-TYAPKIN: The Judge has read five or six books and so considers himself something of a free-thinker. He is fond of philosophic discussion, carefully weighing each word. Speaks with a bass voice and prolonged drawl, clearing his voice beforehand like an old clock that buzzes before it strikes.

COMMISSIONER OF CHARITIES: Very fat, slow and awkward; still he's an intriguing rascal, obliging but officious.

POSTMASTER: An artless simpleton.

The other characters require no special explanation since their prototypes can be found almost anywhere.

The performers must pay special attention to the final scene. The last word spoken must strike them like an electric shock, suddenly and simultaneously, and the entire group should fall into a tableau at the same instant. The ladies' cry of astonishment must seem to come from one throat. The neglect of these directions will ruin the entire effect.

ACT ONE

Scene 1

A room in the MAYOR'S *house, stuffy and over-furnished in heavy furniture and bibelots of the period. The entrance, center, has double doors; other doors lead to back of house and a side room.*

It is a drowsy afternoon. The COMMISSIONER OF CHARITIES *and* HUBNER, *the doctor, are playing cards mechanically. One* POLICEMAN *is asleep in a chair and snoring; occasionally he moves his hand or twitches his nose to shake off a fly which continues to pester him. Another* POLICEMAN *is leaning against the center doorway. The* JUDGE *is staring vacantly at the ceiling of the room. The* COMMISSIONER OF SCHOOLS *has a large ledger in one hand and a sheaf of papers in the other; as he swiftly skims through the papers he checks off names in the ledger. Papers fall to the floor but he doesn't bother to pick them up.*

The Center doors are pushed open and the MAYOR *enters, breathing heavily and obviously flustered. The* POLICEMAN *doesn't move. Nobody looks up. The* MAYOR *slaps a table heavily to get their attention. The* POLICEMAN *slowly, eyes still shut, shuffles to the door and leans against it to balance his partner on the other side.*

MAYOR. I've called you to my house, gentlemen, to warn you! An Inspector General is coming here!

JUDGE. What? An Inspector?

COMMISSIONER OF CHARITIES. An Inspector?

MAYOR. Yes, an Inspector from St. Petersburg. Incognito! With *secret* instructions!

JUDGE. What a despicable trick!

COMMISSIONER OF CHARITIES. Well, our district has escaped so far. Now it's our turn to catch hell.

COMMISSIONER OF SCHOOLS [*appalled*]. Good God! *Secret* instructions?

MAYOR. I knew this would happen, I knew it! All last night I had a dream about two monster rats! I've never seen anything like them—so huge and all *black!* They came into my room, sniffed around, then vanished.

JUDGE. Two *black* rats you say? But there is only one inspector. Possibly he has blacked up his face to hide—?

MAYOR [*ignoring him*]. I have a letter here from Andrei Chmikov. [*To* COMMISSIONER OF CHARITIES.] You know him . . . he's reliable. [*He reads.*] "My dear friend and benefactor . . ." [*He mutters through a few lines.*] ah, here it is—"an official has been sent out with instructions to inspect the entire province and especially your district. [*Points a finger significantly.*] I know from reliable sources that he will pretend to be just a private citizen. And so, since you're a sensible man and don't let any little graft slip through your fingers. . . ." [*Looks up, irritably.*] People shouldn't send that kind of joke through the mails. [*Reading.*] "He might come any day—if he's not already there—and remember, he's incognito. My cousin has grown very fat and now he has trouble sticking his fiddle under his chin. . . ." Well, there you are. This is a real trap!

JUDGE. Extraordinary! Most extraordinary! There must be some hidden motive behind all this.

COMMISSIONER OF SCHOOLS. Of course! Why should *we* in particular be cursed with an Inspector?

MAYOR [*sighing*]. It's the heavy hand of God!

JUDGE. It is my opinion that this is a subtle political move. It means . . . let me think now . . . that Russia wants—yes, that's it! Russia is about to declare war! And the government has sent a secret agent to sniff out disloyalty here.

MAYOR. Oh, what a brain! What good could an enemy spy do here? We're not on the border—you could gallop for three years before you hit a border!

JUDGE. Disloyalty knows no borders! The government may be far away in St. Petersburg but its eyes are everywhere, watching, lurking. . . .

MAYOR [*disturbed*]. Maybe so, maybe so. Anyhow, gentlemen, I've warned you. I've taken steps to straighten out my office, and you'd better do the same. [*To* COMMISSIONER OF CHARITIES.] And especially you. I'll bet the first thing the Inspector wants to see is the hospital. Better clean it up fast. Get the patients into some presentable nightgowns. And scrub up the wretches a little. I don't want them to look like they've been sleeping in a blacksmith's shop.

COMMISSIONER OF CHARITIES [*irritably*]. All right, all right. I'll have some nightgowns washed.

MAYOR. I can't even recognize any of those people. [*To* DOCTOR.] You ought to have a little card over the bed, in Latin or German or whatever language you doctors use, with the name of the patient, his disease and so on. And if any of them are dead, I want them taken out right away! [DOCTOR *doesn't answer*. MAYOR *turns to* COMMISSIONER OF CHARITIES.] Another thing. You have too damn many patients. The Inspector will say that's bad management. You'll have to—[*waves his hand*.] lose some of them somehow.

COMMISSIONER OF CHARITIES. I assure you, we don't waste expensive medicines on those cases. We prefer nature's own remedies. If they die, they die. If they live—we are proved right. . . . Unfortunately, it's hard for the patients to explain their symptoms to the doctor.

MAYOR. Why?

COMMISSIONER OF CHARITIES. All he can speak is German.

[*The* DOCTOR *grunts unintelligibly. The* MAYOR *throws up his hands*.]

MAYOR [*to* JUDGE]. And you, Ammos Fyodorovich, you ought to spend a little more time in the Court House. Have you been in the lobby lately? Some of your clever attendants are raising geese there! And the goslings go poking their beaks under the women's skirts. It's not respectable! And all those feathers floating around! . . . [*Wearily*.] I was going to mention it to you before but somehow I forgot.

JUDGE. Very well. I shall order the attendants to take the geese over to my kitchen today. Would you like to come to dinner tonight?

MAYOR. Not tonight! . . . And what about that relative of yours, that assessor? He reeks of liquor, as though he's just come out of a distillery—and he probably has. There must be some way to get rid of that stink.

JUDGE. He claims that's the way he has always smelled.

MAYOR. Tell him to cover it up with onions or garlic or something. Can't the Doctor give him some pills?

[*The* DOCTOR *grunts*.]

JUDGE [*shrugs*]. My cousin swears his nurse dropped him when he was a baby, and ever since he's smelled of vodka.

MAYOR. My God! I'm surrounded by idiots! That reminds me.

I know no man is free of sin—God made him that way—but starting today no one is to accept any bribes! Is that clear? No one!

JUDGE. What do you mean by sin? There are small sins and there are great sins. I admit I take gifts, but what kind? Greyhound puppies. That's a small sin.

MAYOR. I don't care if it's a small puppy or a big dog, that's a sin.

JUDGE. Just a moment. Let us examine the evidence. Suppose the defendant receives a cloak, worth 500 rubles, or your wife, say, gets a fancy shawl . . .

MAYOR [angrily]. Are you making me a defendant? You're a great one to be arguing about sin. You're an atheist! You've never been inside a church. At least I attend service every Sunday. When I hear you talking about Original Sin, it just makes my hair curl! God will punish you for this.

JUDGE. At least I thought it all out with my own brain—it's not dogma—

MAYOR. That's the trouble—everybody is *thinking* around here! [He turns on the COMMISSIONER OF SCHOOLS.] You better watch those teachers in your schools. I know a few of them have gone to the university and they're damned queer. That fat-faced one—I forget his name—why is he always screwing up his mug like this? [He imitates a monster.] Then he starts clawing at his necktie and scratching his chin. I don't care if he makes faces at the pupils—maybe they need it—but if he sticks out his tongue at the Inspector he may take it personally and there'll be hell to pay.

COMMISSIONER OF SCHOOLS [a martyr]. I've told him time and again. What can I do? I keep getting complaints from people about the revolutionary notions being planted in the children's heads.

MAYOR. That's all I need now—bomb-throwers in the schools! And what about that history teacher? He looks smart, all right, but when he starts lecturing he goes absolutely crazy! I heard him once. As long as he was on the Assyrians and the Babylonians, he was fine. But when he got to Alexander the Great—good God! He threw books around and smashed his chair on the floor and broke it into little pieces. Alexander the Great is a hero, but does your madman have to break up the furniture to prove it? That's state property, and some day somebody will have to pay for it.

COMMISSIONER OF SCHOOLS [*resigned*]. I've spoken to him about the damages several times. All he says is—"In the cause of learning I will even sacrifice my life!"

MAYOR [*sighs*]. It's a strange law of heaven—your scholar is either a drunkard or an anarchist!

COMMISSIONER OF SCHOOLS [*fervently*]. God preserve us from the influence of books!

MAYOR [*suddenly remembering*]. God preserve us from this Inspector! He'll put his head in here suddenly: "Aha! so you're all together, my friends? And who's the Judge?" he'll say. "Lyapkin-Tyapkin." "Well, ship Lyapkin-Tyapkin away," he'll order. "And who is the Commissioner of Charities?" "Zemlyanika." "Take Zemlyanika, too!" That's what's so terrifying—we don't know when he'll pop in!

[*At this instant, the* POSTMASTER *rushes in, frightening all of them.*]

POSTMASTER. Am I too late? Who's coming? I heard something from Bobchinski at the post office.

MAYOR. *You're* the postmaster. What do you think about these reports?

POSTMASTER [*thinking hard*]. What do *I* think? Why, there'll be war with the Turks for sure.

JUDGE [*to the group*]. That is exactly what I said.

MAYOR. The Turks? It's *us* who're going to be shot at, not the Turks. I've got a letter that proves it.

POSTMASTER. Ah, good. Then we *won't* go to war with the Turks.

MAYOR [*restraining himself*]. What do you feel about all this?

POSTMASTER [*slyly*]. How do *I* feel? The important thing is—how do *you* feel?

MAYOR. I'm not afraid of anything . . . but those crafty shopkeepers bother me. I'm sure they've drawn up some complaints against me. God knows, if I've put pressure on them for contributions now and then, I've done it without any personal spite. I don't have any grudge against them. [*Takes* POSTMASTER *by the lapels and draws him aside.*] Listen, Ivan, couldn't you open every letter that comes into the post office—just a little? [POSTMASTER *is shocked.*] It's really a public service—to see if it has any lies about me. If it's all right, paste it up again.

POSTMASTER [*amiably*]. Oh, you don't have to teach me *that* trick. I like to know what's going on in the world. And it sure is interesting, I tell you! Sometimes I come across a love letter with some hot little tidbits . . .

MAYOR. Have you read anything lately about an official from St. Petersburg?

POSTMASTER. No, but lots about Kostroma and Saratov. Too bad you don't get to read 'em, mayor. Some great stuff there. I remember one an artillery lieutenant wrote to a friend about a dance. "I live in paradise," he writes. "Lots of music, girls—all well fortified. Let me tell you about the breastworks . . ." Oh, it would make your mouth water. I kept that letter—would you like to read it?

MAYOR. Not now . . . [*Wearily.*] If only I knew what that damned Inspector looks like! I expect the door to open and all of a sudden—

[*The door flies open and* BOBCHINSKI *and* DOBCHINSKI *tumble in, out of breath. The* MAYOR *chokes as if God is about to strike him dead.*]

BOBCHINSKI. What a fantastic thing just happened!

DOBCHINSKI. Incredible!

ALL. What is it? What happened?

DOBCHINSKI. Who would have expected it? We go into the inn—

BOBCHINSKI [*interrupting*]. Yes, he and I go into the inn—

DOBCHINSKI. All right, Peter Ivanovich, just let *me* tell it.

BOBCHINSKI. No, no. Let me—let me! . . . You don't know the first thing about telling a story—

DOBCHINSKI. Oh, you'll just get mixed up and won't remember anything.

BOBCHINSKI. Oh no, I won't! Now don't interrupt me, damn it! Please, gentlemen, tell Dobchinski to keep quiet!

MAYOR. Well, tell it, for God's sake. My heart's in my mouth. Sit down, gentlemen—take a chair. Here's one for you, Bobchinski. [*They all sit around* BOBCHINSKI *and* DOBCHIN-SKI.]

BOBCHINSKI [*to* MAYOR]. . . . As soon as I left you—after you got that letter that worried you so much—I ran right out. . . . Now, please stop trying to interrupt, Dobchinski. I know all the details, I assure you. . . . So, as I was saying, I ran out to see Karobkin. But since he wasn't home, I dashed off to find Rastakovski. And since *he* wasn't home either, I went to see the Postmaster to tell *him* of the news you'd received. Ah yes, and going on from there I ran into Dobchinski—

DOBCHINSKI [*breaking in*]. Near the stall, where they sell cakes—

BOBCHINSKI [*grimly*]. —near the stall where they sell cakes. Well, I meet Dobchinski and I say, "Have you heard the news our Mayor got?" But he had already heard it [*To* MAYOR.] from your housekeeper who'd been sent to Philip Antonovich Pachechuyev . . . only I can't remember why—

DOBCHINSKI. You see why I should tell it? [*Triumphantly*.] It was for a bottle of French brandy—

BOBCHINSKI. Oh yes, French brandy—will you stop butting in, Peter Ivanovich? Damn it!—So we both rush off to Pachechuyev's, but on the way Dobchinski says, "Let's stop at the inn. I haven't eaten anything since morning . . . there's such a rumbling inside me!" Yes sir, right in his belly—

JUDGE. Spare us the details!

BOBCHINSKI. "They've just delivered some fresh salmon at the inn," he says. "So we can have a nice snack." Well, we hadn't been inside the inn for a minute when in comes this young fellow—

DOBCHINSKI. Rather good-looking and well-dressed—

BOBCHINSKI [*firmly*]. *Plain*-looking and well-dressed, he walks into the room with such a look on his face—important!— and what style—and a really distinguished forehead, that I had a hunch. I say to Dobchinski, "Aha! There's *something going on here!*" Oh, yes! And Dobchinski calls over Vlas, the innkeeper, you know [*To* MAYOR.] three weeks ago his wife presented him with a baby—what a fine, active boy—when he grows older he'll be just like his dad and keep an inn—

MAYOR. We'll all grow old before you come to the point!

BOBCHINSKI. Well, we calls over Vlas, and Dobchinski asks him quietly, "Who," says he, "is that young fellow?" And Vlas answers, "That," says he, "is"—don't interrupt me, Peter Ivanovich! Please! Good God you can't tell a story, you never could! You just can't speak clearly, you lisp! Yes you do! You've got one tooth in your mouth and that one whistles.

COMMISSIONER OF CHARITIES [*To* DOBCHINSKI]. Really? I never noticed that. Let's see—

MAYOR [*about to explode*]. For the love of God—go on!

BOBCHINSKI. Well, Vlas says, "That young fellow is an official"—yes, sir! "who has come from St. Petersburg. And his name," says he, "is Ivan Alexandrovich Hlestakov. And he's on his way," says he, "to the governor of Saratov, and he acts very strange—he's stayed here over two weeks, he doesn't leave the inn and he charges everything! He doesn't pay a single kopek!" When he told me that, it dawned on me at last! And I said to Peter Ivanovich, "Aha!—"

DOBCHINSKI. No, *I* said "Aha!"

BOBCHINSKI. Well, first *you* said it and then *I* did. "Aha! Why does he hang around here when he's on the way to Saratov, huh?" Yes sir—that official is the *one!*

MAYOR [*exploding*]. *What* one?

BOBCHINSKI. The official you were warned about—the Inspector General!

MAYOR [*in a panic*]. What are you talking about? It *can't* be!

DOBCHINSKI. It *is!* He won't pay for anything and he doesn't stick his nose outside the inn. What else could he be but an Inspector?

BOBCHINSKI [*exultantly*]. It's him, it's him! Good God! It's him! He sees everything. He noticed that Dobchinski and I were eating salmon—all on account of Dobchinski's stomach, you know—and he snooped right into our plates like this [*Imitating the action.*] Oh, I choked!

MAYOR. May God have mercy on sinners like us! What room is he in?

DOBCHINSKI. Number five, first floor.

BOBCHINSKI [*eagerly*]. That's the same room where the officers had that brawl last year—

MAYOR. How long has he been there?

DOBCHINSKI. Two weeks or more. He came on St. Vasili's—

MAYOR. *Two weeks!* Holy father and saints, save us! He's had time to find out about the sergeant's wife who was flogged! And the prisoners haven't been fed! And people staggering drunk in the streets—and the streets full of filth! What a scandal! [*To* BOBCHINSKI.] You say he's a *young* fellow?

BOBCHINSKI. Well, about twenty-three or four.

MAYOR. It'll be easier to feel him out. It's tough when you've got a sly old buzzard to deal with, but a young fellow is more transparent. Now you men run and straighten out your departments, while I go around by myself—or with Dobchinski here—and have a little look [*With a wink.*] to see that visitors to our town are treated with proper consideration. [*He calls to one of the* POLICEMEN.] Svistunov!

SVISTUNOV. Yes, sir?

MAYOR. Run to your Superintendent—no, no. I'll need you here. Tell somebody to send him here on the double, and then you come right back. [SVISTUNOV *runs out.*]

COMMISSIONER OF CHARITIES [*to* JUDGE]. Let's go, let's go. All sorts of devilment may have broken out.

JUDGE. What are *you* afraid of? Cover the patients with some clean gowns and you're clear.

COMMISSIONER OF CHARITIES. Gowns, hell! I had orders from St. Petersburg to give the patients oatmeal porridge. And who snatched the oatmeal? [*He indicates the* MAYOR.] So I had to switch to cabbage. Now there's such a stink of cabbage in my corridors, you'd think you were drowning in a tub of borscht!

JUDGE. I don't worry. If the Inspector ever peeps into the pile of documents in my court, he'll be more confused than I am. I've been sitting on that bench for fifteen years and I've never opened a single statement of charges.

[*The* JUDGE, COMMISSIONER OF CHARITIES, COMMISSIONER OF SCHOOLS *and* POSTMASTER *go out. The* POLICEMAN *bumps violently into them as he dashes in.*]

MAYOR. Well, is the carriage ready?

SVISTUNOV. Yes, sir.

MAYOR. Go into the street—no, stop! go and bring . . . Where are the other men? Didn't I give orders for Prokhorov to come here? Where is he?

SVISTUNOV. Prokhorov is in the police station. He can't go on duty right now.

MAYOR. Why not?

SVISTUNOV. They carried him in this morning, dead drunk. His head's in a bucket of water, but he hasn't sobered up yet.

MAYOR [*tearing his hair*]. Oh, my God! Run to my room fast and get my new hat and sword! [POLICEMAN *runs out.*] [*To* DOBCHINSKI.] Let's be off.

BOBCHINSKI. And me? Me, too! Let me come along.

MAYOR. Oh no, Bobchinski. There's no room in the carriage.

BOBCHINSKI. I don't care. I'll run along behind the carriage. I just want to peep through the door, to see what that Inspector acts like.

[POLICEMAN *returns with ceremonial sword and hatbox.*]

MAYOR [*to* POLICEMAN *as he straps on the sword*]. Run and get the street cleaners together. Let each one take a—oh,

look how this sword is rusted! That fatbelly shopkeeper
Abdulin knows the Mayor's sword is all banged out of
shape, but does he supply me with a new one? Oh, no! The
stingy crook! [*To* POLICEMAN.] I want each of the cleaners
to take hold of a street—damn, I mean a broom—and
sweep all of the street that leads to the inn. Sweep it clean,
do you hear? And you'd better watch out, too. I know your
little tricks. You worm your way into my kitchen by
fondling the cook, and slip silver spoons into your boots.
And how about that shopkeeper Chornyaiev, hm? He
donated two yards of cloth for your uniform, but you stole
the entire bolt. Watch yourself! Don't steal any more than
your job entitles you to. Get out!

[POLICEMAN *runs out, just as* POLICE SUPERINTENDENT *rushes
in. They collide.*]

MAYOR. Where in hell have you been? What kind of invisible
Police Superintendent are you?

SUPERINTENDENT. I was just outside the door all the while.

MAYOR. Listen, Ukhavyortov. That spy is here from St. Petersburg. What arrangements have you made?

SUPERINTENDENT. Just as you ordered. I've dispatched the
sweepers to clean the streets.

MAYOR. But where is Derzhimorda?

SUPERINTENDENT. Uh, he's driven off with the fire pump. . . .

MAYOR [*betrayed*]. But you told me the wheel was broken?

SUPERINTENDENT. He had to see his poor old mother and
father.

MAYOR. You idiot! What if there's a fire?

SUPERINTENDENT. Oh, his father is a blacksmith—he'll *fix* the
wheel.

MAYOR. I'm surrounded by traitors! . . . Well, here's what
you have to do. The police lieutenant—tell him to stand
on the bridge. He's tall—that will make a good impression.
Then that old fence, near the shoemaker's, I want you to
tear it down and scatter the boards around and then put up
a pole with a sign on it: NEW STREET UNDER CONSTRUC-
TION. The more destruction we have, the more it'll show
we're building! The best thing would be to tear down the
whole damn town! . . . Good God!—I forgot! That fence!
There are about forty cartloads of rubbish dumped behind
it. . . . What a filthy town this is! No matter where you
put a fence or even a monument, somebody always collects
rubbish and dumps it there! Where in hell do they find it

all? . . . Listen, if the Inspector asks any of my officials if they're satisfied with conditions, they're to say, "Perfectly, your honor." And if anybody is *not* satisfied, I'll give him something to be dissatisfied about! [*Sighs wearily.*] Oh, I'm a sinner, a terrible sinner! [*Takes the hatbox instead of his hat.*] Heaven only grant that I get out of this trap, and I'll give a candle for a thank-offering such as our cathedral has never seen before. Every goddamn merchant in town will donate a hundred pounds of wax for that candle! . . . Oh, God, God! . . . Let's be off, Dobchinski. [*Puts on the hatbox instead of the hat.*]

SUPERINTENDENT. That's not your hat!

MAYOR [*throwing the box down*]. Damn it—I know *that*. . . . And another thing.—If the Inspector asks why the hospital chapel was never built—the money was appropriated five years ago—everybody has to say the building was started all right, but it burned down. Don't you remember? I drew up the report on the fire myself! . . . Come on, come on, Dobchinski. [*He rushes out, and runs back in again.*] And another thing—I don't want those soldiers running around in the streets half-dressed. Those rookies put on their jackets over their shirts, all right, but then they're too lazy to put on their pants! It looks sloppy, damn it!

[*All go out.* ANNA ANDREYEVNA *and* MARYA ANTONOVNA *hurry in from another door.*]

ANNA. Where are they, where are they? Oh, my goodness! [*Opening another door.*] Husband! Anton! Where are you? [*To* MARYA.] It's all your fault, fussing around—"I need a pin, I want a handkerchief!" [*Runs to window and yells out.*] Anton! Where are you going? Has he come—the Inspector? What does he look like? Does he have a mustache?

VOICE OF THE MAYOR. Later, dear—wait a while.

ANNA. What do you mean, wait? I want only one word out of you—is he a general or not? [*Disgusted.*] There you are— he's gone! Oh, he won't get away with *that*! [*To* MARYA]. And *you*! Primping and chattering: "Mamma, dear, wait a minute while I pin my scarf; I'll be ready in a moment!" Moment my foot! It's all your fault we've missed this big news. Vanity, sheer vanity! You heard the Postmaster was here, so you had to preen in front of the mirror, and stare at yourself this way and that way. You really think he's sweet on you! Why, you silly girl, he smirks as soon as you turn your back.

MARYA. There's no need to go on screaming, Mamma. We'll get all the details in an hour or so.

ANNA. An *hour* or so! That's a *great* answer!—We'll know it all in a month, you mean. [*She leans out the window.*] Oh, Avdotya dear! . . . Have you heard anything about a stranger in town, sweetie? . . . No? Well, that shows what a fool you are. You should have asked. . . . What? They went off in a hurry? Well, you should have run after the carriage! Go right now, do you hear? Run and ask everybody you meet—but do it discreetly—and find out all about him—what sort of eyes he has, if they're black or what. And come back here right away, you understand . . . sweetie? [*Aside.*] What a stupid moron! . . . Hurry up, hurry up!

[*She continues shouting and they both stand at the window as the scene ends.*]

Scene 2

HLESTAKOV'S *tiny room at the inn, furnished with a broken-down bed, table and chair. A satchel, empty bottles, books, clothes brush are scattered around the room.*

OSIP [*lounging on his master's bed*]. I'm so hungry there's a barrage in my belly like a whole battery of cannon! Two months since we left St. Pete and I'm damned if I see how we'll ever get back. He threw away all his cash on this trip, that dumb dog, and now he's stuck here—with his tail between his legs. We had enough to take care of the fare, but oh no! He has to put on a big show in every town, high-class style. [*Imitating Hlestakov.*] "Oh, I say, Osip! Engage the best lodgings they have. And order the most exquisite meal on the menu. You know, I can't endure anything cheap or shoddy." The boy's lost his head—he's only a pencil-pusher, fourteenth rank, in the Civil Service. If they had a fifteenth, he'd be it. And he picks up pals on the road, and he has to play cards—and gets gypped, naturally. I'm sick of this crazy life. It was a lot better in my hick town—not so much going on, but there's a lot less to worry you. You lay around all day near the stove and eat hot rolls. . . . Ah, but there's nothing like life in St. Pete, that's a fact, and I can't kid myself. All you need is money, and you live like a noble—theatres, dancing dogs, any little thing you want. And everybody so polite. If you go to the bazaar, the shopkeepers call you My Lord. . . . Then some old officer's wife tries to pick you up, or a pretty chamber-maid gives you a wink. Oh, you gay dog! [*Smirks and wags his head.*] If you're tired of walking, why you rent a carriage and ride around like a real gent. And if you don't feel like paying—every house has an open door; you sneak in one and out the other so fast the devil himself couldn't grab you. Only trouble is, sometimes you eat first-class and sometimes you starve, like now. The old man sends him money—enough to get by—and what happens? He goes on a binge, and in a week I have to sell his new coat. Such beautiful English cloth! Every suit costs him a hundred and fifty rubles, and he lets it go for twenty. All because he never goes to his office! Instead of sticking to his job, he's out following women on the boulevards or he sneaks off to play cards. Oh, if your old man ever finds out! He'll lift your little shirt-tail and spank you so hard you wouldn't sit at a card table for a week. . . . Now the innkeeper says he won't let us have one bone to chew unless that dumb dog pays in advance—and what's going to happen if he *don't* pay? [*With a sigh.*] Oh, Christ, if I only had a little borscht! I'll bet everybody else in this dump is eating except me. . . . Oh, oh! He's coming. . . . [*He jumps off the bed just as* HLESTAKOV *comes in.*]

HLESTAKOV. Here, take these. [*Hands his hat and cane to* OSIP.] So you've been rolling around on my bed again?

OSIP. Me? Roll on your bed? What for?

HLESTAKOV. Stop lying. Look how it's all wrinkled.

OSIP. I've got two legs—I can stand on them. What do I need your bed for?

HLESTAKOV [*searching the room*]. Is there any tobacco left?

OSIP. Tobacco? You know you smoked it all four days ago!

HLESTAKOV [*pacing up and down, biting his lip, then loudly and peremptorily*]. Listen, Osip. Are you listening to me?

OSIP. What do you want?

HLESTAKOV [*less sure of himself*]. I want you to go down there . . .

OSIP. Down where?

HLESTAKOV [*almost pleading*]. Down to the dining room. . . . tell them, uh . . . we need some food. . . .

OSIP. Oh no, I won't.

HLESTAKOV. What? You dare disobey me, you blockhead!

OSIP. You watch who you call a blockhead! . . . What's the

use? . . . if I go down there, they wouldn't serve you
nothing. The boss says your food is cut off.

HLESTAKOV. He wouldn't dare say that!

OSIP. Is that so? He said, "I'm going to see the Mayor. This
is the third week your master hasn't paid his bill. You're a
couple of fakers, and what's more—your master is a good-
for-nothing bum!" That's what he said.

HLESTAKOV. You don't have to look so happy about it!

OSIP. That's not all. He said, "Yah, I know that kind. They
come around here, make themselves at home, run up a big
bill and then I can't collect. I'm not kidding," he says. "I'm
going to sign a complaint and have him thrown right into
jail."

HLESTAKOV. Now stop talking like a fool. Just go and speak
to the proprietor nicely—that foul-mouth pig!

OSIP. Maybe I oughtta call him and let *you* talk.

HLESTAKOV. I wouldn't talk to him! You go—you understand
him. . . .

OSIP [*innocently*]. But I wouldn't know what to say.

HLESTAKOV. Oh, damn it! Call him—see if I care!

[OSIP *shuffles out.*]

HLESTAKOV. I'm starving to death! I'll just lie down and die.
I took a little walk to take my mind off my appetite, but it's
worse now. My stomach's full of flapping vultures! . . .
That infantry captain in Penza certainly cleaned me out!
Didn't take him more than fifteen minutes to pluck me like
a chicken. I wish I could take him on again—with *my*
cards. But I suppose I never will now. . . . What a beastly
little town this is! They won't give you any food on credit.
[*He whistles an incomprehensible tune.*] The innkeeper will
never come. Nobody wants to climb all the way up here.

[OSIP *and a sullen* WAITER *enter.*]

WAITER. Boss wants to know what's on your mind.

HLESTAKOV. Ah, good day, my friend. And how are you?
How's business? Doing nicely?

WAITER. Very nice.

HLESTAKOV. Plenty of guests?

WAITER. We got enough.

HLESTAKOV. Look here, my friend. My dinner hasn't been
sent up yet, so would you please hurry it? I have an important engagement immediately after dinner.

WAITER. Boss says you don't get no more service. He was going to see the Mayor today with a complaint.

HLESTAKOV. A complaint? About *me*? Whatever for? . . . Now, my good fellow, if this dreadful service continues, I shall dissolve into a skeleton. I'm not joking any more with your boss. . . .

WAITER. He ain't jokin' either. Boss says, "No dinner till he coughs up for what he swallowed already."

HLESTAKOV. Tell him it's a matter of life or death! He seems to think that because he's a peasant who can go all day without food—everybody can. That sort of thinking will ruin his business.

[WAITER *shrugs and goes out with* OSIP.]

HLESTAKOV. What a way to die—by slow starvation! I can feel the wings of the angel of death hovering over me! Wonder if I could pawn my pants? . . . No, I'd rather starve than come home without style. . . . I really ought to drive into St. Petersburg in an elegant hired rig, with the carriage lamps glowing and Osip behind, in livery. Oh, how the society belles will flutter with excitement! "Who's *that*? How handsome!" Then my footman goes up in his gold livery [*Draws himself up to imitate him.*] and announces, "Ivan Alexandrovich Hlestakov!" And then I glide up to the prettiest girl and murmur, "How charmed I am, my dear. *Charmant!*" [*Bows as if kissing a hand, then catches at his stomach.*] Oh, my God! I'm sick! I'm really going to die!

[OSIP *enters happily, followed by the* WAITER.]

HLESTAKOV [*to* OSIP]. I forbid you to be so damned cheerful!

OSIP. He got your dinner.

HLESTAKOV [*claps his hands and sits quickly in his chair*]. Aha! Dinner! Dinner! Haha!

WAITER [*with plates and a napkin*]. This is the last time the boss is feeding you.

HLESTAKOV. The boss? My good fellow, I spit on your boss! Now, what have you brought me?

WAITER. Soup and roast beef.

HLESTAKOV. Only two courses?

WAITER. That's all.

HLESTAKOV. I won't put up with it! What does he mean by this? It's not enough.

WAITER. Boss says it's too much.

HLESTAKOV. But there isn't even a sauce!

WAITER. That's right.

HLESTAKOV. No cutlets—no salmon?

WAITER. No pay—no salmon.

HLESTAKOV. [*tastes the soup*]. Do you call that chicken soup? They just poured lukewarm water in a pot and let a chicken walk through with boots on! Bring some other soup!

WAITER. All right, I'll take it away. Boss says, if you don't like it, you can lump it.

HLESTAKOV [*holding onto his plate*]. If that's his attitude, I'll show him. I reject his insults! I'll eat this soup! And *you!* You may be a smart-aleck with other guests but don't try it on me. [*Swallowing soup hungrily.*] My God! what slop! Here are some feathers floating around! [*Comes across a tiny bit of chicken.*] Well, well!—a piece of chicken! That poor bird must have slipped. . . . Hand me the roast beef. There's some soup left, Osip. Possibly you can stomach it. [*Cuts the meat.*] Is *that* what you call roast beef?

WAITER. Yeh. What do you think it is?

HLESTAKOV. It's more like cold armor plate. [*Eats.*] Crooks and scoundrels! The slop they dish out! Why one mouthful is enough to make my jaw ache. [*Picks his teeth with his finger.*] Can't get it out—it's like iron filings! [*Wipes mouth with napkin.*] What else do you have?

WAITER. That's all.

HLESTAKOV. There should have been some pastry! So this is how you fleece your guests! Robber!

[WAITER *removes the dishes and goes out, followed by* OSIP.]

HLESTAKOV. I swear, I feel as if I hadn't eaten at all: it only sharpened my appetite. If I only had a few kopeks I'd send out for a roll.

OSIP [*returning*]. The Mayor just showed up—I can't figure why—and he's asking about you.

HLESTAKOV [*alarmed*]. *What?* There you are! That louse of an innkeeper has gone and turned me in! . . . What if they really haul me off to jail? I'll go—but with elegant style . . . like a French aristocrat, standing erect in the tumbril as he goes to the guillotine? . . . Oh, no! I couldn't. I've already caught the eye of a rich man's daughter—it would ruin the match. . . . Who in hell does that innkeeper think he is? He's got a lot of nerve treating me as if I were some shopkeeper or ditch-digger. [*Draws himself up to his full height.*] I'll just stand up to him and say, "How dare you try—"

[*The door handle is rattled.* HLESTAKOV *pales; his courage collapses. The* MAYOR *and* DOBCHINSKI *enter, the* MAYOR *leading. The* MAYOR *fumbles with his hat and stares from* DOBCHINSKI *to* HLESTAKOV, *afraid to begin.*]

MAYOR [*gathering his courage, stands at attention*]. I hope you are well, sir.

HLESTAKOV [*bowing*]. How do you do, sir.

MAYOR. Excuse the intrusion . . .

HLESTAKOV. Oh, don't mention it . . .

MAYOR. It is my duty, as chief magistrate of this town, to take proper measures to see that travelers and important persons don't suffer any inconvenience . . .

HLESTAKOV [*warily at first but gathering confidence as he goes along*]. Well, what was I to do? . . . It's not *my fault* . . . I assure you, I am . . . going to pay . . . I'm about to receive a remittance from home. [BOBCHINSKI *peeps in through open door.*] *He's* the one to blame! He sends me beef as stiff as cast iron! And the soup! I had to pour it out the window. . . . And the tea is most peculiar—it stinks of fish. And the fish has the consistency of tea! . . .

MAYOR [*nervously*]. I assure you it was not my fault! Our town market receives the best beef. I'm sure I don't know where the innkeeper gets his meat. But if anything's unsatisfactory, please come with me and we'll find better quarters.

HLESTAKOV. Oh, no I won't! I know exactly what "better quarters" means. It's another word for jail! . . . And what right have you? . . . How dare you? Why, I'm a government official from St. Petersburg. [*Defiantly.*] Yes, I am! I—I—

MAYOR [*aside*]. Oh, my God! How angry he is! He knows everything! Those pig shopkeepers must have squealed!

HLESTAKOV [*aggressively, snaps his fingers*]. *That's* for you and your whole gang! I will not go with you. I will go straight to the Prime Minister! [*Bangs fist on table.*] What do you say to that?

MAYOR [*quivering all over*]. Take pity on me! I have a wife and small children! Don't ruin me!

HLESTAKOV. Do you expect me to go to Siberia just because you have a wife and small children? Oh, I like that—that's just lovely! [BOBCHINSKI *peeps in again, then disappears in terror.*] Oh no—thank you very much, but I will not budge!

MAYOR [*quaking*]. It was just my inexperience—so help me!—
just my inexperience . . . and inadequate funds. Judge
for yourself—the salary I get is hardly enough for tea and
sugar. And if I've taken any, ah . . . contributions, they
were *tiny* ones—something for the table, or possibly a coat
—a *short* coat. As for that sergeant's wife they say I had
flogged—she was whoring without a permit. But it's all a
lie anyhow—she never was flogged. My enemies made that
up! They're just waiting to murder me in cold blood.

HLESTAKOV [*bewildered*]. I don't know why you're rattling
on about your enemies or your affair with that sergeant's
widow. . . . But don't you dare try to flog *me!* I'll pay—
I'll pay the bill. But at the moment I'm strapped for cash.
Yes—that's the only reason I'm staying here—I find myself
temporarily short of funds.

MAYOR [*aside, relieved*]. What a sly operator! I don't know
where to start working on him. Well, it won't hurt to make
a wild stab. . . . [*Aloud.*] Ah, my friend, if you're so short
of cash, allow me to help you out—immediately. It's . . .
ah, my civic duty to assist gentlemen travelers.

HLESTAKOV [*eagerly*]. Then lend me—oh, a pittance—just
enough to settle with my host. I'll need two hundred rubles,
more or less.

[*The* MAYOR *immediately presses a wad of bills into his hand.*]

MAYOR. Exactly two hundred. You don't even have to count it.

HLESTAKOV. I'm very obliged to you! I'll return it as soon as
I arrive at my country house. . . . Just a case of stupidity
on the part of my financial secretary. You are, indeed, a
great gentleman. Everything's quite satisfactory now.

MAYOR [*aside*]. Well, thank God, he took the money. I guess
now it'll all be smoothed over . . . but maybe I was a
little too eager to slip him four hundred instead of two. . . .

HLESTAKOV. Say, Osip! [OSIP *enters.*] Call the waiter. [*To*
MAYOR *and* DOBCHINSKI.] But why are you still standing?
Please, take a seat.

MAYOR. Oh, no . . . we'll just stand.

HLESTAKOV. Please, please be seated. I see now your utter
generosity and sincerity. I must confess I thought when
you first came in you intended to—[*To* DOBCHINSKI.] Take
a chair—I insist!

[MAYOR *and* DOBCHINSKI *finally sit down.* BOBCHINSKI *looks
in at the door and listens.*]

MAYOR [*aside*]. He wants to keep his incognito. All right. [*Aloud.*] I was just going around inspecting, with Peter Dobchinski—he's a landowner here—and we stopped at this inn to see how travelers are treated. I'm not like other mayors who don't pay attention to these important details. But aside from that, out of pure Christian charity, I want every human being to be well treated. And you see? . . . as a reward for doing good, I have the opportunity to make such a pleasant acquaintance!

HLESTAKOV. I'm delighted, too. Without your kind help, I must confess, I might have been trapped here for days. I hadn't the foggiest notion of how I would raise the cash.

MAYOR [*aside*]. Listen to that! Didn't know how he was going to pay! Ha! [*Aloud.*] May I ask where you are going from here?

HLESTAKOV. I am on my way to Saratov province, to my own estate.

MAYOR [*aside, with deep irony*]. To Saratov province! Oh, I'll bet you are! And he doesn't even blush. You have to keep a sharp eye on this fellow. [*Aloud.*] I'm sure you'll enjoy the trip. It's a most pleasant way to stretch your mind. You're traveling for your own amusement, I suppose?

HLESTAKOV. Oh no, it's my father's idea. The old man is mad because, so far, I haven't climbed very high in the civil service. He thinks that the minute you get to St. Petersburg, they hang a medal on you. I'd like to send *him* there, see how fast he gets shoved around in a government office.

MAYOR [*aside*]. Just listen to that fairy tale—and he has to drag in his old father, too. [*Aloud.*] May I ask, are you going to stay there for a while?

HLESTAKOV. I really don't know. You see, the old man is as stubborn as a chunk of wood. I intend to make it quite clear: "You can do as you please, father, but I absolutely cannot live away from St. Petersburg!" Why should I receive a life sentence to rot away among the yokels? That's not *living*—my soul demands the civilized world.

MAYOR [*aside*]. This fellow is a virtuoso—he's the *liar's* liar! But he's sure to make a little slip. I'll just give him more rope. . . . [*To* HLESTAKOV.] You're right—my friend. What can any man with brains accomplish in a provincial town? You work and sweat for the good of your country, you lie awake at night *thinking*, and what reward do you get?— complete misunderstanding! [*Looks about the room.*] Rather damp here, isn't it?

HLESTAKOV. Yes, it is a shabby hole. And the bugs! I've never seen anything like them—they bite like dogs.

MAYOR. Oh, no! Tsk, tsk. What a way to treat a distinguished visitor! To welcome him with disgusting insects, that shouldn't even be alive! And I suppose this room is dark, too?

HLESTAKOV. The innkeeper has a quaint custom of refusing me candles. Now and then I want to read—or work on my novel—but, oh what a bore—it's dark as a well-hole.

MAYOR. I wonder if I could ask you—oh, no! I'm not worth it. . . .

HLESTAKOV. What do you mean?

MAYOR. No, no. I don't deserve the honor. . . .

HLESTAKOV. What honor?

MAYOR. I hope you won't think I'm being presumptuous but . . . I have a charming little room at home you might like . . . comfortable and full of light . . . but it's too great an honor. Don't be offended, sir— I only wanted to help. . . .

HLESTAKOV. Why, of course! I'll accept with pleasure. I know I'll be much more comfortable in a private home than in this pest house.

MAYOR. Oh, thank you, bless you! My wife will be delighted. It's a little failing I have—I always was hospitable, even when I was a child. Especially when my guest is so distinguished and civilized. And don't think I say this just to butter you up. Oh no—I don't have *that* vice. I welcome you from the bottom of my heart.

HLESTAKOV. Thank you so much. I hate two-faced people. I'm impressed with your plain speaking and generosity, and I assure you I don't expect much. All I ask is to be treated with consideration and . . . a bit of respect. Yes, that's all—a bit of respect.

[*Enter the* WAITER, *escorted by* OSIP. BOBCHINSKI *peeps in again.*]

WAITER. What'd you want?

HLESTAKOV. The bill.

WAITER. I gave you a bill.

HLESTAKOV. Oh, I can't remember your idiotic figures! Just tell me the total. [*Brings out the wad of bills the* MAYOR *gave him.*]

MAYOR. Don't let it upset you. [*To* WAITER.] Get out! The money will be sent to you.

HLESTAKOV. That's the way to handle 'em. Yes, you're quite right! [*He puts the bills back in his pocket. The* WAITER *goes out.* BOBCHINSKI *looks in again.*]

MAYOR. Would you like to inspect a few of our town's high spots? Such as the hospital?

HLESTAKOV. Hospital? What would I see there?

MAYOR. You'll see how we manage things . . . our smooth system.

HLESTAKOV. Oh, certainly, certainly . . . [BOBCHINSKI *puts his head in again.*]

MAYOR. Afterward you might like to look in at the town jail—

HLESTAKOV [*uneasy*]. The jail? Why go there?

MAYOR. To see how we take good care of criminals.

HLESTAKOV. No, let's just look into the hospital.

MAYOR. Whatever you wish. Do you prefer to ride in your carriage—or in mine?

HLESTAKOV. In yours, by all means.

MAYOR [*to* DOBCHINSKI.] I'm afraid there's no room for you.

DOBCHINSKI. Oh, I can squeeze in.

MAYOR [*aside to* DOBCHINSKI]. Listen, I want you to run as fast as you can with a couple of notes—to the hospital and my wife. [*To* HLESTAKOV.] Do you mind if I send a word to my wife now, so that she can prepare to receive her honored guest?

HLESTAKOV. But why all this fuss? . . . There's the ink. I don't know about paper, though . . . [*Looks around room.*] How about this bill? [*Hands him the paper previously left by the* WAITER.]

MAYOR. That's just the thing! [*Talks to himself as he writes.*] We'll see how things go after lunch and a nice fat bottle or two. We'll have some local wine—not much to look at but it can roll a mule under the table. Then maybe I'll find out who he really is—and how much he knows.

[*He hands the notes to* DOBCHINSKI, *who runs to the door just as it suddenly breaks off its hinges.* BOBCHINSKI, *who has been eavesdropping behind it, falls on the floor atop the door, his arms outstretched. Cries of surprise.* BOBCHINSKI *slowly picks himself up.*]

HLESTAKOV. What's this? Are you hurt?

BOBCHINSKI. Oh, nothing, nothing, sir. Nothing to worry about—just a little crack on the nose. [*Smiles wanly.*] I'll run over to Doctor Hubner—he has some special plaster. I'll live.

MAYOR [*gesturing angrily to* BOBCHINSKI *as he talks to* HLESTAKOV]. Oh, it doesn't matter, sir. If you're ready, let's be off. Your man can bring your bags over. [*To* OSIP.] Take everything over to my house—the Mayor's. Just ask anybody—they'll show you. [*He makes way for* HLESTAKOV.] After you, sir, after you. [*As soon as* HLESTAKOV *exits, he turns angrily on* BOBCHINSKI.] You muttonhead! Did you have to break down the door? What if you had landed on the Inspector? . . . Oh, God help me—I'm surrounded by assassins!

[*He pushes* BOBCHINSKI *out ahead of him.*]

Scene III

ANNA *and* MARYA *are standing at the window in the Mayor's house, in the same position as at the end of Scene I.*

ANNA. We've been waiting a whole hour, all because of your stupid vanity! You were all dressed but still you had to dawdle around. . . . Oh, dear! And what's become of Avdotya? I send her on an important mission and she's probably gossiping in the square. How exasperating! . . . Not a soul in sight. It looks as if the whole town has been hit by a plague.

MARYA. Now, now, Mamma. We'll know all about it in a minute or two. Avdotya *has* to come back. [*Looks out window and squeals.*] Oh, Mamma, Mamma! See! Someone is coming—way down there at the end of the street!

ANNA. Who's coming? Where? You're always seeing things! . . . Ah, yes . . . Now, who can it be? He's short—in a dress coat. How frustrating? Who the devil is it?

MARYA. It's Dobchinski, Mamma.

ANNA. Dobchinski? Another one of your wild visions! It certainly is *not* Dobchinski. [*Waves her handkerchief.*] I say there—you! Come here—quick.

MARYA. Mamma, it really *is* Dobchinski.

ANNA. Must you contradict me every time? I've told you, it is *not* Dobchinski!

MARYA. Mamma, can't you see? It *is* Dobchinski.

ANNA. Oh, so it is . . . but why did you have to argue about it? [*Shouts out the window.*] Hurry up! My, how slow you walk! Well, where are they? You can tell me from where you are. What? Has he been tough? Eh? . . . [*Moves away from the window, disgusted.*] What a pretentious creature! He won't say a word till he comes in! [DOBCHINSKI *runs in, breathless.*] Now, aren't you ashamed of yourself? I used to think you were the only one in the group who's a gentleman. Then they all dash off—and *you* after them. I've been marooned here for ages, without a soul to tell me what's going on! You've been just horrid. I was godmother to your little Ivan and Lisa, and this is the way you repay me!

DOBCHINSKI. I swear, dear lady. I ran so fast to pay my respects that I'm all out of breath. [*He takes a deep breath and bows formally.*] I have the honor to greet you, Marya Antonovna.

MARYA. Good afternoon to you, Peter Ivanovich.

ANNA. Tell me, tell me! What's happened?

DOBCHINSKI. Your husband sent this note.

ANNA. But what is he—a general?

DOBCHINSKI. Not quite—but just as important. What manners—what dignity!

ANNA. That's just what Chmikov's letter to my husband said.

DOBCHINSKI. Exactly. And, remember, Bobchinski and I were the first to spot him.

ANNA. Good for you. Now tell me about it.

DOBCHINSKI. I will . . . God help us, everything's smoothed out now. At first he was really rough with your husband. Believe me, madame, he was *angry*. He said the inn was shabby and he wouldn't go to your house, either, and then he swore he wouldn't go to Siberia for your husband. But when he found out how innocent your husband was, he changed his mind and then, thank God, everything went well. They're out inspecting the hospital now. . . . I have to admit your husband thought a secret complaint had been filed against him. I was a little scared myself.

ANNA. You're not an official. Why should you be scared?

DOBCHINSKI. That's how I am—sympathetic.

ANNA. Well, the most important thing is—what does he look like? Is he young or old?

DOBCHINSKI. Oh, young. Very young—about twenty-three. But he speaks like a mature man of the world. "All I ask," he says, "is to be treated with a little respect." [*Gesticulating.*] All this with a most aristocratic poise. "Now and then I like to read—or work on my novel, but oh, what a bore," he says, "my room is as dark as a well-hole!" [MARYA *gasps.*]

ANNA. But what does he *look* like—dark or fair?

DOBCHINSKI. Sort of in between. His eyes flash like a wild beast's—they made me jittery.

ANNA. Hm . . . let's see what Anton's note says. [*She reads.*] "I want you to know, dear, that I was in a tight hole, but relying on the mercy of God, two pickles on the side and a half portion of caviar—one ruble 25 kopeks—" [*Baffled.*] What the devil is he babbling about—God and pickles . . . ?

DOBCHINSKI. Anton wrote it on the back of the waiter's bill.

ANNA. Lately he doesn't make sense, either . . . [*Reads on.*] "But relying on the mercy of God . . . it's all right now. Get a room ready right away—the one with the gold wallpaper—for our distinguished guest. Don't bother to lay out anything extra for dinner; we'll have lunch at the hospital with Artemi Philippovich. But order some domestic wine. Tell Abdulin to send his best or I'll smash his whole cellar. I kiss your hand, my dear, and so on." Oh, my God! Not a minute to lose! [*She calls.*] Mishka!

DOBCHINSKI. [*runs to door and shouts*]. Mishka! Hey, Mishka!

[*The boy* MISHKA *shuffles in.*]

ANNA. Now, listen. Run over to Abdulin's. Wait, I'll give you a note. [*Writes and talks at the same time.*] Give this note to the coachman; he's to run with it to Abdulin's and pick up the wine. Then you come right back and get the gold room ready for our guest. Put in a bed, washstand, and everything. And don't forget to sweep off the mattress.

DOBCHINSKI. Well, I'll run along and see how the inspection is coming.

ANNA. Yes, by all means. [DOBCHINSKI *goes out.*] Now, Marya, we have to figure out our ensembles. He's a young dandy from the capital; we don't want to look small-townish, God forbid. So you'd better put on your blue dress with the little flounces.

MARYA [*exasperated*]. Oh, no, Mamma! The *blue?* I hate it! Old Lady Lyapkin-Tyapkin wears blue, and so does Zemlyanika's daughter. I want to put on my light pink.

ANNA. Your light pink? You're just trying to start an argument again! You'll look much better in blue because I intend to wear my best shade—buttercup yellow.

MARYA. Oh, Mamma, buttercup doesn't do anything for you at all!

ANNA [*temper rising*]. My buttercup doesn't do anything?

MARYA. It won't be right. Your eyes would have to be very dark to go with buttercup.

ANNA. How do you like *that!* Do you mean to say my eyes are
not dark? They're dark enough for all normal purposes!
How can they help not being dark? When I tell fortunes
with cards, don't I always draw the queen of *clubs?*

MARYA. I don't care. Your best color is the queen of *hearts.*

ANNA. Oh, pishtosh! I never was a queen of hearts! [*They go
out, but she can still be heard offstage.*] Queen of hearts!
Where do you get those stupid ideas? Certainly not from
your mother. . . .

[*As they go out, the door of side room opens and* MISHKA
appears, sweeping the dust. He sweeps it right into the face of
OSIP *who enters at center, carrying bags on his head.*]

OSIP [*angrily*]. Where's this go?

MISHKA. Here, Pop—this way. [*But he doesn't help with bags.*]

OSIP. Don't call me Pop. Hold it—let me catch my breath.
What a lousy life . . . on an empty stomach, every load feels
like your own coffin.

MISHKA. Say, Pop—is the general coming soon?

OSIP. What general?

MISHKA. Your boss.

OSIP. My boss a general? [*He bellows with laughter.*]

MISHKA. Ain't he a general?

OSIP. Oh, sure.

MISHKA. Is he higher or lower than Inspector General?

OSIP. He's both.

MISHKA. No wonder the old lady's raising hell today.

OSIP. I can see you're a real smart kid. How about slipping me
something to eat?

MISHKA. For a bigshot like you, Pop, nothin's ready that's
good enough. You wouldn't want the plain food. When your
boss sits down at the table, they'll toss you a bone.

OSIP [*restraining himself*]. Just tell me what that plain food is.

MISHKA. Borscht, kasha and meat pies.

OSIP. I'll take the borscht, kasha and meat pies. Now give me
a hand with the bags.

MISHKA [*blankly*]. Huh?

OSIP [*with a* HLESTAKOV *gesture*]. I'll take care of you later,
my boy. [*They carry the bags into the side room.*]

[*Both doors of the entrance are pushed open by the two*
POLICEMEN. HLESTAKOV *enters. After him come the* MAYOR,
COMMISSIONER OF CHARITIES, COMMISSIONER OF SCHOOLS, *and*
BOBCHINSKI *with a plaster on his nose. The* MAYOR *angrily*

indicates a scrap of paper on the floor to the POLICEMEN.
They rush about to pick it up and bump into each other.]

HLESTAKOV. Splendid institutions in this town. I'm charmed
by the way you show strangers everything! In other places
they didn't show me a single thing.

MAYOR. In other towns—if I may say so—the administrators
and officials are only concerned with their own advance-
ment. But here, I must admit, there is only one rule—to win
the recognition of St. Petersburg by good order and vigi-
lance.

HLESTAKOV. That was indeed a gourmet lunch. I'm afraid I
may have overeaten a bit. Do you have a banquet like that
every day?

MAYOR. Oh, no. It was in honor of our lovable guest.

HLESTAKOV. I certainly enjoyed that lunch. What does any
man live for but to pluck the flowers of pleasure! . . .
What was that fish called?

COMMISSIONER OF CHARITIES [*stepping forward*]. Salted cod.

HLESTAKOV. It was exquisite! And where did we lunch—in
the hospital?

COMMISSIONER OF CHARITIES. Exactly right, sir. In one of our
sick rooms.

HLESTAKOV. Oh, of course. I remember—there were beds. But
where were the patients? I didn't see many.

COMMISSIONER OF CHARITIES. Oh, about ten—no more. The
rest have all recovered. You see, the hospital is so well-
organized it operates almost by itself. . . . It may seem incredible to you, sir, but ever since I became Commissioner,
the sick recover like . . . flies. We carry the patients in and
—as soon as they see the sick ward, they're well again.

MAYOR. And I'd like to point out what a nightmare job the
Mayor has. Every problem that comes to him has so many
ramifications, such as sanitation and repairs and street improvements. It's just one sewer after another . . . even a
man of superhuman knowledge could get into the most
hopeless snarl. But, God be thanked, everything here operates smoothly. Other mayors, I'm sure, are only lining
their own pockets with graft. But, believe me, when I lie
down to sleep, my only prayer is: "O Lord, my God, please
grant that the Government will see my zeal and be satisfied!" They may not reward me—that's up to them, of
course—but, my conscience is clear. When there's law and
order all through the town, when the streets are swept spot-

less, and the jailbirds are safely locked up, when you can count the drunkards on one hand—what more can I ask? I don't want any medals. They are alluring, I'm sure, but to the upright man they are as dust!

COMMISSIONER OF CHARITIES [*aside*]. Listen to that old crook pour it on! It's a gift from heaven. . . .

HLESTAKOV [*awed*]. How true. I don't mind saying I also have a bent for philosophy. Sometimes it's in prose—and sometimes I toss off verses.

BOBCHINSKI [*to* DOBCHINSKI]. Did you hear that? How very well that was put.

DOBCHINSKI. What insight! Oh, you can see he's been to the university.

HLESTAKOV. Oh, I say—do you have any amusements here? Places where, for instance, one could relax with a spot of cards?

MAYOR [*aside*]. Ah, my little pigeon . . . I can see where you're aiming. . . . [*Aloud.*] Heaven forbid! Why, we've never heard of a card club here. I've never dealt a hand of cards in my life . . . I can't even stand to *look* at cards! Why, if I ever happen to see a king of diamonds or something like that—in someone's house—I'm overcome by such a feeling of disgust, I have to spit! [*Shudders.*] I remember one time, just to please the children, I built them a little house of cards. And, do you know what? All night those cursed images made me toss and groan in my sleep!

COMMISSIONER OF SCHOOLS [*aside*]. Why, that sharper took me for a hundred at faro yesterday!

HLESTAKOV. Oh, we mustn't sneer at cards—actually they're like a mathematics exercise.

[ANNA *and* MARYA *bustle in.*]

MAYOR. May I take the liberty of introducing my wife and daughter?

HLESTAKOV [*bowing to each*]. How fortunate I am, madame, to have this pleasure of meeting you.

ANNA. Meeting such a distinguished person is a far greater pleasure for *us*.

HLESTAKOV [*with a gallant gesture*]. Oh, no. I insist—the pleasure is much more mine.

ANNA. Oh, impossible, sir. You're just saying that to be gallant. It's my pleasure! Please, do sit down.

HLESTAKOV. To stand near you is happiness enough. However,

if you insist, I will sit. What a lucky man I am to sit by your side!

ANNA. Oh, sir. I don't dare take that as anything more than big city flattery. . . . I suppose you've found traveling quite unpleasant after the gay life of the capital?

HLESTAKOV. Terribly. After being accustomed, *comprenez-vous,* to high society, to find myself thrust into filthy inns, in the depths of barbarism . . . I must admit, if it weren't for the luck . . . [*Stares meaningfully at* ANNA.] which repays me for all that—

ANNA. How dreadfully unpleasant it must have been!

HLESTAKOV. Oh, but madame, right now I find it quite pleasant.

ANNA. Oh, sir, you do me too much honor. I don't deserve it.

HLESTAKOV. Why not? If I say it, you deserve it.

ANNA. Even if I only live in . . . barbarian country?

HLESTAKOV. Oh, the country has its own charm—hills and dales you know. Of course, you simply can't compare it to St. Petersburg. Ah, Petersburg—what a life! You might think I'm just a minor cog there but, on the contrary—I'm on the friendliest terms with the chief of my department. Why, he slaps me on the back and says, "Come on, let's have lunch, my friend!" I look into the place only a few minutes now and then, just to give a few orders, "Do it this way—phrase it that way . . ." And then my clerk—what a mouse he is!—scribbles away for dear life. [*He imitates a pen scratching paper.*] Why, they even wanted to make me an assistant bureau chief—it's quite obvious I'm the fair-haired boy. And the porter runs after me on the stairs with a brush: "Oh, allow me, sir, to shine your boots." [*To* MAYOR.] But why do you stand, gentlemen? Please, sit down.

MAYOR. Oh, we don't rank that high—we'll stand.

COMMISSIONER OF CHARITIES. I'd feel better standing. . . .

COMMISSIONER OF SCHOOLS. Oh, don't worry about us!

HLESTAKOV. No ceremony! I insist—sit down! [*They sit slowly.*] I don't like protocol. On the contrary, I always try to avoid stiff state functions. But it's impossible to hide oneself. Quite impossible. No matter where I go, they call out, "There goes Ivan Alexandrovich!" Once they even took me for the Commander in Chief. All the soldiers rushed out of the guardhouse and saluted! Yes, sir, one officer, whom I knew very well, said to me afterward, "I could have sworn you were the Commander in Chief."

ANNA. You don't say!

HLESTAKOV. I'm quite close to most of the pretty, up-and-coming actresses—you see, I write all sorts of sketches for the stage. I'm on the inner circle of the literary set. Why, Pushkin and I are old pals. I often say to him, "Well, how's it going, Pushkin, old boy?" Oh, he's a rare bird, that one.

ANNA. You *write,* too? How delightful! Do you write for the papers?

HLESTAKOV. Oh, I toss off some things for them, too. I write in so many fields . . . operas—*Marriage of Figaro* . . . *Robert the Devil* . . . *Norma*—and some others I've forgotten about. I somehow fell into it. I didn't want to fool around with the stage, but a manager I knew kept bothering me, "Come on, write something for me, old boy!" So I thought, "Why not?" I dashed off "Figaro" in one day. Or was it two? . . . Oh, I have a prolific flow of ideas. I also work under the name of Baron Brambeus for the Moscow *Telegraph*—

ANNA. So *you're* Brambeus!

HLESTAKOV. Of course. And you know that sensational novel, *The Frigate of Hope?* It came out under the pseudonym Marlinski. That was me—I mean, I. As for most of the top-rank poets—why Smirdin, the publisher, pays me forty thousand a year to polish their stuff.

ANNA. Then *you* must have written *Yuri Miroslavski.*

HLESTAKOV. One of my minor efforts.

ANNA. I knew it right away!

MARYA. But Mamma, it says on the title page the author is Zagoskin.

ANNA. There you go again—trying to start an argument . . .

HLESTAKOV. That's true. There is a *Yuri Miroslavski* by a Zagoskin. He stole my title.

ANNA. I'm sure I read *yours.* What lovely writing.

HLESTAKOV. My salon is the most exquisite and famous in St. Petersburg. Everyone tries to crash it. Because of my cutting wit, I'm called . . . Ivan the Terrible! [*Suddenly, to the group.*] If any of you ever visit St. Petersburg, you must be sure to visit me. I insist on it. . . . I give lavish fancy dress balls, too.

ANNA. I can imagine the good taste and magnificence!

HLESTAKOV. Really impossible to describe. The centerpiece, for example, is a watermelon made into a fountain, with bubbling watermelon juice! It sets me back seven hundred rubles. The soup comes straight from Paris by steamer in my own tureen. Oh, there's nothing in the world to compare with the aroma! I'm forced to go out in the social whirl every evening. And we have our whist club . . . the Foreign Minister . . . the French Ambassador . . . the German Ambassador, myself. Oh, it can be an exhausting bore. They insist on fighting duels with me because of their poor luck . . . and so the government has to put up with a constant flow of new ambassadors. . . . Most nights, it's all I can do to stagger home, and up four flights of stairs, and murmur, "Here, Mavrusha, take my coat before I expire!" Did I say fourth floor? I live on the first floor, of course. . . . You see, I'm still in a daze from my harsh travels. Why, that staircase alone cost me—it's simply priceless! It's studded with my coat of arms in precious stones. . . . And you really ought to see my waiting room: counts and princes jostling and hovering around there like bees. All you can hear is buzz, buzz, buzz. Why, once the Prime Minister was there! . . . [*The* MAYOR *and others rise out of their chairs, alarmed.*] Why, one time I took charge of an entire Department. That was an amusing story. The Director had gone off somewhere—disappeared —nobody knew where. Naturally, people began to whisper: how could his job be filled? Who would be the unlucky man? I say unlucky, because any number of generals tried it and flopped. It looked easy enough, but when they got right down to it, it was fiendishly complicated. The upshot was—I was the government's last resort. They had to come to *me*. Instantly the streets were choked with messengers, and messengers and more messengers! How's that for a crisis? "Ivan Alexandrovich," they begged me, "you must come and take over the Department!" I admit, I was a little hesitant. I went out to address them in my dressing gown, and I was all set to refuse, but then it occurred to me: what if the Emperor hears of this? And it won't look good on my service record, either. "Very well!" I said. "I'll *take* the job. I'll accept. But, remember—no nonsense from anybody! You'll have to be sharp! Sharp's my motto—sharp!" And that's the way it was. Every time I inspected the department, it was like an earthquake: they all shivered and shook like aspen leaves. [*The* MAYOR *and others quake with terror.* HLESTAKOV *is transported by his own vehemence.*] Oh, I don't fool around with them, I tell you! I give those clowns hell! Even the Imperial Council is afraid of me. And why shouldn't they be? I am Ivan the Terrible! I don't attack any one man—I slash them all! I say, "Nobody can stop me! Nobody! I know my duty! I know my power!" My eyes are everywhere—*everywhere*! Every day I visit the Palace. Why, if I wanted it, they would make me a field marshal tomorrow—[*He slips off his chair and sprawls on the floor. The officials respectfully help him up.*]

MAYOR [*trembling all over*]. But your ex-ex—[*He chokes with fear.*]

HLESTAKOV [*sharply*]. What's the matter with you?

MAYOR. Your ex-ex—

HLESTAKOV. I can't understand a word you say. Don't talk nonsense.

MAYOR. Your Excellency . . . Your Highness. Wouldn't you like to take a little . . . rest? Your room is ready and—

HLESTAKOV. Rest? How dare you intimate I am drunk! [*He draws himself up erect.*] Your lunch, gentlemen, was excellent. I am delighted. [*He gives a stiff military salute.*] To salted cod! It was cod! Cod by God!

[*He bows low to the ladies and collapses. But* OSIP *is waiting right behind him, and catches him under the arms before he reaches the floor.*]

ALL [*in despair and surprise*]. Oh, heaven help us now! . . . Is he poisoned? . . . We are all destroyed! . . . Who got him drunk? . . . Anton! It's all Anton's doing! Anton made him sick. . . .

[*All eyes turn to the* MAYOR *and there is a moment of deathly silence.*]

MAYOR [*in anguish, shivering*]. I feel the cold wind of Siberia! . . . [*He sinks to his knees to pray.*]

ACT TWO

Scene 1

The same scene, a few moments later. The MAYOR, HLESTAKOV *and* OSIP *have disappeared.*

BOBCHINSKI. I nearly fainted from fright!

DOBCHINSKI. Let's go quick and warn the Judge and Karobkin! Good afternoon, Anna Andreyevna!

BOBCHINSKI. Good afternoon, my dears! [*Both run out.*]

COMMISSIONER OF SCHOOLS [*to* COMMISSIONER OF CHARITIES]. I could smell disaster coming! This fellow not only reads books—he *writes* them! The first thing he'll do when he wakes up is write a report to St. Petersburg. [*Suddenly.*] And we're not even in dress uniform! Oh, God help us!

COMMISSIONER OF CHARITIES. Perhaps we should have a formal reception for him. If he sees us all in uniform he will realize we are not barbarians.

COMMISSIONER OF SCHOOLS. Ah, yes. I'd better go now and have my uniform repaired. The cursed mice have nibbled away the seat of my pants.

COMMISSIONER OF CHARITIES [*groaning*]. We may never survive tomorrow!

COMMISSIONER OF SCHOOLS *and* COMMISSIONER OF CHARITIES [*to* ANNA, *as they hurry out*]. Good day, madam!

ANNA [*to* MARYA]. What an utterly charming young man that Inspector is!

MARYA. How delightful!

ANNA. What refinement! You can see he's spent his entire life in society. That dignity and everything. . . . Oh, how elegant! I'm easy prey for young men like that—I'm afraid he's swept me off my feet. I'm sure I made a hit with *him*, too. You noticed how he kept staring at me all the time?

MARYA. Oh, Mamma dear. He was staring at *me!*

ANNA. There you go, arguing again! *When* did he look at you, for goodness sake? *Why* should he ever look at you?

MARYA. Really, Mamma, he gave me the eye all night. When he started to talk about literature he was practically *hypnotizing* me, and when he told how he played whist with the ambassadors, I felt his eyes going up and down—Oh! [*She almost swoons.*]

ANNA. Well, maybe he did turn to you once or twice, but that was only to make it look right. He must have thought, "I'd better throw her a glance, just to protect Anna!"

MAYOR [*tiptoes in from* HLESTAKOV'S *room*]. Sh . . . sh . . .

ANNA. Well, well?

MAYOR. I'm worried—he really sopped up that wine. . . . If even half of what he claimed is true, we're in deep trouble. [*Thoughtfully.*] When a man is in his cups everything comes out. What's in his heart flies right to his tongue. . . . So he plays whist with ambassadors and hangs around the palace? . . . Damn it, the more I think about it—I feel as dizzy as if I were standing on top of a steeple—or [*Frightened.*] on a gallows and they were about to hang me.

ANNA. I didn't feel nervous at all. I merely saw in him an educated, polished, well-bred young man.

MAYOR. That's just like a woman! What could they do to you? —just flog you, that's all. But your poor husband—I may be sent away and never heard of again. And all the while you, my darling, treated this high official as if he was some old pal, another Dobchinski.

ANNA. You don't have to worry in that department. We know how to take care of him. [*Glances significantly at daughter.*]

MAYOR. Your kind of help I can only wish on my enemies! [*He opens door and calls off.*] Mishka, get those policemen —Svistunov and Dherzimorda. They're leaning on the gate. [*Closes door, pauses.*] What a mixed-up world this is! You should be able to tell if a man is important by his appearance. But no—this miserable, skinny kid! How can anyone figure out who he is? With a military man, it's easy —when he puts on civilian clothes he looks like a fly with its wings clipped. Well anyhow, before he passed out, he *looked* happy. . . .

[OSIP *enters from* HLESTAKOV'S *room. All run to him.*]

ANNA. Come over here, friend.

MAYOR. Ssh . . . Is he—is he still sleeping?

OSIP. Nah, he's stretching.

ANNA. Tell me. What's your name?

OSIP. Osip, ma'am.

MAYOR [*to wife and daughter*]. All right. That's enough now. [*To* OSIP.] My dear friend, did they take good care of you in the kitchen?

OSIP. Yes sir. I did all right. Thank you very much.

ANNA. Tell me, do a lot of counts and princes call on your master?

OSIP [*aside*]. Maybe if I say yes, I'll eat better. [*Aloud.*] Oh, yes, ma'am. Lots of counts come around. Counts . . . dukes . . . kings. . . .

MARYA. How handsome your master is!

ANNA. Tell me, please, how does he—?

MAYOR. You're only getting in my way with that fool talk. Now listen, my friend—

ANNA. But what is your master's rank?

OSIP. Oh, the regular rank . . .

MAYOR. Oh, good God! Must you rattle on with this stupid cross-examination? You don't make one point that could uncover anything. . . . Now, my good man. What is your master like? Strict, huh? Does he scold you, or beat you?

OSIP. Oh, yah. He likes everything in order. He wants everything just so.

MAYOR. You know, I like your face, Osip. I can see that you're a man I can trust. Now, what—

ANNA. Listen, Osip, what does your master wear in town— a dress uniform or—?

MAYOR. What a blabbermouth! I tell you, this is a matter of life and death. . . . [*To* OSIP.] Yes, sir. I like you a lot. I know an extra cup of tea on a trip is always welcome. And it's so cold now . . . how about a couple of rubles for tea?

OSIP [*taking the money*]. Yes, sir. Thank you kindly. God give you good health, you're a holy sight for a poor man's eyes.

MAYOR. It gives me great pleasure to help you. Now, my friend, what—?

ANNA.—color eyes does your master like best?

MARYA. Oh, Osip—your master has the most exciting little turned-up nose!

MAYOR. If you don't shut up, you'll have the reddest, turned-up bottom! [*To* OSIP.] Tell me, my good man where exactly does your master inspect— I mean, what pleases him most on his trips?

OSIP. Oh, he likes to see everything. Most of all, he likes to be glad-handed . . . you know, taken care of right.

MAYOR. Taken care of?

OSIP. Yah. I mean, I'm only a serf, see, but he makes sure I'm fixed up right. Let me tell you! We go some place, he says, "Well, Osip, how'd they take care of you?" And I comes right back with, "Oh, shabby, your excellency. Shabby." "Aha" he says. "Our host rates down at the bottom in my book. You remind me about that when we visit next time." And I thinks to myself, "God help that one!"

MAYOR. You speak right to the point. What I gave you before was for tea. Now here's something extra for cakes.

OSIP. Oh, you're too good, your highness. [*Pockets the money.*] I'll make sure I spend this drinking toasts to you.

ANNA. Come to me, Osip, and you'll get something more.

MARYA. Osip, dear, kiss your master for me!

[HLESTAKOV *is heard coughing in the next room.*]

MAYOR. Ssh! [*Walks on tiptoe; rest of scene is played in low voices.*] Good God, don't make a sound! [*To* ANNA.] That's enough. You can get out now.

ANNA. Let's go, Marya. I want to tell you something I noticed about our guest that I can only say in private. [*They go out.*]

MAYOR. Oh, they're at it again! You listen to them and you'd have to stop up your ears fast to keep from getting nauseous. [*To* OSIP.] Now that we're alone, my dear friend—

[*Enter* DERZHIMORDA *and* SVTSTUNOV.]

MAYOR. Sssh! Damn bowlegged bears, stomping around! You sound like you're throwing a body into the police wagon! What in hell took you so long?

DERZHIMORDA. My orders was—

MAYOR. Sssh! [*Puts hand over his mouth.*] My orders was!— for God's sake! Do you have to bellow like a bull in heat? [*To* OSIP.] Now, my good man, you can go and freshen up . . . order anything you want—the house is yours. [OSIP *goes out.*] Now you two bums. You stand on the front steps and don't budge. Don't let any stranger in the house—especially no shopkeepers. If you just let one slip past, I'll flog your skin off! And remember, if anybody comes up with a complaint, or even *without* one—if he only looks like the kind who *might* complain—you kick him right out! Headfirst! Like this! [*He demonstrates.*] You understand? Now ssh! [*He sighs worriedly, exits on tiptoe, following the* POLICEMEN.]

Scene II

The MAYOR'S *house, the next morning.*

Enter cautiously, the JUDGE, *the* COMMISSIONER OF CHARITIES, *the* COMMISSIONER OF SCHOOLS, *the* POSTMASTER, DOBCHINSKI *annd* BOBCHINSKI. *All are in full dress uniform. The scene is played in hushed voices.*

JUDGE [*arranging them in a semicircle*]. For God's sake, gentlemen, take your places quickly, and let's have some semblance of order! Good heavens, he knows everybody at the Court, and he bullies the Imperial Council! Line up with military precision. Chin up, pull your stomachs in! . . . Bobchinski, you stand there. Dobchinski—there! [*They run to their assigned places.*]

COMMISSIONER OF CHARITIES. But, Judge, we certainly should try something *positive*.

JUDGE. Positive?

COMMISSIONER OF CHARITIES. You know, a little palm oil.

JUDGE. He's liable to kick up a storm. After all, he's a State official. I believe it might better take the form of a testimonial from the nobility and the gentry. Some sort of souvenir.

POSTMASTER. How about, say—there's some money arrived at the post office—and we don't know who it's for?

COMMISSIONER OF CHARITIES. These matters should be arranged more smoothly in a well-run town. What's a whole regiment doing here? We ought to approach him individually . . . and conduct our business in private, so that nobody knows anything about anything. That's how a well-organized community operates. Judge—you ought to go first.

JUDGE. It would be more correct if it were *you*. The illustrious visitor broke bread at *your* hospital.

COMMISSIONER OF CHARITIES. No. No! It should be Luka Lukich, the man who enlightens youth.

COMMISSIONER OF SCHOOLS. I can't, gentlemen. Really I can't. I've had an unfortunate education. If anyone a single degree in rank above me, addresses me—my tongue seems to be stuck in glue. No, gentlemen, I really must be excused.

COMMISSIONER OF CHARITIES. You see, the only one who can bring it off is you, Judge. Why, your every word sounds as if Cicero himself were talking.

JUDGE. Nonsense! Cicero indeed! Just because one now and

then discourses on housedogs or greyhound puppies . . . ?

ALL [*surrounding him*]. Not just dogs! . . . You could have made sense out of the Tower of Babel, too! . . . Oh, no, Judge. Don't desert us. . . . We need a great mind to lead us! . . . Don't abandon us, Lyapkin-Tyapkin!

JUDGE. Let go of me, gentlemen!

[HLESTAKOV *is heard stumbling about in his room; he coughs and mumbles.* ALL *rush to the center door, squeezing and pushing to get out.*]

BOBCHINSKI'S VOICE. Owh! Dobchinski, you're standing on my corn!

COMMISSIONER OF CHARITIES. I'm smothering, smothering! Give me air before I pass out!

[*More cries of despair and pain until they all push out. The room is empty for a moment.* HLESTAKOV *comes out, yawning and sleepy.*]

HLESTAKOV. I must have had a pretty long snooze. . . . What a lovely featherbed! . . . Oh, my tongue, it feels like the dragoons have been marching over it. . . . I *like* this kind of hospitality. . . . That Mayor's daughter, she's not bad at all. And his wife, I mustn't neglect her, either. This sort of life just suits me perfectly. . . .

JUDGE [*enters, his eyes turned up to heaven*]. Oh, Lord, Lord! I know I've made some foolish statements about You before but, as one judge to another, You can't let me down. At least, stop my knees from knocking! [*Draws himself up and leans on his sword to steady himself.*] I have the honor to present myself: Judge of the District Court and College Assessor Lyapkin-Tyapkin.

HLESTAKOV. Do sit down. So, you are the judge here?

JUDGE [*sitting*]. I was chosen for that position for three years by the nobility and gentry in 1816—and I've continued in that office ever since.

HLESTAKOV. I dare say, you find the position . . . profitable?

JUDGE. After nine years, I was decorated with the Order of St. Vladimir, Fourth Class, with a commendation from my superiors. [*Aside.*] This money is burning a hole through my hand!

HLESTAKOV. Well, I *like* the Vladimir. It has much more color than the Anna of the Third Class.

JUDGE [*thrusting his clenched fist forward, as if in pain; aside*]. Oh, good Lord! I feel as if I'm sitting on hot, burning coals!

HLESTAKOV. What have you got in your hand?

JUDGE [*shaken, dropping money on the floor*]. Oh, no-nothing, Sir!

HLESTAKOV. Nothing? You've dropped some money.

JUDGE [*shaking all over*]. I?—impossible, sir! [*Aside.*] Oh, Lord! Now I'm in front of the judge. They've got the cart ready to take me to the hangman!

HLESTAKOV [*picking up the money*]. Why, so it is—it's money!

JUDGE. It's all over, now. I'm doomed, doomed!

HLESTAKOV. I wonder—could you *lend* me this?

JUDGE [*eagerly*]. If you wish, sir, if you would condescend to . . . with the greatest of pleasure! [*Aside.*] Stand by me, Holy Mother!

HLESTAKOV. I'm a bit low in cash—spent it all on the road for one thing or another . . . However, I'll reimburse you as soon as I reach my estate.

JUDGE. Oh, don't give it a second thought. The honor of serving you is enough. . . . Indeed, though my powers are feeble, still with all zeal and loyalty . . . I shall endeavor to serve. . . . [*Rises and stands at attention, hands at his sides.*] I will not presume to disturb you further with my presence. . . . Will there be any orders?

HLESTAKOV. Orders? What kind of orders?

JUDGE. I mean, will you issue any orders for the District Court?

HLESTAKOV. Why? I have nothing to say to your Court. Now, thank you very much.

JUDGE [*bowing as he exits, aside.*] Now the town is ours again!

HLESTAKOV. Good man—a gentleman of the old school.

[*POSTMASTER enters in full regalia, sword in hand. He comes to attention.*]

POSTMASTER. I have the honor to present myself: Postmaster and Court Councilor Shpyokin.

HLESTAKOV. Welcome! How nice to have so many callers so early. Have a seat. . . . So, you've always lived here?

POSTMASTER. Yes, sir.

HLESTAKOV. You know, I like this little town. Of course, it's not overly populated—but what of it? It's not the capital. Eh—that's true, isn't it—it's *not* the capital?

POSTMASTER. That's true. Exactly.

HLESTAKOV. It's only in the capital that one finds the *bon ton*, and escapes the country clodhoppers. What do you think?

POSTMASTER. You're exactly right, sir.

HLESTAKOV. After all, what does a man want out of life? In my opinion, all one wants is to have people respect one, and sincerely like one. Isn't that so?

POSTMASTER. Absolutely. Exactly.

HLESTAKOV. I'm glad we think the same way. I suppose some people may consider me eccentric—but that's the way I am. [*Aside.*] I might as well put the touch on him, too. [*Aloud.*] A strange thing happened to me on the way into town— I spent my last kopek. Could you lend me 300 rubles?

POSTMASTER. Of course! It will give me the greatest happiness. Here you are—take it, sir. Please . . . delighted to be of service.

HLESTAKOV. Thank you very much. You see, I have a dreadful fear of cramping myself when I'm traveling—and anyhow, why the devil should I? Isn't that right?

POSTMASTER. Oh, exactly. Yes, sir! [*Rises and comes to attention, hand on sword.*] I won't presume to disturb you further with my presence. . . . Do you have any suggestions . . . random thoughts on the postal administration?

HLESTAKOV. Not a single one.

[POSTMASTER *bows and exits.*]

HLESTAKOV [*lighting a cigar*]. The Postmaster seems to be very obliging, too. That's the kind of man I like.

[*There is a commotion offstage, and a voice is heard: "Go on, what are you afraid of?" A door is opened and the* COMMISSIONER OF SCHOOLS *is pushed into the room.*]

COMMISSIONER OF SCHOOLS [*saluting frantically, his hand on his sword*]. I have the honor to present myself: Commissioner of Schools and Honorary Councilor Hlopov!

HLESTAKOV. Ah, how do you do. Have a seat. Take a chair. Will you have a cigar? [*Offers one to him.*]

COMMISSIONER OF SCHOOLS [*Aside*]. I never thought of *that!* Should I take it?

HLESTAKOV. Take it, take it. It's not a bad brand. Of course, it's not what I'm accustomed to. In St. Petersburg I smoke only imported tobacco; when you inhale a puff you float up to heaven with the angels. Here's a match—light up. [*Gives him a match.* COMMISSIONER, *shaking all over, lights it*]. You're lighting the wrong end.

COMMISSIONER OF SCHOOLS [*throws cigar down, spits. Aside*]. Damn it—my nervousness ruins me every time!

HLESTAKOV. I see you're not very fond of cigars. Well, I admit they're one of my weaknesses. Not the only one, though. I'm rather susceptible to the charm of the fair sex. What's your taste—brunette or blonde?

[COMMISSIONER OF SCHOOLS *is stunned.*]

HLESTAKOV. Come on, out with it—brunette or blonde?

COMMISSIONER OF SCHOOLS. I wouldn't dare have an opinion.

HLESTAKOV. Oh, now, don't weasel out of it that way. I'm interested in *your* taste.

COMMISSIONER OF SCHOOLS. I'm too shy, Your Nob . . . Excell . . . enity! [*Aside.*] My confounded tongue has betrayed me for sure!

HLESTAKOV. Too shy? Well, let me help you overcome that shyness . . . a funny thing happened to me on the way here. I ran out of cash. Could you lend me three hundred?

COMMISSIONER OF SCHOOLS [*aside, fumbling with his purse*]. Oh, oh! Do I have that much? . . . Ah, I do, I do! [*Takes out some bills and, trembling, hands them to* HLESTAKOV.]

HLESTAKOV. I'm deeply indebted to you.

COMMISSIONER OF SCHOOLS. I won't presume to disturb you further with my presence.

HLESTAKOV. Good-bye, then.

COMMISSIONER OF SCHOOLS [*sotto voce as he runs out*]. Thank heaven! He won't poke around the schools now.

[*Enter the* COMMISSIONER OF CHARITIES. *He stands at attention, his hand on his sword.*]

COMMISSIONER OF CHARITIES. I have the honor to present myself: Commissioner of Charities and Court Councilor Zemlyanika.

HLESTAKOV. How do you do. Won't you take a seat?

COMMISSIONER OF CHARITIES. I had the honor of personally conducting you through the charitable institutions in my charge.

HLESTAKOV. Ah, yes: Salted cod. You made an excellent impression. But I could have sworn you were . . . *shorter* yesterday.

COMMISSIONER OF CHARITIES [*agreeably*]. It's very possible. [*After a short silence.*] I spare no effort to perform my duties with zeal and dispatch. [*Draws his chair closer to* HLESTAKOV *and speaks confidentially.*] Now, this Postmaster. He does absolutely nothing. The Post office is falling apart . . . letters are lost, packages break open mysteriously. It's something you should look into. As for the Judge, he hunts rabbits while the court is in session, and he kennels his dogs in the Courthouse! And his behavior in general—well, he's a friend of mine, but I must do this for the good of the country. There's a certain landowner around here—Dobchinski, you've possibly met him —well, as soon as Dobchinski goes out to collect his rent, the Judge hops into bed with his wife! I'll swear it on the Bible! The five children, all the way down to the youngest girl, look exactly like the Judge.

HLESTAKOV [*delighted*]. Well, well! Who would have thought it!

COMMISSIONER OF CHARITIES. Then there's the Commissioner of Schools. I can't understand how the government ever appointed him. He's worse than an anarchist, and he poisons the minds of the youngsters with revolutionary doctrines I don't even understand myself. Would you like me to put all this down on paper?

HLESTAKOV. By all means. It'll be something amusing to read when I'm bored. . . . By the way, what is your name? I keep forgetting.

COMMISSIONER OF CHARITIES. Zemlyanika.

HLESTAKOV. Ah, of course. Zemlyanika.

COMMISSIONER OF CHARITIES. I will not presume to disturb you further with my presence, or take up the time which you devote to performing your duties . . . [*Bows, prepares to leave*].

HLESTAKOV [*accompanying him out*]. Oh, I assure you, what you've told me was a great treat. [*Closes door, then remembers. He reopens door, yells out.*] Oh, I say there! What is your *first* name?

COMMISSIONER OF CHARITIES [*returning*]. Artemi. Artemi Philipovich.

HLESTAKOV. Well, Artemi, somehow or other, I've lost all my money. This town is full of thieves. Do you happen to have four hundred to lend me?

COMMISSIONER OF CHARITIES. Why yes, I believe I do. [*Gives packet of bills to him.*]

HLESTAKOV. My, that *is* lucky. Thank you, most sincerely.

[COMMISSIONER OF CHARITIES *goes out.*]

HLESTAKOV [*calling through door*]. Next!

[BOBCHINSKI *and* DOBCHINSKI *stumble in.*]

BOBCHINSKI. I have the honor to present myself: Peter Ivanovich Bobchinski, a citizen of this town.

DOBCHINSKI. And I am Pyotr Ivanovich Dobchinski, land-owner.

HLESTAKOV. Oh, yes. I've met you before—when you fell in. And how is your nose?

BOBCHINSKI. Quite well, thank you. It's swollen up nicely, don't you think? I'm very pleased with it.

HLESTAKOV. It's a lovely job. If only your money could double so quickly. . . . [*Suddenly.*] By the way, do you have any of it on you?

DOBCHINSKI. Any of what?

HLESTAKOV. Money. Lend me a thousand.

BOBCHINSKI. A thousand? Good God, I don't have that much. Maybe you do, Pyotr?

DOBCHINSKI. I? Oh, no. I'm completely in hock to the damned shysters.

HLESTAKOV. Well, if not a thousand—say, a hundred rubles?

BOBCHINSKI [*rummaging through his pockets*]. You must have a hundred, Dobchinski? All I can find is forty.

DOBCHINSKI. I never carry more than twenty-five.

BOBCHINSKI. Why don't you take another look? I know you have a hole in your right pocket—some might have dropped through.

DOBCHINSKI [*firmly*]. I'm positive there's nothing in the hole.

BOBCHINSKI. Of course, there's nothing *there!* That's why it's called a hole. Maybe it dropped into your—lining—

HLESTAKOV. Never mind. I'll manage with sixty-five. It's quite all right. [*He takes the bills*]. Good-bye.

DOBCHINSKI. I was going to ask you a favor in a very delicate matter—

HLESTAKOV. Well, what is it?

DOBCHINSKI. It's very, very delicate. My oldest son, you see, was born just a few days before I got married—

HLESTAKOV. Oh?

DOBCHINSKI. I don't think a few days, more or less, should matter, in the date of the registration. I want him to be called Dobchinski, just like me. I wouldn't trouble you, sir, but it would be a great pity since the boy has so many talents. He has so much promise. He's memorized entire poems by heart, and if he picks up a knife, he'll immediately carve a little toy droshky as quick as a magician. Bobchinski will testify to that.

BOBCHINSKI. The boy is a genius.

HLESTAKOV. Very well. Let him be called Dobchinski.

DOBCHINSKI. Don't I need some sort of . . . document?

HLESTAKOV. If I say he's a Dobchinski, he's a Dobchinski! By God, just let anybody try to question it! [*To* BOBCHINSKI *grandly.*] Don't you have something you'd like me to do for you?

BOBCHINSKI. Ah, yes. A very small favor.

HLESTAKOV. Certainly. What is it?

BOBCHINSKI. I beg you, sir, when you return to St. Petersburg and tell all the notables there, all those councilors and admirals, about your visit, just say, "In that town, Your Excellency or Your Highness, in that very town lives Peter Ivanovich Bobchinski." That's all. Just say, "Peter Ivanovich Bobchinski lives there."

HLESTAKOV. Why not? And when I call on the Emperor, I'll slip it into the conversation, "It's the town, Your Imperial Majesty, where Peter Ivanovich Bobchinski lives."

BOBCHINSKI. Oh, God bless you!

DOBCHINSKI and BOBCHINSKI [*together*]. And pardon us for giving you so much trouble with our presence.

HLESTAKOV. Not at all! It was a great pleasure. [*He conducts them out. Alone*]. I've really fallen into a barrel of butter! . . . What a bunch of idiots! . . . I think I'll write Tryapichkin about this. He scribbles for the St. Petersburg papers . . . this might give him a little comic inspiration. Hey, Osip! Bring some ink and paper!

OSIP [*putting his head in the door*]. Yes, sir.

HLESTAKOV. This ought to hit Tryapichkin right in the funny-bone. He'd sell his own father for a joke. . . . First, let's add up the take: Three hundred from the Judge and three hundred from the Postmaster . . . Six . . . seven . . . eight hundred—what a greasy bill! . . . Eight hundred, nine hundred . . . Oh, my! It comes out to over a thousand . . . Now, where's that light-fingered captain? Just let me catch you now, with *my* cards! [OSIP *enters with inkwell and paper and pen.*] Well, you old windbag, you see how well they treat me? [*Begins to write.*]

OSIP. Yeh, thank God for that. Only, you know what . . . ?

HLESTAKOV. What?

OSIP. I think we better get the hell out of here. Fast!

HLESTAKOV [*writing*]. Nonsense! Why should I?

OSIP. You been having a high old time here for two days. All right. That's enough, ain't it? What do you want to hang around for? Spit on 'em! How do you know who's gonna show up here tomorrow and spill the beans? They've got fast horses here—they go like lightning.

HLESTAKOV. I've decided to accept a bit more of their hospitality. We might leave tomorrow.

OSIP. Tomorrow? Christ, we better get outta here right now! It's a big honor for you, and all that, but don't overdo it. They musta took you for somebody else, but your old man won't believe it—you'll catch hell for taking so long. . . . Since you're such a big shot, they'll give you the best horses. Come on, let's beat it.

HLESTAKOV [*still writing*]. Very well then. But first take this letter and then get an order for post-horses. Tell the drivers I'll give them a ruble each if they bring horses that run like the Imperial Couriers'. And I want the drivers to sing for me, too. [*Continues writing.*] There. Tryapichkin ought to die laughing—

OSIP. I'll send it with this man here. I better pack up so's we don't lose any time.

HLESTAKOV. Very good. But bring me a candle.

OSIP [*goes off and is heard yelling*]. Hey, you there! Get ready to run a letter to the post office. And tell 'em to send their best troika—a courier's troika, you understand?—and my boss don't pay. He travels at government expense. And tell 'em they better look alive, or my boss'll get mad. . . . Ah, wait a minute. The letter ain't ready yet.

HLESTAKOV [*goes on writing*]. I wonder where he's living now . . . Post Office Street or Peas Street? He likes to change his room regularly—saves paying rent. I'll take a chance on Post Office Street. [*Folds the letter and addresses it.*]

[OSIP *brings the candle.* HLESTAKOV *seals the letter.*]

DERZHIMORDA'S VOICE [*offstage*]. Where are you goin', Black Beard? I told you—orders is orders. Nobody goes in!

HLESTAKOV [*gives letter to* OSIP]. There, send it out.

SHOPKEEPER'S VOICE. Come on, be a good fellow. . . . You can't stop us—we're here on business!

DERZHIMORDA. Get out, get out! He ain't receivin' nobody. He's sleepin'. [*The noise increases.*]

HLESTAKOV. What is it, Osip? What's that uproar?

OSIP [*looking out window*]. Some shopkeepers want to come in, but the cop won't let 'em. They're wavin' papers—they must want to see you.

HLESTAKOV [*at window*]. What do you want, my friends?

SHOPKEEPERS' VOICES. We throw ourselves at your mercy! Your Lordship, please receive our petition.

HLESTAKOV. Let them in! Let them all in, Osip. [OSIP *exits.*

HLESTAKOV *accepts some petitions through the window; he turns them over and reads:*] "To His High Well-Born Illustrious Lord of Finance, from Abdulin the Merchant—" damned if I know what this is all about! But what a title!

[*The* SHOPKEEPERS *push in, carrying sugar loaves and bottles of wine in a basket.*]

HLESTAKOV. Now, now, my friends. What is all this?

SHOPKEEPERS. We beg your indulgence!

HLESTAKOV. Well, tell me what you want?

SHOPKEEPERS. Save us from bankruptcy, Your Lordship! We are grievously and unjustly oppressed.

HLESTAKOV. By who—whom?

ABDULIN. The Mayor. It's all because of the Mayor of this town. You never saw such a Mayor! Who can describe the outrages he commits? He billets so many of his visiting relatives in our houses, we're bankrupt. We might as well end the misery by hanging ourselves! And if he doesn't like your looks, he grabs you by the beard and calls you a Mongolian dog! My God! as if we didn't pay him enough respect! We've never refused anything his wife or daughter might pick out to wear. But no, that's not enough for him! He'll see a piece of cloth, and he'll say, "Ah, my friend, that's a nice little piece of material. Just send it over to my house." And the piece can be 50 yards long.

HLESTAKOV. My, what sticky fingers!

A SHOPKEEPER. Yes, by God! Nobody can remember another mayor like this in the whole history of this town! Whenever we see him coming, we cover up everything in the shop. He'll take any kind of junk. I had some prunes laying around in a barrel seven years—even my helper-boy wouldn't eat them—but this Mayor stuffs a whole fistful into his pocket. He claims his name-day is the feast of St. Anthony, so you've got to bring him gifts. And then, next month, he decides St. Onufri's is another name-day of his, so you have to contribute again!

HLESTAKOV. Why, he's no better than a pirate!

ANOTHER SHOPKEEPER. That's right. But just you try to cross him, and he'll quarter a whole regiment of soldiers in your house. And if you bar the door to him, he'll say, "I won't subject you to corporal punishment or torture—that is forbidden by law." But, my dear fellow, it'll be worse than swallowing herring without water!

HLESTAKOV. What a hypocrite! He ought to be ashamed of himself.

ABDULIN. Your Lordship, if you can just remove him, we'll be able to breathe again. And please accept a little token of our hospitality—these sugar-loaves and wine.

HLESTAKOV. Now, now! Don't even think of that. I never accept bribes. However, if you offered me a loan of, say, three hundred rubles, that would be an entirely different matter. I could accept that.

SHOPKEEPERS. Take it, noble lord! [*They produce bags of coins.*] But three hundred may not be enough. . . . Better have five hundred. Just help us!

HLESTAKOV. If you wish . . . as long as it's a loan, I can't refuse. I'll take it.

ABDULIN [*offering money on a silver tray*]. Please accept the tray, too.

HLESTAKOV. Why, yes. How thoughtful of you.

ANOTHER SHOPKEEPER [*bowing*]. Take the sugar loaves, too.

HLESTAKOV. Oh, no. That would be an out-and-out bribe.

OSIP. Your Highness, please accept it. It'll make these gents feel better. And it can be mighty useful on the trip . . . [*To* SHOPKEEPERS.] Give me the loaves and the basket—I hate waste. What's this? Rope? Let's have that, too—everything comes in handy on the road.

SHOPKEEPERS. Please grant us this favor, Your Lordship. If you don't come to our rescue, we just don't know which way to turn—

ABDULIN. We'll hang ourselves!

HLESTAKOV. Of course, I will. Of course. I'll do my best.

[THE SHOPKEEPERS *go out.*]

WOMAN'S VOICE [*off*]. Don't you dare stop me, you bum! Don't shove me!

HLESTAKOV. Who's there? [*Goes to window.*] Well, what's the trouble, madam?

VOICES OF TWO WOMEN. Take pity on us, sir! Say that you'll listen to us!

HLESTAKOV [*at window*]. Let them in.

[*Enter the* LOCKSMITH'S WIFE, *an old harridan, and* SERGEANT'S WIFE.]

LOCKSMITH'S WIFE [*bowing to the ground*]. Have pity on me!

SERGEANT'S WIFE. Have pity on me, too!

HLESTAKOV. Who are you?

SERGEANT'S WIFE. I'm Sergeant Ivanov's wife.

LOCKSMITH'S WIFE. I live here, sir. I'm the locksmith's wife, Fevronya Pyetrova Pashlyopkina—

HLESTAKOV. One at a time! [*To* LOCKSMITH'S WIFE.] What do you want?

LOCKSMITH'S WIFE. Beggin' your mercy, I want to complain against the Mayor! I hope the Lord curses him with every kind of disease he can dig up, so that crook and his children and his uncles and his aunts never have any luck in anything!

HLESTAKOV. Really? Why?

LOCKSMITH'S WIFE. Why, that grafter stuck my man into the army—and it ain't his turn yet! Besides, it's against the law because my man's *married!* To me!

HLESTAKOV. But how could the Mayor do that?

LOCKSMITH'S WIFE. He done it anyhow, the swindler. He just done it! I hope God blasts him good in this world *and* the next! And his aunt—if he *had* an aunt—let every kind of sickness shrivel her up! And his father—if he *had* a father and he's alive—let him rot to death, the rat! I hope he chokes forever and ever, that thief! They shoulda took the tailor's son, the drunk, but his family slipped the Mayor a big bribe. So he snatched Panteleyeva's son, but his old lady sent around three bolts of cloth to the Mayor's wife. So he picks on *me!* "What do you need a husband for?" he says. "He's no use to you." Well, *I'm* the one that oughta know if he's any use or not! Then he says, "Your husband is a crook. It don't matter if he ain't stole nothin' yet, he sure will someday. So what's the difference if they take him now or next year?" What am I gonna do without my dear husband? You stinkin' Mayor! I hope not one of your family wakes up tomorrow to see God's blessed light. And your mother-in-law—if you *have* a mother-in-law—

HLESTAKOV. Now, now! That's enough! [*He dismisses her. To the other.*] Now, what do you have to complain about?

LOCKSMITH'S WIFE [*as she goes out*]. Don't forget me, little father. And bless you.

SERGEANT'S WIFE. I want justice from the Mayor!

HLESTAKOV. Well, what is it? Make it short.

SERGEANT'S WIFE. He had me flogged by mistake!

HLESTAKOV. How can that happen?

SERGEANT'S WIFE. Well, a couple of us girls was arguing in the marketplace, strictly a private thing. And the cops come up and grab me. I don't know why—and next thing I know, I can't sit down for two days.

HLESTAKOV. What do you expect me to do about it now?

SERGEANT'S WIFE. I know you can't take back the flogging. I just want him to pay me compensation. I took a terrible beating for nothing.

HLESTAKOV. You can go now—I'll take care of everything.

[*Hands with petitions are thrust in through the window.*]

What? They're still coming! [*Goes to window.*] No, no! I can't take care of any more. Impossible, impossible! [*Turning away from window.*] They certainly are pests, damn them! Don't let any more in, Osip.

OSIP [*calling out the window*]. Break it up! . . . Beat it, I said! That's all. Come back tomorrow.

[MARYA ANTONOVNA *enters from another door.*]

MARYA [*in mock surprise*]. Oh, dear me!

HLESTAKOV. Why are you so frightened, mademoiselle?

MARYA. Oh, I wasn't frightened.

HLESTAKOV [*strutting*]. Forgive me if I say so, my dear girl, but I'm quite pleased to think you have taken me for the kind of man who. . . . May I ask where you were going?

MARYA. Actually, I was not going anywhere.

HLESTAKOV. Well then, might I ask *why* you were not going anywhere?

MARYA. I wondered if Mamma was here. . . .

HLESTAKOV. I really would like to know why you were not going anywhere?

MARYA. Oh, I'm interrupting you. You were in the middle of important business.

HLESTAKOV [*the lady-killer*]. But just a glance from your eyes is more important to me than any business! . . . *You* could never interrupt me. On the contrary, just to see you gives me the greatest pleasure.

MARYA. Ah, you toss compliments around just like they do in the capital.

HLESTAKOV. That's the only proper way to address an entrancing creature such as you. Dare I offer you a chair? Alas, you should have not a chair but a throne!

MARYA. I really don't know . . . I ought to be going. . . .

[*Takes seat.*]

HLESTAKOV. What an enchanting scarf!

MARYA. Oh, now! You're making fun. You're just laughing at us small-towners.

HLESTAKOV. Oh, mademoiselle, how I wish I were that scarf, so that I could wrap myself around your lily neck!

MARYA. I really don't understand what you mean. . . . Isn't this unusual weather we're having?

HLESTAKOV. For your little lips, my dear, I would come running through the most unusual weather in the world!

MARYA. You do say the strangest things. . . . I was going to ask you to write some poetry in my souvenir album. You must know a lot of poems.

HLESTAKOV. For you, mademoiselle, I will compose an entirely original one. Just command me—what kind shall it be?

MARYA. I don't know . . . as long as it's now.

HLESTAKOV. Let me think a moment—my head is simply swarming with rhymes. Would you like this little thing I dashed off:

> Goodnight, good night, parting is such sweet sorrow,
> I shall say good night till it's tomorrow . . .

MARYA [*clutching him*]. Oh, don't go! . . . How lovely that is!

HLESTAKOV. Well, I have others, even better. I just can't recall them now. . . . What does it matter? Instead of my verses, I give you my love! Ever since your first smile . . . [*Moves his chair closer.*]

MARYA. Love? I've never understood just what it is. . . . [*She moves her chair away.*]

HLESTAKOV. Why move your chair away? It's far better that we sit closer together.

MARYA [*moves farther away*]. Why closer? It's better to sit farther!

HLESTAKOV [*moves toward her*]. Why farther? It's better to sit closer.

MARYA. But why do you do that?

HLESTAKOV [*edging nearer*]. So that I can only *seem* to be close to you. Actually, I am far, far away. . . .

MARYA [*mollified, looks out window*]. What was that flying by? A magpie?

HLESTAKOV [*kisses her on the shoulder*]. Just the wings of a bird. . . .

MARYA [*rises indignantly*]. That was not a bird—that was you! . . . How bold!

HLESTAKOV [*holding her back*]. Can you blame me, mademoiselle? I did it in the heat of love. Love for *you!*

MARYA. So you think I'm some kind of country . . . milkmaid!

[*Struggles to free herself.*]

HLESTAKOV [*still holding her*]. I was driven mad by love, really. Just love! Marya Antonovna, don't be angry! I'm ready to get down on my knees to beg your pardon. [*Falls on his knees.*] You see? Now, will you pardon me?

[ANNA ANDREYEVNA *enters.*]

ANNA. My, what a position!

HLESTAKOV [*rising, exasperated*]. Doesn't anyone ever knock?

ANNA [*turning on her daughter*]. As for you, young lady, what is the meaning of this?

MARYA. Mamma, dear, I—

ANNA. Leave the room! Do you hear me? March right out of here and don't you dare show your face to me again. [MARYA *runs out in tears.*] Excuse me, sir, but I'm so shocked by all this . . .

HLESTAKOV [*aside*]. Well, this one isn't too bad-looking. . . . [*Throws himself at her feet.*] Madam, you see before you a man burning with love. For *you!*

ANNA. What are you doing on your knees again? Oh, get up, sir, get up. The floor's quite dirty.

HLESTAKOV. No, I insist. I will stay on my knees until I learn my fate. What will it be—life or death?

ANNA. Sir, I don't understand what you're talking about. If my eyes didn't deceive me, you were just now making a proposal to my daughter.

HLESTAKOV. No, I am in love with *you!* My life hangs on a thread! If you will not crown my eternal burning love, then I cannot endure existence on earth! While the flame licks at my heart, I beg for your hand!

ANNA. But, sir, I must mention that I am, so to speak . . . well, actually I *am* married!

HLESTAKOV. What does that matter? Love does not recognize such trifles. Didn't Karamazin say, "It's only the law that condemns." We will fly away together, under the canopy of heaven. Your hand. I must have your hand—!

[*Suddenly,* MARYA *runs in.*]

MARYA. Papa wants you to—[*Finally realizes* HLESTAKOV *is on his knees again.*] My, what a position!

ANNA. Well, what do *you* want? Leaping around like a cat in a fit! What's so surprising about what you've seen? You act like a three-year-old, not at all like a girl of eighteen! Not at all! When will you ever learn good manners in front of a gentleman?

MARYA [*through her tears*]. Honest, Mamma dear, I didn't know—

ANNA. There's a constant draft blowing through your head!

HLESTAKOV [*seizing* MARYA'S *hand but talking to* ANNA]. Do not oppose our happiness. Give your blessing to our eternal, burning love!

ANNA [*astounded*]. So it's *her* you want—?

HLESTAKOV. Decide my fate—is it love or death?

ANNA [*recovering, to* MARYA]. There now, you silly girl. Now you see it was all on your account that our guest had to fall on his knees. And then you suddenly barge in as if you'd gone crazy. It would serve you right if I refused permission—you're really not worth such good fortune.

[MAYOR *runs in, out of breath.*]

MAYOR. I'll never do it again, Your Excellency. Don't ruin me, don't destroy me!

HLESTAKOV. What's the matter with you?

MAYOR. So the shopkeepers have been complaining about me! I swear, on my honor, not half of what they say is true. *They* are the ones who cheat and rob the people. That sergeant's wife lied when she told you I flogged her. It's a damned, dirty lie, by God! She flogged herself!

HLESTAKOV. Oh, who cares about the sergeant's wife?

MAYOR. Don't you believe 'em—not for a minute. They're such liars . . . not even a baby would trust them.

ANNA. Anton, shut up! Ivan Alexandrovich has asked for our daughter's hand!

MAYOR. What's that? You're mad, woman! . . . Don't be alarmed, Your Excellency, she has a few screws loose in her head—takes after her mother.

HLESTAKOV. But I really do ask for her hand! I am in love! Madly!

MAYOR. I can't quite believe it, Your Excellency—?

ANNA. Not even when he *tells* you?

HLESTAKOV. I am not joking. I am madly in love with your daughter.

MAYOR. I just can't believe it—you must be joking, Excellency?

ANNA. You numskull! How many times does he have to say it?

MAYOR. No—it's incredible!

HLESTAKOV. You must give me your consent! I'm a desperate man—capable of anything. If I blow my brains out, you will be held responsible in court.

MAYOR. Court? Oh, my God! I am innocent, body and soul! Don't be angry, I beg you! Do whatever you want! My head is going round and round. . . .

ANNA. There now, give them your blessing.

[HLESTAKOV *and* MARYA *come to him.*]

MAYOR. May the Lord bless you—but I swear I'm innocent! [HLESTAKOV *kisses* MARYA. *The* MAYOR *at last realizes this is not some plot.*] What the devil! . . . They really are—! [*Rubs his eyes.*] They're really kissing each other—just as if they were engaged! Haha! What a barrel of luck! Well, I *am* blessed!

[OSIP *enters.*]

OSIP. The horses are here.

HLESTAKOV. I'll be out in a minute.

MAYOR. You're leaving?

HLESTAKOV. Of course.

MAYOR. But just when . . . after you condescended to . . . hint . . . I thought . . . at marriage?

HLESTAKOV. I'm only going for a day to pay my respects to my uncle—he's a rich old fellow. I'll be back tomorrow.

MAYOR. Then we certainly don't want to detain you. Take our blessings for a safe return.

HLESTAKOV. Thank you, thank you. I'll be right back. [*To* MARYA.] Good-bye, my love—no, I can't bear to say that!—au revoir, my dearest darling. [*Kisses her hand.*]

MAYOR. Do you need anything for the trip? You were good enough to say that you were a . . . little short of cash?

HLESTAKOV. Oh, no. It's quite all right . . . [*Reflects.*] But, since you do insist—

MAYOR. How much would you want?

HLESTAKOV. Well you know, you've already lent me two hundred. Oh, no—it was actually four hundred—let's keep our accounts clear—so if you'd like to make it a nice easy-remembered sum, make it another four hundred.

MAYOR. Certainly! [*He takes the bills out of his purse.*] There, just as if I'd been thinking of you—brand, new bills!

HLESTAKOV [*examines bills*]. Ah, so they are! That's wonderful. They say new bills mean new luck.

MAYOR. So they do, sir. Exactly right.

HLESTAKOV. Well, good-bye, Anton Antonovich. I am deeply grateful for your hospitality. I've never been so well treated—anywhere. Goodbye, Anna Andreyevna! Au revoir, Marya, my darling!

[*They start off.* OSIP *goes out.*]

HLESTAKOV. Farewell, Marya Antonovna, angel of my soul!

MAYOR [*looking out window*]. What's that—you're riding in a broken-down post-carriage? Without springs?

HLESTAKOV. I prefer that. Springs bounce, they give me a headache.

DRIVER'S VOICE. Whoa, there!

MAYOR. Let's make it comfortable. A rug? Won't you let me give you a rug?

HLESTAKOV. Oh, it's a bother . . . still, if you like, let's have the rug.

MAYOR [*calling off*]. Hey, Avdotya! Run to the closet and get the best rug—the Persian with the blue background. Hurry up!

DRIVER. Whoa, there! Ho!

HLESTAKOV. Good-bye, Anton Antonovich! [MAYOR *embraces him.*]

MAYOR. Goodbye, Your Excellency.

ANNA [*tearfully*]. Au revoir, Ivan Alexandrovich!

HLESTAKOV. Au revoir, dear Mamma! [*He kisses her in a long embrace.* MAYOR *and* MARYA *stare perplexedly at each other.* HLESTAKOV *runs out, blowing kisses to the group.*]

MARYA. What a cute little nose!

OSIP'S VOICE. We've got the rug, Your Honor. Let's beat it!

DRIVER. Giddyap, my beauties!

[*Bells tinkle as the horses slowly trot away. The* WOMEN *wipe away a few furtive tears*]

MAYOR [*roaring with pleasure*]. Well, Anna! How do you like that masterstroke, eh? Now admit it—never in your whole life did you ever dream of such a prize! Just a Mayor's wife but look what we hooked—an aristocrat! a holy terror, by Christ!

ANNA. *We?* It took *you* a long time to catch on.

MAYOR. I'll make it hot for all those bloodsuckers who were so free and easy with their petitions! [*Puts head out door.*]

Hey, who's out there? [*The policeman* PUGOVKIN *enters.*] Call those shopkeepers in here! I'll give it to you hyenas! Squeal on *me*, will you? Just wait, you damned pack of traitors! I've been too easy on you before—now I'll really use the whip! [*To* POLICEMAN.] Make a list of all those that complained—especially the scribblers with the goddamned petitions. And be sure to let 'em all know what an honor heaven has sent down for me, the Mayor! He's going to marry his daughter—not to a hayseed nobody—but to a gentleman, a man as big as anybody in the whole empire, a man who can fix everything—everything—everything! Yell that out so everybody can hear it—ring the bells! It's my hour of triumph and, so help me, Christ, I'm going to enjoy it! [POLICEMAN *goes out.*] Now, Anna, we have to think about where we're going to live. Here or in St. Pete?

ANNA. Oh, St. Petersburg, of course. How could we remain here?

MAYOR. All right! St. Pete it is! Now we're really going straight to the top! Since he's such a pal of the ministers and hangs around the Court, he'll get me promoted fast. In no time at all, I ought to be right up there with the generals! How about that, Anna? How would I look as a general?

ANNA. Beautiful, just beautiful.

MAYOR. They'll hang a ribbon across my shoulder. Which do you like best—the red one for the Order of St. Anne or the blue for the White Eagle?

ANNA. Oh, I adore blue.

MAYOR. Well, the red one is pretty high, too! Do you know why everybody wants to be a general? When you travel anywhere, you have couriers and orderlies galloping ahead, ordering up horses, so nobody else can get them. And everybody has to wait for you—all the councillors and big shots! You dine with the governors and snub the mayors. [*Roars with laughter.*] That's what I call living, by Christ!

ANNA. Sure. Anything coarse like that makes you happy. But just remember, we'll have to change our whole way of living. You can't run around with that dog-loving Judge, chasing rabbits, or with slobs like Zemlyanika. Oh no! From now on, all our friends must be people of distinction—counts and society people. . . . Only I'm a little worried about you. You're liable to open your big mouth and let out some dirty word.

MAYOR. I can be just as clean-minded as you pretend to be.

. . . You know, in St. Pete you can get all sorts of fresh fish—eels and smelts. My mouth's watering already!

ANNA. Is that all you can think about at a time like this—fish?

[*The* SHOPKEEPERS *file in, bowing very low*.]

MAYOR [*pleasantly*]. Ah, good afternoon, my little pigeons.

SHOPKEEPERS. Good health to you, Little Father.

MAYOR [*sweetly*]. How are you getting along? How's business? [*Roaring.*] So you thought you'd get rid of me, huh? You tea-guzzlers, you mother-peddlers! You would, would you! —you fat-belly skunks, you bloodsuckers, you beetle-headed pimps! *You* complain about blackmail! So you thought, here's a chance to toss our pal into jail! May the seven fiends and a witch grab you—

ANNA. Heavens—what language!

MAYOR [*impatiently*]. This is no time to be particular! [*To* SHOPKEEPERS.] Don't you know the very official you complained to is now engaged to my daughter? I'll take care of you! . . . Why you gyp the whole country! . . . You make a contract with the government and cheat it out of a hundred thousand with your rotten cloth. And then, if I ask you to contribute fifteen or twenty yards, you expect a monument in the square. If the government only knew all your thievery, they'd crack down so hard! . . . And how you stick your belly out so proud—"I'm a merchant, you can't touch me! I rank just as high as any gentleman," you say. Ha! A gentleman has an education, you apes! I'm sure you were all properly flogged at school, but it didn't help. What did you learn—the ABC's of swindling? While you're still kids, you may not know the Lord's Prayer, but Goddamn it, you sure know how to mix the sand in with the pepper. And then, when your belly swells out and your purse swells up, don't you put on the airs! Just because you drink up sixteen samovars a day, that makes you gentlemen? Those fancy airs really stink! Phew! I can't stand you!

SHOPKEEPERS [*bowing low*]. We are all guilty, Anton Antonovich. We are guilty. Forgive us.

MAYOR. You complained about *me!* Who closed his eyes when you built that bridge and charged twenty thousand for less than a hundred rubles worth of lumber? It was *me*—you flea-infested goat's-beard!

ABDULIN. God knows, we are guilty. But it's not our fault— the devil tempted us. We'll never complain again. Tell us what the fine will be . . . but don't be mad at us.

MAYOR [*roaring*]. Don't be mad! If you were in my position, you'd stick me feet-first into the mud and drive me in with a sledge-hammer!

SHOPKEEPERS [*prostrating themselves*]. Spare us, Anton Antonovich!

MAYOR [*waves his hand condescendingly*]. All right, I'm not spiteful. There will be no fine. Just stay in line. . . . And remember, I'm not giving my daughter to any ordinary small-town yokel. So the presents better be appropriate. And no dried fish! . . . You may go now, gentlemen, and God be with you. [*The* SHOPKEEPERS *exit gratefully through center door. The* JUDGE, COMMISSIONER OF CHARITIES *and, afterward,* RASTAKOVSKI *come in through another*]

JUDGE [*as he enters*]. What's this I hear, Anton Antonovich? An extraordinary piece of good fortune has come your way?

COMMISSIONER OF CHARITIES. I have the honor to congratulate you on your great good fortune. [*Kisses* ANNA'S *hand.*] Anna Andreyevna! [*Kisses* MARYA'S.] Marya Antonovna!

RASTAKOVSKI [*entering*]. Congratulations, Anton! God grant you long life, and the same to the bridal couple. May they bless you with grandchildren and great-grandchildren and many others. Anna Andreyevna! [*Kisses her hand.*] Marya Antonovna! [*Kisses her hand.*]

[KAROBKIN *and his wife enter with* LYULYUKOV.]

KAROBKIN. I have the honor to congratulate Anton Antonovich! Anna Andreyevna! . . . Marya Antonovna! [*Kisses their hands.*]

KAROBKIN'S WIFE. I heartily congratulate you, Anton Antonovich, on your good fortune!

LYULYUKOV. I have the honor to congratulate you, Anna Andreyevna! [*He kisses her hand, and turns to the audience to smack his lips with gusto.*] Marya Antonovna! I have the honor. [*Goes through the same business.*]

[*A number of visitors, who have entered before, now shake* ANNA'S *hand and then* MARYA'S, *exclaiming "Anna Andreyevna!" and "Marya Antonovna!"* BOBCHINSKI *and* DOBCHINSKI *rush in.*]

BOBCHINSKI. I have the honor to congratulate you . . .

DOBCHINSKI. Anton Antonovich, I have the honor to congratulate you!

BOBCHINSKI. . . . on this happy occasion.

DOBCHINSKI. Anna Andreyevna!
BOBCHINSKI. Anna Andreyevna!

[*They both try to kiss her hand and bump foreheads.*]

DOBCHINSKI. Marya Antonovna! [*Kisses her hand.*] I have the
honor to congratulate you. May you enjoy the best of all
happiness, and dress in cloth of gold and eat all kinds of
beautifully-spiced soups. . . .

BOBCHINSKI [*interrupting*]. Marya Antonovna, I have the
honor to congratulate you. May God bring you all sorts of
wealth and gold pieces and a baby boy as tiny as this—
[*Measures with hand.*] Just big enough to sit in the palm
of your hand. Yes! And may the little darling cry with joy
all the time! [*He mimics a happy cry.*] Wah, wah, wah!

[*Enter* COMMISSIONER OF SCHOOLS *and his* WIFE.]

COMMISSIONER OF SCHOOLS. I have the honor—

HIS WIFE [*running ahead of him*]. I congratulate you, Anna
Andreyevna! [*They kiss each other.*] I am so delighted,
really I am! When they told me of the engagement, I was
so carried away I couldn't talk. All I could do was cry. I
cried and cried—I really sobbed! Then Lukanchik says,
"What are you sobbing for, Nastenka?" And I say, "How
should I know?" but the tears keep flowing like a river!
[*She cries.*]

MAYOR. Please sit down, everybody! Mishka, bring some more
chairs. [*The visitors take seats.*]

[*The* POLICE SUPERINTENDENT *enters.*]

SUPERINTENDENT. I have the honor to congratulate you, your
honor.

MAYOR. Thanks, thanks. Please be seated, gentlemen. [*They
sit.*]

JUDGE. Now tell us, how it all happened. Give us the complete
history of the case.

MAYOR. It was very unusual—he condescended to make the
proposal himself.

ANNA. In a most respectful and dignified way. He put it so
sweetly: "You have simply made a conquest of me, Anna
Andreyevna!"

MARYA. Mamma, now really! That's what he said to *me!*

ANNA. Oh, no doubt he meant it for you, too. Did I say not?

MAYOR. And how he frightened us! "If you refuse me," he
screamed, "I'll shoot myself! I'll blow my brains out!"

VISITORS [*ad lib*]. Goodness! . . . You don't say!

JUDGE. That's evidence of strong character!

KAROBKIN. May I ask where our distinguished guest is now?

MAYOR. He has gone away for the day on very important business—

ANNA. To see an uncle and ask for his blessing.

MAYOR. Yes, to ask for his blessing, but tomorrow— [*He sneezes; everyone choruses "Bless you!"*] Thanks. As I said, he'll be back again to—[*Sneezes again; again a chorus of "Bless You!" During this, the following voices are heard:*]

SUPERINTENDENT OF POLICE. Good health, your honor.

BOBCHINSKI. A sack of gold pieces and a hundred years!

DOBCHINSKI. May the Lord stretch it to a thousand.

COMMISSIONER OF CHARITIES [*aside*]. I hope you go straight to hell!

KAROBKIN'S WIFE [*aside*]. Drop dead!

MAYOR. Thank you all, and the same to you!

ANNA. We intend to move to St. Petersburg . . . The air here is too . . . too rural! And my husband—he'll be promoted to general.

MAYOR. Yes, gentlemen. I have a consuming ambition to be a general.

JUDGE [*nodding*]. A great voyage demands a great ship.

COMMISSIONER OF CHARITIES. It's the least you deserve for your unselfish service.

JUDGE [*aside*]. Why a general's uniform fits him like a saddle fits a cow. Now, my friend, that's going too far.

COMMISSIONER OF CHARITIES [*aside*]. General? Well, I'll be Goddamned! But he's stupid enough to make it. [*To* MAYOR.] When you're a general, don't forget us!

JUDGE. And if any little opening appears, one in which you'll need a talented administrator, don't hesitate—

MAYOR. Of course, of course.

ANNA. There you go again, handing out promises. How can you weigh yourself down with so many obligations?

MAYOR. Promises never hurt anybody.

ANNA. But you can't go on, tying yourself up with nobodies!

KAROBKIN'S WIFE [*aside*]. Did you hear what she called us?

LADY VISITOR. Oh, I *know* her! Just let her have a seat at the table and she'll put her big feet up on it!

[POSTMASTER *runs in, out of breath, waving an opened letter.*]

POSTMASTER. Say, here's a funny thing! That man we took for the Inspector—he's not an Inspector!

ALL. What! Not an Inspector?

POSTMASTER. No Inspector at all. I found it out from the letter.

MAYOR [*outraged*]. What? What do you mean? What letter?

POSTMASTER. From the letter he wrote. They bring me a letter to send off. I look at the address and I see "Post Office Street." You could have knocked me over with a stamp! I figures, he's found out something in the Post Office, and he's turning me in. So I take the letter and . . . and open it . . .

MAYOR [*outraged*]. How *could* you?

POSTMASTER. I don't know—some little voice inside kept saying, "Go ahead, open it!" And then a voice came in the other ear, "Stop before you're ruined!" And then back came the other voice, "Open it just a little. . . ." So I broke the seal—Oh, my veins were on fire. But after I read it, they froze, by God! They froze!

MAYOR. How dare you open the letter of such an important official?

POSTMASTER. That's what's so funny. He isn't important or official!

MAYOR. You idiot! Don't you know he's going to marry my daughter? I'm going to be a general! I'll ship you straight to Siberia!

POSTMASTER. Ech! That Siberia is a long way off. . . . Let me read you this letter.

ALL. Yes, read it! Hurry up!

POSTMASTER [*reading with great difficulty*]. ". . . just to let you know hastily, my dear Tryapichkin, all my adventures. On the way here, an infantry captain had cleaned me out completely, so the keeper of the local flea-bag wanted to throw me into jail. Then all of a sudden—due to my St. Petersburg clothes and aristocratic manner—the entire town assumed I was an Inspector General! At the moment, I am living in style at the Mayor's mansion. It's really open house. I'm flirting madly with the mayor's wife *and* daughter. I can't decide which to start on first. I think the old lady would be more grateful. . . . And everybody lends me as much money as I ask for! They're a ridiculous bunch—feel free to use them in any comic sketches you may want to write. First, there's the Mayor. He's stupid as a mule—

MAYOR. Impossible! That can't be in there!

POSTMASTER [*showing the line*]. Read it yourself!

MAYOR [*reading*]. . . . "stupid as a mule." *You* wrote it!

POSTMASTER. Me? I'm lucky I can *read!*

COMMISSIONER OF CHARITIES [*impatiently*]. All right, read!

COMMISSIONER OF SCHOOLS. Read it, read it!

POSTMASTER [*resuming*]. . . . "The Mayor. He's stupid as a mule—"

MAYOR. Damn it! Do you have to keep repeating it?

POSTMASTER [*continues*]. . . . hmmmmm . . . hmmmmm . . . "as a mule. The Postmaster is a pretty good fellow" . . . hmmmm . . . hmmmm . . .

MAYOR. Well, what does it say?

POSTMASTER. Something dirty about me.

MAYOR. Damn it, if you can read dirty things about me, you can read them about yourself!

COMMISSIONER OF CHARITIES. Let me try. [*Puts on his spectacles and reads.*] The Postmaster is like our porter Mikheyev—drinks like a fish."

POSTMASTER [*to the group*]. Why, the lousy brat ought to be flogged!

COMMISSIONER OF CHARITIES [*continuing*]. "The Charity Commissioner . . . eh . . . hmmm . . . hmmm . . . [*hesitates.*]

KAROBKIN. What are you stopping for?

COMMISSIONER OF CHARITIES. I can't decipher the writing.

KAROBKIN. Let me try. I have perfect eyesight. [*Grabs for letter.* COMMISSIONER *holds it back.*]

COMMISSIONER OF CHARITIES. It's easier to read farther on . . .

MAYOR. Read it all! If one person can be insulted, everybody can be insulted!

KAROBKIN [*reading*]. "The Charity Commissioner, Zemlyanika, is a regular pig in a skull-cap—"

COMMISSIONER OF CHARITIES [*appealing to the group*]. That's supposed to be witty? Who ever saw a pig in a skull-cap?

KAROBKIN [*continues*]. "The Commissioner of Schools stinks of onions . . ."

COMMISSIONER OF SCHOOLS [*to others*]. So help me, no onion has ever touched my lips!

KAROBKIN. ". . . the Judge—"

JUDGE [*quickly*]. I think this letter is irrelevant. What's the point of reading all that rubbish?

COMMISSIONERS OF SCHOOLS, CHARITIES *and* POSTMASTER [*together*]. Get on with it . . . Read it through!

KAROBKIN. . . . "Lyapkin-Tyapkin is really *mauvais ton.* [*He pronounces it moves tun, then stops, puzzled.*] That must be some dirty French word.

JUDGE. Devil knows what it means! If it means *swindler*—
I'll take him to court!

KAROBKIN [*reading on*]. "Au revoir my dear Tryapichkin. It's
such a bore to live as I do—marooned, without sustenance
for the intellect" . . .

MAYOR [*in panic*]. He's cut my throat! I'm assassinated—
dead! After him, I say! Catch him! [*Staring wildly.*] Holy
Christ! All I can see are pigs' snouts! I'm surrounded by
pigs' snouts!

POSTMASTER. How are ya gonna catch him? I told the stable
to give him the best troika and horses! God must be laughing at us!

KAROBKIN'S WIFE [*delighted*]. What a mess! I've never heard
of anything as awful as this!

JUDGE [*dazed*]. Not only that—he borrowed three hundred
from me!

COMMISSIONER OF CHARITIES. And three hundred from *me*.

POSTMASTER [*groaning*]. And me, too.

BOBCHINSKI. And Dobchinski and I were taken for sixty-five—
in bills!

MAYOR [*beating himself on the forehead*]. How could I *do* it?
I must be senile! My brains have turned to mush! Thirty
years in the government—not one shopkeeper or con-
tractor could ever gyp me! I outsmarted one slick crook
after another! Three governors—themselves the greatest
grafters in the empire!—could never find a shred of evidence against me! And now, this simpering little punk! [*He
chokes up with wrath.*]

ANNA [*soothingly*]. Oh, it can't be. He's engaged to Machen-
ka! . . .

MAYOR [*furiously*]. Engaged! Your stupidity has even infected
me! [*In desperation.*] Look at me, world! All of Christen-
dom—look at me, see how the Mayor's made an ass of himself! Featherbrain! Butter-fingers! [*Shakes fist at himself.*]
Oh, you hayseed! Taking a brat, a kid in diapers, for a
gentleman of rank! And I'm sure some pen-pusher, some
paper-stainer will go and put him in a play! He won't spare
your rank or profession and everybody will roar and clap
their hands! It's driving me mad! . . . Who are you laughing
at? Laugh at yourself! [*Stamps on the ground ferociously.*]
That's what I'd do to the whole pack of scribblers! Ugh,
you damned liberals—devil's bastards! I'd scrag you all—
grind you to powder! You'd make a great dish for the foul
fiend! [*Shakes his fist and grinds his heel into the floor.*

After a pause.] I'd better pull myself together. It's true, who God will punish he first drives mad. . . . But that little fathead didn't even *look* like an Inspector! Who was it first said he's the Inspector, huh? Tell me!

COMMISSIONER OF CHARITIES. Our wits were befogged—it was the devil who did it.

JUDGE. Who started the whole idea? Why there they are—those two enterprising connivers—Dobchinski and Bobchinski!

BOBCHINSKI. I swear it never occurred to me—

DOBCHINSKI. I *hated* even to think of it—

COMMISSIONER OF SCHOOLS. They ran like mad from the inn—[*Mimicking them.*] "He's here! He doesn't pay any money!" What a rare, stinking bird you discovered!

MAYOR. Sure it was you—you snooping old biddies, you goddamned lousy liars! All you do is run around town and stick your pigs' snouts into everything, you blabbermouths—

JUDGE. You cursed Mongolian idiots!

COMMISSIONER OF SCHOOLS. Filthy sausage-heads!

COMMISSIONER OF CHARITIES. Fat-nose dribblers!

MAYOR. Scandal-farters!

[ALL *crowd around them threateningly.*]

BOBCHINSKI. By heaven, it wasn't *me!* It was Dobchinski!

DOBCHINSKI. Oh, now, Peter! You certainly were first—

BOBCHINSKI. Don't blame me! *You* began it!

[A POLICEMAN *enters.*]

POLICEMAN [*loudly, slowly like a court chamberlain*]. Gentlemen! On orders of the Emperor, the Inspector-General has arrived!

[*In stalks a tall, imperious figure in magnificent uniform, with glowering eyes and fierce mustache. From the group come simultaneous cries of amazement and fear.* ALL *freeze into position.*]

TABLEAU

[*The* MAYOR *stands at center, stiff as a post, arms outstretched as if begging for mercy, his head bent back. At his right are his angry wife and daughter, turning on him. Beyond them the* POSTMASTER *is turned out to audience with a question on his lips; behind him is the* COMMISSIONER OF SCHOOLS, *completely innocent. At the outer edge of the scene are three lady visitors, sneering at the* MAYOR *and his family. On* MAYOR'S

left is ZEMLYANIKA, *his head slightly to one side as if eavesdropping. Behind him the* JUDGE *shrugs, lips pursed, his
shoulders bent low, as if to say, "Here comes the hangman!"
Next to him is* KAROBKIN, *winking at the audience and gesturing contemptuously at the* MAYOR. *Outside the group,* BOB-
CHINSKI *and* DOBCHINSKI *stare at each other, open-mouthed.
All guests stand motionless as statues. They maintain positions
for a minute or so.*]

THE CURTAIN FALLS

THE IMPORTANCE
OF BEING EARNEST

by Oscar Wilde

The Importance of Being Earnest was first performed at the St. James Theatre, London, February 14, 1895. It was a hilarious success with the audience and almost all the critics.

THE CAST

JOHN WORTHING, J.P.
ALGERNON MONCRIEFF
REV. CANON CHASUBLE, D.D.
MERRIMAN [*Butler*]
LANE [*Manservant*]
LADY BRACKNELL
HON. GWENDOLEN FAIRFAX
CECILY CARDEW
MISS PRISM [*Governess*]

SCENES

ACT ONE
Algernon Moncrieff's Flat in Half-Moon Street, W.
ACT TWO
The Garden at the Manor House, Woolton
ACT THREE
Drawing-room of the Manor House, Woolton
Time, 1895.   Place, London.

ACT ONE

Morning-room in ALGERNON'S *flat in Half-Moon Street. The room is luxuriously and artistically furnished. The sound of a piano is heard in the adjoining room.* [LANE *is arranging afternoon tea on the table, and after the music has ceased,* ALGERNON *enters.*]

ALGERNON. Did you hear what I was playing, Lane?

LANE. I didn't think it polite to listen, sir.

ALGERNON. I'm sorry for that, for your sake. I don't play accurately—anyone can play accurately—but I play with wonderful expression. As far as the piano is concerned, sentiment is my forte. I keep science for Life.

LANE. Yes, sir.

ALGERNON. And, speaking of the science of Life, have you got the cucumber sandwiches cut for Lady Bracknell?

LANE. Yes, sir. [*Hands them on a salver.*]

ALGERNON [*inspects them, takes two, and sits down on the sofa*]. Oh! . . . by the way, Lane, I see from your book that on Thursday night, when Lord Shoreman and Mr. Worthing were dining with me, eight bottles of champagne are entered as having been consumed.

LANE. Yes, sir; eight bottles and a pint.

ALGERNON. Why is it that at a bachelor's establishment the servants invariably drink the champagne? I ask merely for information.

LANE. I attribute it to the superior quality of the wine, sir. I have often observed that in married households the champagne is rarely of a first-rate brand.

ALGERNON. Good Heavens! Is marriage so demoralizing as that?

LANE. I believe it *is* a very pleasant state, sir. I have had very little experience of it myself up to the present. I have only been married once. That was in consequence of a misunderstanding between myself and a young woman.

ALGERNON [*languidly*]. I don't know that I am much interested in your family life, Lane.

LANE. No, sir; it is not a very interesting subject. I never think of it myself.

ALGERNON. Very natural, I am sure. That will do, Lane, thank you.

LANE. Thank you, sir. [LANE *goes out*.]

ALGERNON. Lane's views on marriage seem somewhat lax. Really, if the lower orders don't set us a good example, what on earth is the use of them? They seem, as a class, to have absolutely no sense of moral responsibility.

[*Enter* LANE.]

LANE. Mr. Ernest Worthing.

[*Enter* JACK. LANE *goes out*.]

ALGERNON. How are you, my dear Ernest? What brings you up to town?

JACK. Oh, pleasure, pleasure! What else should bring one anywhere? Eating as usual, I see, Algy!

ALGERNON [*stiffly*]. I believe it is customary in good society to take some slight refreshment at five o'clock. Where have you been since last Thursday?

JACK [*sitting down on the sofa*]. In the country.

ALGERNON. What on earth do you do there?

JACK [*pulling off his gloves*]. When one is in town one amuses oneself. When one is in the country one amuses other people. It is excessively boring.

ALGERNON. And who are the people you amuse?

JACK [*airily*]. Oh, neighbours, neighbours.

ALGERNON. Got nice neighbours in your part of Shropshire?

JACK. Perfectly horrid! Never speak to one of them.

ALGERNON. How immensely you must amuse them! [*Goes over and takes sandwich*.] By the way, Shropshire is your county, is it not?

JACK. Eh? Shropshire? Yes, of course. Hallo! Why all these cups? Why cucumber sandwiches? Why such reckless extravagance in one so young? Who is coming to tea?

ALGERNON. Oh! merely Aunt Augusta and Gwendolen.

JACK. How perfectly delightful!

ALGERNON. Yes, that is all very well; but I am afraid Aunt Augusta won't quite approve of your being here.

JACK. May I ask why?

ALGERNON. My dear fellow, the way you flirt with Gwendolen is perfectly disgraceful. It is almost as bad as the way Gwendolen flirts with you.

JACK. I am in love with Gwendolen. I have come up to town expressly to propose to her.

ALGERNON. I thought you had come up for pleasure? . . . I call that business.

JACK. How utterly unromantic you are!

ALGERNON. I really don't see anything romantic in proposing. It is very romantic to be in love. But there is nothing romantic about a definite proposal. Why, one may be accepted. One usually is, I believe. Then the excitement is all over. The very essence of romance is uncertainty. If ever I get married, I'll certainly try to forget the fact.

JACK. I have no doubt about that, dear Algy. The Divorce Court was specially invented for people whose memories are so curiously constituted.

ALGERNON. Oh! there is no use speculating on that subject. Divorces are made in Heaven—[JACK *puts out his hand to take a sandwich.* ALGERNON *at once interferes.*] Please don't touch the cucumber sandwiches. They are ordered specially for Aunt Augusta. [*Takes one and eats it.*]

JACK. Well, you have been eating them all the time.

ALGERNON. That is quite a different matter. She is my aunt. [*Takes plate from below.*] Have some bread and butter. The bread and butter is for Gwendolen. Gwendolen is devoted to bread and butter.

JACK [*advancing to table and helping himself*]. And very good bread and butter it is, too.

ALGERNON. Well, my dear fellow, you need not eat as if you were going to eat it all. You behave as if you were married to her already. You are not married to her already, and I don't think you ever will be.

JACK. Why on earth do you say that?

ALGERNON. Well, in the first place girls never marry the men they flirt with. Girls don't think it right.

JACK. Oh, that is nonsense!

ALGERNON. It isn't. It is a great truth. It accounts for the extraordinary number of bachelors that one sees all over the place. In the second place, I don't give my consent.

JACK. Your consent!

ALGERNON. My dear fellow, Gwendolen is my first cousin. And before I allow you to marry her, you will have to clear up the whole question of Cecily. [*Rings bell.*]

JACK. Cecily! What on earth do you mean? What do you mean, Algy, by Cecily? I don't know anyone of the name of Cecily.

[*Enter* LANE.]

ALGERNON. Bring me that cigarette case Mr. Worthing left in the smoking-room the last time he dined here.

LANE. Yes, sir. [LANE *goes out.*]

JACK. Do you mean to say you have had my cigarette case all this time? I wish to goodness you had let me know. I have been writing frantic letters to Scotland Yard about it. I was very nearly offering a large reward.

ALGERNON. Well, I wish you would offer one. I happen to be more than usually hard up.

JACK. There is no good offering a large reward now that the thing is found.

[*Enter* LANE *with the cigarette case on a salver.* ALGERNON *takes it at once.* LANE *goes out.*]

ALGERNON. I think that is rather mean of you, Ernest, I must say. [*Opens case and examines it.*] However, it makes no matter, for, now that I look at the inscription, I find that the thing isn't yours after all.

JACK. Of course it's mine. [*Moving to him.*] You have seen me with it a hundred times, and you have no right whatsoever to read what is written inside. It is a very ungentlemanly thing to read a private cigarette case.

ALGERNON. Oh! it is absurd to have a hard-and-fast rule about what one should read and what one shouldn't. More than half of modern culture depends on what one shouldn't read.

JACK. I am quite aware of the fact, and I don't propose to discuss modern culture. It isn't the sort of thing one should talk of in private. I simply want my cigarette case back.

ALGERNON. Yes; but this isn't your cigarette case. This cigarette case is a present from someone of the name of Cecily, and you said you didn't know anyone of that name.

JACK. Well, if you want to know, Cecily happens to be my aunt.

ALGERNON. Your aunt!

JACK. Yes. Charming old lady she is, too. Lives at Tunbridge Wells. Just give it back to me, Algy.

ALGERNON [*retreating to back of sofa*]. But why does she call herself little Cecily if she is your aunt and lives at Tunbridge Wells? [*Reading.*] "From little Cecily with her fondest love."

JACK [*moving to sofa and kneeling upon it*]. My dear fellow, what on earth is there in that? Some aunts are tall, some aunts are not tall. That is a matter that surely an aunt may be allowed to decide for herself. You seem to think that every aunt should be exactly like your aunt! That is absurd!

For Heaven's sake give me back my cigarette case. [*Follows* ALGERNON *round the room.*]

ALGERNON. Yes. But why does your aunt call you her uncle? "From little Cecily, with her fondest love to her dear Uncle Jack." There is no objection, I admit, to an aunt being a small aunt, but why an aunt, no matter what her size may be, should call her own nephew her uncle, I can't quite make out. Besides, your name isn't Jack at all; it is Ernest.

JACK. It isn't Ernest; it's Jack.

ALGERNON. You have always told me it was Ernest. I have introduced you to everyone as Ernest. You answer to the name of Ernest. You look as if your name was Ernest. You are the most earnest looking person I ever saw in my life. It is perfectly absurd your saying that your name isn't Ernest. It's on your cards. Here is one of them. [*Taking it from case.*] "Mr. Ernest Worthing, B 4, The Albany." I'll keep this as a proof your name is Ernest if ever you attempt to deny it to me, or to Gwendolen, or to anyone else. [*Puts the card in his pocket.*]

JACK. Well, my name is Ernest in town and Jack in the country, and the cigarette case was given to me in the country.

ALGERNON. Yes, but that does not account for the fact that your small Aunt Cecily, who lives at Tunbridge Wells, calls you her dear uncle. Come, old boy, you had much better have the thing out at once.

JACK. My dear Algy, you talk exactly as if you were a dentist. It is very vulgar to talk like a dentist when one isn't a dentist. It produces a false impression.

ALGERNON. Well, that is exactly what dentists always do. Now, go on! Tell me the whole thing. I may mention that I have always suspected you of being a confirmed and secret Bunburyist; and I am quite sure of it now.

JACK. Bunburyist? What on earth do you mean by a Bunburyist?

ALGERNON. I'll reveal to you the meaning of that incomparable expression as soon as you are kind enough to inform me why you are Ernest in town and Jack in the country.

JACK. Well, produce my cigarette case first.

ALGERNON. Here it is. [*Hands cigarette case.*] Now produce your explanation, and pray make it improbable. [*Sits on sofa.*]

JACK. My dear fellow, there is nothing improbable about my explanation at all. In fact it's perfectly ordinary. Old Mr.

Thomas Cardew, who adopted me when I was a little boy, made me in his will guardian to his granddaughter, Miss Cecily Cardew. Cecily, who addresses me as her uncle from motives of respect that you could not possibly appreciate, lives at my place in the country under the charge of her admirable governess, Miss Prism.

ALGERNON. Where is that place in the country, by the way?

JACK. That is nothing to you, dear boy. You are not going to be invited. . . . I may tell you candidly that the place is not in Shropshire.

ALGERNON. I suspected that, my dear fellow! I have Bunburyed all over Shropshire on two separate occasions. Now, go on. Why are you Ernest in town and Jack in the country?

JACK. My dear Algy, I don't know whether you will be able to understand my real motives. You are hardly serious enough. When one is placed in the position of guardian, one has to adopt a very high moral tone on all subjects. It's one's duty to do so. And as a high moral tone can hardly be said to conduce very much to either one's health or one's happiness, in order to get up to town I have always pretended to have a younger brother of the name of Ernest, who lives in the Albany, and gets into the most dreadful scrapes. That, my dear Algy, is the whole truth pure and simple.

ALGERNON. The truth is rarely pure and never simple. Modern life would be very tedious if it were either, and modern literature a complete impossibility!

JACK. That wouldn't be at all a bad thing.

ALGERNON. Literary criticism is not your forte, my dear fellow. Don't try it. You should leave that to people who haven't been at a University. They do it so well in the daily papers. What you really are is a Bunburyist. I was quite right in saying you were a Bunburyist. You are one of the most advanced Bunburyists I know.

JACK. What on earth do you mean?

ALGERNON. You have invented a very useful younger brother called Ernest, in order that you may be able to come up to town as often as you like. I have invented an invaluable permanent invalid called Bunbury, in order that I may be able to go down into the country whenever I choose. Bunbury is perfectly invaluable. If it wasn't for Bunbury's extraordinary bad health, for instance, I wouldn't be able to dine with you at Willis's to-night, for I have been really engaged to Aunt Augusta for more than a week.

JACK. I haven't asked you to dine with me anywhere tonight.

ALGERNON. I know. You are absolutely careless about sending out invitations. It is very foolish of you. Nothing annoys people so much as not receiving invitations.

JACK. You had much better dine with your Aunt Augusta.

ALGERNON. I haven't the smallest intention of doing anything of the kind. To begin with, I dined there on Monday, and once a week is quite enough to dine with one's own relatives. In the second place, whenever I do dine there I am always treated as a member of the family, and sent down with either no woman at all, or two. In the third place, I know perfectly well whom she will place me next to, tonight. She will place me next to Mary Farquhar, who always flirts with her own husband across the dinner-table. That is not very pleasant. Indeed, it is not even decent . . . and that sort of thing is enormously on the increase. The amount of women in London who flirt with their own husbands is perfectly scandalous. It looks so bad. It is simply washing one's clean linen in public. Besides, now that I know you to be a confirmed Bunburyist I naturally want to talk to you about Bunburying. I want to tell you the rules.

JACK. I'm not a Bunburyist at all. If Gwendolen accepts me, I am going to kill my brother, indeed I think I'll kill him in any case. Cecily is a little too much interested in him. It is rather a bore. So I am going to get rid of Ernest. And I strongly advise you to do the same with Mr. . . . with your invalid friend who has the absurd name.

ALGERNON. Nothing will induce me to part with Bunbury, and if you ever get married, which seems to me extremely problematic, you will be very glad to know Bunbury. A man who marries without knowing Bunbury has a very tedious time of it.

JACK. That is nonsense. If I marry a charming girl like Gwendolen, and she is the only girl I ever saw in my life that I would marry, I certainly won't want to know Bunbury.

ALGERNON. Then your wife will. You don't seem to realize, that in married life three is company and two is none.

JACK [*sententiously*]. That, my dear young friend, is the theory that the corrupt French Drama has been propounding for the last fifty years.

ALGERNON. Yes; and that the happy English home has proved in half the time.

JACK. For heaven's sake, don't try to be cynical. It's perfectly easy to be cynical.

ALGERNON. My dear fellow, it isn't easy to be anything now-adays. There's such a lot of beastly competition about. [*The sound of an electric bell is heard.*] Ah! that must be Aunt Augusta. Only relatives, or creditors, ever ring in that Wagnerian manner. Now, if I can get her out of the way for ten minutes, so that you can have an opportunity for proposing to Gwendolen, may I dine with you to-night at Willis's?

JACK. I suppose so, if you want to.

ALGERNON. Yes, but you must be serious about it. I hate people who are not serious about meals. It is so shallow of them.

[*Enter* LANE.]

LANE. Lady Bracknell and Miss Fairfax. [ALGERNON *goes forward to meet them. Enter* LADY BRACKNELL *and* GWEN-DOLEN.]

LADY BRACKNELL. Good afternoon, dear Algernon, I hope you are behaving very well.

ALGERNON. I'm feeling very well, Aunt Augusta.

LADY BRACKNELL. That's not quite the same thing. In fact the two things rarely go together. [*Sees* JACK *and bows to him with icy coldness.*]

ALGERNON [*to* GWENDOLEN]. Dear me, you are smart!

GWENDOLEN. I am always smart! Aren't I, Mr. Worthing?

JACK. You're quite perfect, Miss Fairfax.

GWENDOLEN. Oh! I hope I am not that. It would leave no room for developments, and I intend to develop in *many directions.* [GWENDOLEN *and* JACK *sit down together in the corner.*]

LADY BRACKNELL. I'm sorry if we are a little late, Algernon, but I was obliged to call on dear Lady Harbury. I hadn't been there since her poor husband's death. I never saw a woman so altered; she looks quite twenty years younger. And now I'll have a cup of tea, and one of those nice cucumber sandwiches you promised me.

ALGERNON. Certainly, Aunt Augusta. [*Goes over to tea-table.*]

LADY BRACKNELL. Won't you come and sit here, Gwendolen?

GWENDOLEN. Thanks, mamma, I'm quite comfortable where I am.

ALGERNON [*picking up empty plate in horror*]. Good heavens! Lane! Why are there no cucumber sandwiches? I ordered them specially.

LANE [*gravely*]. There were no cucumbers in the market this morning, sir. I went down twice.

ALGERNON. No cucumbers!

LANE. No, sir. Not even for ready money.

ALGERNON. That will do, Lane, thank you.

LANE. Thank you, sir. [*Goes out.*]

ALGERNON. I am greatly distressed, Aunt Augusta, about there being no cucumbers, not even for ready money.

LADY BRACKNELL. It really makes no matter, Algernon. I had some crumpets with Lady Harbury, who seems to me to be living entirely for pleasure now.

ALGERNON. I hear her hair has turned quite gold from grief.

LADY BRACKNELL. It certainly has changed its colour. From what cause I, of course, cannot say. [ALGERNON *crosses and hands tea.*] Thank you. I've quite a treat for you to-night, Algernon. I am going to send you down with Mary Farquhar. She is such a nice woman, and so attentive to her husband. It's delightful to watch them.

ALGERNON. I am afraid, Aunt Augusta, I shall have to give up the pleasure of dining with you to-night after all.

LADY BRACKNELL [*frowning*]. I hope not, Algernon. It would put my table completely out. Your uncle would have to dine upstairs. Fortunately he is accustomed to that.

ALGERNON. It is a great bore, and, I need hardly say, a terrible disappointment to me, but the fact is I have just had a telegram to say that my poor friend Bunbury is very ill again. [*Exchanges glances with* JACK.] They seem to think I should be with him.

LADY BRACKNELL. It is very strange. This Mr. Bunbury seems to suffer from curiously bad health.

ALGERNON. Yes; poor Bunbury is a dreadful invalid.

LADY BRACKNELL. Well, I must say, Algernon, that I think it is high time that Mr. Bunbury made up his mind whether he was going to live or to die. This shilly-shallying with the question is absurd. Nor do I in any way approve of the modern sympathy with invalids. I consider it morbid. Illness of any kind is hardly a thing to be encouraged in others. Health is the primary duty of life. I am always telling that to your poor uncle, but he never seems to take much notice . . . as far as any improvement in his ailments goes. I should be much obliged if you would ask Mr. Bunbury, from me, to be kind enough not to have a relapse on Saturday, for I rely on you to arrange my music for me. It is my last reception and one wants something that will encourage conversation, particularly at the end of the season when

everyone has practically said whatever they had to say,
which, in most cases, was probably not much.

ALGERNON. I'll speak to Bunbury, Aunt Augusta, if he is still
conscious, and I think I can promise you he'll be all right
by Saturday. You see, if one plays good music, people don't
listen, and if one plays bad music people don't talk. But I'll
run over the programme I've drawn out, if you will kindly
come into the next room for a moment.

LADY BRACKNELL. Thank you, Algernon. It is very thoughtful
of you. [*Rising, and following* ALGERNON.] I'm sure the programme will be delightful, after a few expurgations. French
songs I cannot possibly allow. People always seem to think
that they are improper, and either look shocked, which is
vulgar, or laugh, which is worse. But German sounds a
thoroughly respectable language, and indeed, I believe is so.
Gwendolen, you will accompany me.

GWENDOLEN. Certainly, mamma. [LADY BRACKNELL *and* AL-
GERNON *go into the music-room,* GWENDOLEN *remains
behind.*]

JACK. Charming day it has been, Miss Fairfax.

GWENDOLEN. Pray don't talk to me about the weather, Mr.
Worthing. Whenever people talk to me about the weather,
I always feel quite certain that they mean something else.
And that makes me so nervous.

JACK. I do mean something else.

GWENDOLEN. I thought so. In fact, I am never wrong.

JACK. And I would like to be allowed to take advantage of
Lady Bracknell's temporary absence . . .

GWENDOLEN. I would certainly advise you to do so. Mamma
has a way of coming back suddenly into a room that I have
often had to speak to her about.

JACK [*nervously*]. Miss Fairfax, ever since I met you I have
admired you more than any girl . . . I have ever met
since . . . I met you.

GWENDOLEN. Yes, I am quite aware of the fact. And I often
wish that in public, at any rate, you had been more demon-
strative. For me you have always had an irresistible fascination. Even before I met you I was far from indifferent to
you. [JACK *looks at her in amazement.*] We live, as I hope
you know, Mr. Worthing, in an age of ideals. The fact is
constantly mentioned in the more expensive monthly mag-
azines, and has reached the provincial pulpits I am told:
and my ideal has always been to love some one of the name
of Ernest. There is something in that name that inspires

absolute confidence. The moment Algernon first mentioned to me that he had a friend called Ernest, I knew I was destined to love you.

JACK. You really love me, Gwendolen?

GWENDOLEN. Passionately!

JACK. Darling! You don't know how happy you've made me.

GWENDOLEN. My own Ernest!

JACK. But you don't really mean to say that you couldn't love me if my name wasn't Ernest?

GWENDOLEN. But your name is Ernest.

JACK. Yes, I know it is. But supposing it was something else? Do you mean to say you couldn't love me then?

GWENDOLEN [glibly]. Ah! that is clearly a metaphysical speculation, and like most metaphysical speculations has very little reference at all to the actual facts of real life, as we know them.

JACK. Personally, darling, to speak quite candidly, I don't much care about the name of Ernest . . . I don't think that name suits me at all.

GWENDOLEN. It suits you perfectly. It is a divine name. It has a music of its own. It produces vibrations.

JACK. Well, really, Gwendolen, I must say that I think there are lots of other much nicer names. I think, Jack, for instance, a charming name.

GWENDOLEN. Jack? . . . No, there is very little music in the name Jack, if any at all, indeed. It does not thrill. It produces absolutely no vibrations. . . . I have known several Jacks, and they all, without exception, were more than usually plain. Besides, Jack is a notorious domesticity for John! And I pity any woman who is married to a man called John. She would probably never be allowed to know the entrancing pleasure of a single moment's solitude. The only really safe name is Ernest.

JACK. Gwendolen, I must get christened at once—I mean we must get married at once. There is no time to be lost.

GWENDOLEN. Married, Mr. Worthing?

JACK [astounded]. Well . . . surely. You know that I love you, and you led me to believe, Miss Fairfax, that you were not absolutely indifferent to me.

GWENDOLEN. I adore you. But you haven't proposed to me yet. Nothing has been said at all about marriage. The subject has not even been touched on.

JACK. Well . . . may I propose to you now?

GWENDOLEN. I think it would be an admirable opportunity.

And to spare you any possible disappointment, Mr. Worthing, I think it only fair to tell you quite frankly beforehand that I am fully determined to accept you.

JACK. Gwendolen!

GWENDOLEN. Yes, Mr. Worthing, what have you got to say to me?

JACK. You know what I have got to say to you.

GWENDOLEN. Yes, but you don't say it.

JACK. Gwendolen, will you marry me? [*Goes on his knees.*]

GWENDOLEN. Of course I will, darling. How long you have been about it! I am afraid you have had very little experience in how to propose.

JACK. My own one, I have never loved anyone in the world but you.

GWENDOLEN. Yes, but men often propose for practice. I know my brother Gerald does. All my girl-friends tell me so. What wonderfully blue eyes you have, Ernest! They are quite, quite blue. I hope you will always look at me just like that, especially when there are other people present.

[*Enter* LADY BRACKNELL.]

LADY BRACKNELL. Mr. Worthing! Rise, sir, from this semi-recumbent posture. It is most indecorous.

GWENDOLEN. Mamma! [*He tries to rise; she restrains him.*] I must beg you to retire. This is no place for you. Besides, Mr. Worthing has not quite finished yet.

LADY BRACKNELL. Finished what, may I ask?

GWENDOLEN. I am engaged to Mr. Worthing, mamma. [*They rise together.*]

LADY BRACKNELL. Pardon me, you are not engaged to anyone. When you do become engaged to some one, I, or your father, should his health permit him, will inform you of the fact. An engagement should come on a young girl as a surprise, pleasant or unpleasant, as the case may be. It is hardly a matter that she could be allowed to arrange for herself. . . . And now I have a few questions to put to you, Mr. Worthing. While I am making these inquiries, you, Gwendolen, will wait for me below in the carriage.

GWENDOLEN [*reproachfully*]. Mamma!

LADY BRACKNELL. In the carriage, Gwendolen! [GWENDOLEN *goes to the door. She and* JACK *blow kisses to each other behind* LADY BRACKNELL'S *back.* LADY BRACKNELL *looks vaguely about as if she could not understand what the noise was. Finally turns round.*] Gwendolen, the carriage!

GWENDOLEN. Yes, mamma. [*Goes out, looking back at* JACK.]

LADY BRACKNELL [*sitting down*]. You can take a seat, Mr. Worthing. [*Looks in her pocket for note-book and pencil.*]

JACK. Thank you, Lady Bracknell, I prefer standing.

LADY BRACKNELL [*pencil and note-book in hand*]. I feel bound to tell you that you are not down on my list of eligible young men, although I have the same list as the dear Duchess of Bolton has. We work together, in fact. However, I am quite ready to enter your name, should your answers be what a really affectionate mother requires. Do you smoke?

JACK. Well, yes, I must admit I smoke.

LADY BRACKNELL. I am glad to hear it. A man should always have an occupation of some kind. There are far too many idle men in London as it is. How old are you?

JACK. Twenty-nine.

LADY BRACKNELL. A very good age to be married at. I have always been of opinion that a man who desires to get married should know either everything or nothing. Which do you know?

JACK [*after some hesitation*]. I know nothing, Lady Bracknell.

LADY BRACKNELL. I am pleased to hear it. I do not approve of anything that tampers with natural ignorance. Ignorance is like a delicate exotic fruit; touch it and the bloom is gone. The whole theory of modern education is radically unsound. Fortunately in England, at any rate, education produces no effect whatsoever. If it did, it would prove a serious danger to the upper classes, and probably lead to acts of violence in Grosvenor Square. What is your income?

JACK. Between seven and eight thousand a year.

LADY BRACKNELL [*makes a note in her book*]. In land, or in investments?

JACK. In investments, chiefly.

LADY BRACKNELL. That is satisfactory. What between the duties expected of one during one's life-time, and the duties exacted from one after one's death, land has ceased to be either a profit or a pleasure. It gives one position, and prevents one from keeping it up. That's all that can be said about land.

JACK. I have a country house with some land, of course, attached to it, about fifteen hundred acres, I believe; but I don't depend on that for my real income. In fact, as far as I can make out, the poachers are the only people who make anything out of it.

LADY BRACKNELL. A country house! How many bedrooms?

Well, that point can be cleared up afterwards. You have a town house, I hope? A girl with a simple, unspoiled nature, like Gwendolen, could hardly be expected to reside in the country.

JACK. Well, I own a house in Belgrave Square, but it is let by the year to Lady Bloxham. Of course, I can get it back whenever I like, at six months' notice.

LADY BRACKNELL. Lady Bloxham? I don't know her.

JACK. Oh, she goes about very little. She is a lady considerably advanced in years.

LADY BRACKNELL. Ah, nowadays that is no guarantee of respectability of character. What number in Belgrave Square?

JACK. 149

LADY BRACKNELL [*shaking her head*]. The unfashionable side. I thought there was something. However, that could easily be altered.

JACK. Do you mean the fashion, or the side?

LADY BRACKNELL [*sternly*]. Both, if necessary, I presume. What are your politics?

JACK. Well, I am afraid I really have none. I am a Liberal Unionist.

LADY BRACKNELL. Oh, they count as Tories. They dine with us. Or come in the evening, at any rate. Now to minor matters. Are your parents living?

JACK. I have lost both my parents.

LADY BRACKNELL. Both? . . . That seems like carelessness. Who was your father? He was evidently a man of some wealth. Was he born in what the Radical papers call the purple of commerce, or did he rise from the ranks of the aristocracy?

JACK. I am afraid I really don't know. The fact is, Lady Bracknell, I said I had lost my parents. It would be nearer the truth to say that my parents seem to have lost me . . . I don't actually know who I am by birth. I was . . . well, I was found.

LADY BRACKNELL. Found!

JACK. The late Mr. Thomas Cardew, an old gentleman of a very charitable and kindly disposition, found me, and gave me the name of Worthing, because he happened to have a first-class ticket for Worthing in his pocket at the time. Worthing is a place in Sussex. It is a seaside resort.

LADY BRACKNELL. Where did the charitable gentleman who had a first-class ticket for this seaside resort find you?

JACK [*gravely*]. In a hand-bag.

LADY BRACKNELL. A hand-bag?

JACK [*very seriously*]. Yes, Lady Bracknell. I was in a hand-bag—a somewhat large, black leather hand-bag, with handles to it—an ordinary hand-bag in fact.

LADY BRACKNELL. In what locality did this Mr. James, or Thomas, Cardew come across this ordinary hand-bag?

JACK. In the cloak-room at Victoria Station. It was given to him in mistake for his own.

LADY BRACKNELL. The cloak-room at Victoria Station?

JACK. Yes. The Brighton line.

LADY BRACKNELL. The line is immaterial. Mr. Worthing, I confess I feel somewhat bewildered by what you have just told me. To be born, or at any rate bred, in a hand-bag, whether it had handles or not, seems to me to display a contempt for the ordinary decencies of family life that re-mind one of the worst excesses of the French Revolution. And I presume you know what that unfortunate movement led to? As for the particular locality in which the hand-bag was found, a cloak-room at a railway station might serve to conceal a social indiscretion—has probably, indeed, been used for that purpose before now—but it could hardly be regarded as an assured basis for a recognized position in good society.

JACK. May I ask you then what you would advise me to do? I need hardly say I would do anything in the world to en-sure Gwendolen's happiness.

LADY BRACKNELL. I would strongly advise you, Mr. Worthing, to try and acquire some relations as soon as possible, and to make a definite effort to produce at any rate one parent, of either sex, before the season is quite over.

JACK. Well, I don't see how I could possibly manage to do that. I can produce the hand-bag at any moment. It is in my dressing-room at home. I really think that should satisfy you, Lady Bracknell.

LADY BRACKNELL. Me, sir! What has it to do with me? You can hardly imagine that I and Lord Bracknell would dream of allowing our only daughter—a girl brought up with the utmost care—to marry into a cloak-room, and form an al-liance with a parcel? Good morning, Mr. Worthing! [LADY BRACKNELL *sweeps out in majestic indignation.*]

JACK. Good morning! [ALGERNON, *from the other room, strikes up the Wedding March.* JACK *looks perfectly furious, and goes to the door.*] For goodness' sake don't play that ghastly tune, Algy! How idiotic you are! [*The music stops, and* ALGERNON *enters cheerily.*]

ALGERNON. Didn't it go off all right, old boy? You don't mean to say Gwendolen refused you? I know it is a way she has. She is always refusing people. I think it is most ill-natured of her.

JACK. Oh, Gwendolen is as right as a trivet. As far as she is concerned, we are engaged. Her mother is perfectly unbearable. Never met such a Gorgon . . . I don't really know what a Gorgon is like, but I am quite sure that Lady Bracknell is one. In any case, she is a monster, without being a myth, which is rather unfair. . . . I beg your pardon, Algy, I suppose I shouldn't talk about your own aunt in that way before you.

ALGERNON. My dear boy, I love hearing my relations abused. It is the only thing that makes me put up with them at all. Relations are simply a tedious pack of people, who haven't got the remotest knowledge of how to live, nor the smallest instinct about when to die.

JACK. Oh, that is nonsense!

ALGERNON. It isn't!

JACK. Well, I won't argue about the matter. You always want to argue about things.

ALGERNON. That is exactly what things were originally made for.

JACK. Upon my word, if I thought that, I'd shoot myself . . . [*A pause.*] You don't think there is any chance of Gwendolen becoming like her mother in about a hundred and fifty years, do you, Algy?

ALGERNON. All women become like their mothers. That is their tragedy. No man does. That's his.

JACK. Is that clever?

ALGERNON. It is perfectly phrased! and quite as true as any observation in civilized life should be.

JACK. I am sick to death of cleverness. Everybody is clever nowadays. You can't go anywhere without meeting clever people. The thing has become an absolute public nuisance. I wish to goodness we had a few fools left.

ALGERNON. We have.

JACK. I should extremely like to meet them. What do they talk about?

ALGERNON. The fools? Oh! about the clever people, of course.

JACK. What fools!

ALGERNON. By the way, did you tell Gwendolen the truth about your being Ernest in town, and Jack in the country?

JACK [*in a very patronising manner*]. My dear fellow, the truth isn't quite the sort of thing one tells to a nice, sweet, refined girl. What extraordinary ideas you have about the way to behave to a woman!

ALGERNON. The only way to behave to a woman is to make love to her, if she is pretty, and to someone else if she is plain.

JACK. Oh, that is nonsense.

ALGERNON. What about your brother? What about the profligate Ernest?

JACK. Oh, before the end of the week I shall have got rid of him. I'll say he died in Paris of apoplexy. Lots of people die of apoplexy, quite suddenly, don't they?

ALGERNON. Yes, but it's hereditary, my dear fellow. It's a sort of thing that runs in families. You had much better say a severe chill.

JACK. You are sure a severe chill isn't hereditary, or anything of that kind?

ALGERNON. Of course it isn't!

JACK. Very well, then. My poor brother Ernest is carried off suddenly in Paris, by a severe chill. That gets rid of him.

ALGERNON. But I thought you said that . . . Miss Cardew was a little too much interested in your poor brother Ernest? Won't she feel his loss a good deal?

JACK. Oh, that is all right. Cecily is not a silly, romantic girl, I am glad to say. She has got a capital appetite, goes for long walks, and pays no attention at all to her lessons.

ALGERNON. I would rather like to see Cecily.

JACK. I will take very good care you never do. She is excessively pretty, and she is only just eighteen.

ALGERNON. Have you told Gwendolen yet that you have an excessively pretty ward who is only just eighteen?

JACK. Oh! one doesn't blurt these things out to people. Cecily and Gwendolen are perfectly certain to be extremely great friends. I'll bet you anything you like, that half an hour after they have met, they will be calling each other sister.

ALGERNON. Women only do that when they have called each other a lot of other things first. Now, my dear boy, if we want to get a good table at Willis's, we really must go and dress. Do you know it is nearly seven?

JACK [*irritably*]. Oh! it always is nearly seven.

ALGERNON. Well, I'm hungry.

JACK. I never knew you when you weren't. . . .

ALGERNON. What shall we do after dinner? Go to a theatre?

JACK. Oh, no! I loathe listening.

ALGERNON. Well, let us go to the Club?

JACK. Oh, no! I hate talking.

ALGERNON. Well, we might trot round to the Empire at ten?

JACK. Oh, no! I can't bear looking at things. It is so silly.

ALGERNON. Well, what shall we do?

JACK. Nothing!

ALGERNON. It is awfully hard work doing nothing. However, I don't mind hard work where there is no definite object of any kind.

[*Enter* LANE.]

LANE. Miss Fairfax.

[*Enter* GWENDOLEN. LANE *goes out.*]

ALGERNON. Gwendolen, upon my word!

GWENDOLEN. Algy, kindly turn your back. I have something very particular to say to Mr. Worthing.

ALGERNON. Really, Gwendolen, I don't think I can allow this at all.

GWENDOLEN. Algy, you always adopt a strictly immoral attitude towards life. You are not quite old enough to do that. [ALGERNON *retires to the fireplace.*]

JACK. My own darling!

GWENDOLEN. Ernest, we may never be married. From the expression on mamma's face I fear we never shall. Few parents nowadays pay any regard to what their children say to them. The old-fashioned respect for the young is fast dying out. Whatever influence I ever had over mamma, I lost at the age of three. But although she may prevent us from becoming man and wife, and I may marry someone else, and marry often, nothing that she can possibly do can alter my eternal devotion to you.

JACK. Dear Gwendolen.

GWENDOLEN. The story of your romantic origin, as related to me by mamma, with unpleasing comments, has naturally stirred the deeper fibres of my nature. Your Christian name has an irresistible fascination. The simplicity of your character makes you exquisitely incomprehensible to me. Your town address at the Albany I have. What is your address in the country?

JACK. The Manor House, Woolton, Hertfordshire. [ALGERNON,

who has been carefully listening, smiles to himself, and writes the address on his shirt-cuff. Then picks up the Railway Guide.]

GWENDOLEN. There is a good postal service, I suppose? It may be necessary to do something desperate. That, of course, will require serious consideration. I will communicate with you daily.

JACK. My own one!

GWENDOLEN. How long do you remain in town?

JACK. Till Monday.

GWENDOLEN. Good! Algy, you may turn round now.

ALGERNON. Thanks, I've turned round already.

GWENDOLEN. You may also ring the bell.

JACK. You will let me see you to your carriage, my own darling?

GWENDOLEN. Certainly.

JACK [*to* LANE, *who now enters*]. I will see Miss Fairfax out.

LANE. Yes, sir. [JACK *and* GWENDOLEN *go off.* LANE *presents several letters on a salver to* ALGERNON. *It is to be surmised that they are bills, as* ALGERNON, *after looking at the envelopes, tears them up.*]

ALGERNON. A glass of sherry, Lane.

LANE. Yes, sir.

ALGERNON. To-morrow, Lane, I'm going Bunburying.

LANE. Yes, sir.

ALGERNON. I shall probably not be back till Monday. You can put up my dress clothes, my smoking jacket, and all the Bunbury suits . . .

LANE. Yes, sir. [*Handing sherry.*]

ALGERNON. I hope to-morrow will be a fine day, Lane.

LANE. It never is, sir.

ALGERNON. Lane, you're a perfect pessimist.

LANE. I do my best to give satisfaction, sir.

[*Enter* JACK. LANE *goes off.*]

JACK. There's a sensible, intellectual girl! the only girl I ever cared for in my life. [ALGERNON *is laughing immoderately.*] What on earth are you so amused at?

ALGERNON. Oh, I'm a little anxious about poor Bunbury, that's all.

JACK. If you don't take care, your friend Bunbury will get you into a serious scrape some day.

ALGERNON. I love scrapes. They are the only things that are never serious.

JACK. Oh, that's nonsense, Algy. You never talk anything but nonsense.

ALGERNON. Nobody ever does. [*Jack looks indignantly at him, and leaves the room.* ALGERNON *lights a cigarette, reads his shirt-cuff and smiles.*]

CURTAIN

ACT TWO

Garden at the Manor House. A flight of gray stone steps leads up to the house. The garden, an old-fashioned one, full of roses. Time of year, July. Basket chairs, and a table covered with books, are set under a large yew tree.

[MISS PRISM *discovered seated at the table.* CECILY *is at the back watering flowers.*]

MISS PRISM [*calling*]. Cecily, Cecily! Surely such a utilitarian occupation as the watering of flowers is rather Moulton's duty than yours? Especially at a moment when intellectual pleasures await you. Your German grammar is on the table. Pray open it at page fifteen. We will repeat yesterday's lesson.

CECILY [*coming over very slowly*]. But I don't like German. It isn't at all a becoming language. I know perfectly well that I look quite plain after my German lesson.

MISS PRISM. Child, you know how anxious your guardian is that you should improve yourself in every way. He laid particular stress on your German, as he was leaving for town yesterday. Indeed, he always lays stress on your German when he is leaving for town.

CECILY. Dear Uncle Jack is so very serious! Sometimes he is so serious that I think he cannot be quite well.

MISS PRISM [*drawing herself up*]. Your guardian enjoys the best of health, and his gravity of demeanour is especially to be commended in one so comparatively young as he is. I know no one who has a higher sense of duty and responsibility.

CECILY. I suppose that is why he often looks a little bored when we three are together.

MISS PRISM. Cecily! I am surprised at you. Mr. Worthing has many troubles in his life. Idle merriment and triviality would be out of place in his conversation. You must remember his constant anxiety about that unfortunate young man, his brother.

CECILY. I wish Uncle Jack would allow that unfortunate young man, his brother, to come down here sometimes. We might have a good influence over him, Miss Prism. I am sure you certainly would. You know German, and geology, and things of that kind influence a man very much. [CECILY *begins to write in her diary*.]

MISS PRISM [*shaking her head*]. I do not think that even I could produce any effect on a character that, according to his own brother's admission, is irretrievably weak and vacillating. Indeed, I am not sure that I would desire to reclaim him. I am not in favour of this modern mania for turning bad people into good people at a moment's notice. As a man sows so let him reap. You must put away your diary, Cecily. I really don't see why you should keep a diary at all.

CECILY. I keep a diary in order to enter the wonderful secrets of my life. If I didn't write them down I should probably forget all about them.

MISS PRISM. Memory, my dear Cecily, is the diary that we all carry about with us.

CECILY. Yes, but it usually chronicles the things that have never happened, and couldn't possibly have happened. I believe that Memory is responsible for nearly all the three-volume novels that Mudie sends us.

MISS PRISM. Do not speak slightingly of the three-volume novel, Cecily. I wrote one myself in earlier days.

CECILY. Did you really, Miss Prism? How wonderfully clever you are! I hope it did not end happily? I don't like novels that end happily. They depress me so much.

MISS PRISM. The good ended happily, and the bad unhappily. That is what Fiction means.

CECILY. I suppose so. But it seems very unfair. And was your novel ever published?

MISS PRISM. Alas! no. The manuscript unfortunately was abandoned. I use the word in the sense of lost or mislaid. To your work, child, these speculations are profitless.

CECILY [*smiling*]. But I see dear Dr. Chasuble coming up through the garden.

MISS PRISM [*rising and advancing*]. Dr. Chasuble! This is indeed a pleasure.

[*Enter* CANON CHASUBLE.]

CHASUBLE. And how are we this morning? Miss Prism, you are, I trust, well?

CECILY. Miss Prism has just been complaining of a slight headache. I think it would do her so much good to have a short stroll with you in the park, Dr. Chasuble.

MISS PRISM. Cecily, I have not mentioned anything about a headache.

CECILY. No, dear Miss Prism, I know that, but I felt instinctively that you had a headache. Indeed I was thinking about that, and not about my German lesson, when the Rector came in.

CHASUBLE. I hope, Cecily, you are not inattentive.

CECILY. Oh, I'm afraid I am.

CHASUBLE. That is strange. Were I fortunate enough to be Miss Prism's pupil, I would hang upon her lips. [MISS PRISM *glares*.] I spoke metaphorically.—My metaphor was drawn from bees. Ahem! Mr. Worthing, I suppose, has not returned from town yet?

MISS PRISM. We do not expect him till Monday afternoon.

CHASUBLE. Ah yes, he usually likes to spend his Sunday in London. He is not one of those whose sole aim is enjoyment, as, by all accounts, that unfortunate young man, his brother, seems to be. But I must not disturb Egeria and her pupil any longer.

MISS PRISM. Egeria? My name is Lætitia, Doctor.

CHASUBLE [*bowing*]. A classical allusion merely, drawn from the Pagan authors. I shall see you both no doubt at Evensong.

MISS PRISM. I think, dear Doctor, I will have a stroll with you. I find I have a headache after all, and a walk might do it good.

CHASUBLE. With pleasure, Miss Prism, with pleasure. We might go as far as the school and back.

MISS PRISM. That would be delightful. Cecily, you will read your Political Economy in my absence. The chapter on the Fall of the Rupee you may omit. It is somewhat too sensational. Even these metallic problems have their melodramatic side. [*Goes down the garden with* DR. CHASUBLE.]

CECILY [*picks up books and throws them back on table*]. Horrid Political Economy! Horrid Geography! Horrid, horrid German!

[*Enter* MERRIMAN *with a card on a salver.*]

MERRIMAN. Mr. Ernest Worthing has just driven over from the station. He has brought his luggage with him.

CECILY [*takes the card and reads it*]. "Mr. Ernest Worthing, B 4 The Albany, W." Uncle Jack's brother! Did you tell him Mr. Worthing was in town?

MERRIMAN. Yes, Miss. He seemed very much disappointed. I

mentioned that you and Miss Prism were in the garden.
He said he was anxious to speak to you privately for a moment.

CECILY. Ask Mr. Ernest Worthing to come here. I suppose you
had better talk to the housekeeper about a room for him.

MERRIMAN. Yes, Miss. [*Goes off*].

CECILY. I have never met any really wicked person before. I
feel rather frightened. I am so afraid he will look just like
everyone else.

[*Enter* ALGERNON, *very gay and debonair*.]

He does!

ALGERNON [*raising his hat*]. You are my little cousin Cecily,
I'm sure.

CECILY. You are under some strange mistake. I am not little.
In fact, I am more than usually tall for my age. [ALGERNON
is rather taken aback.] But I am your cousin Cecily. You,
I see from your card, are Uncle Jack's brother, my cousin
Ernest, my wicked cousin Ernest.

ALGERNON. Oh! I am not really wicked at all, cousin Cecily.
You mustn't think that I am wicked.

CECILY. If you are not, then you have certainly been deceiving
us all in a very inexcusable manner. I hope you have not
been leading a double life, pretending to be wicked and
being really good all the time. That would be hypocrisy.

ALGERNON [*looks at her in amazement*]. Oh! of course I have
been rather reckless.

CECILY. I am glad to hear it.

ALGERNON. In fact, now you mention the subject, I have been
very bad in my own small way.

CECILY. I don't think you should be so proud of that, though I
am sure it must have been very pleasant.

ALGERNON. It is much pleasanter being here with you.

CECILY. I can't understand how you are here at all. Uncle
Jack won't be back till Monday afternoon.

ALGERNON. That is a great disappointment. I am obliged to
go up by the first train on Monday morning. I have a business appointment that I am anxious . . . to miss.

CECILY. Couldn't you miss it anywhere but in London?

ALGERNON. No; the appointment is in London.

CECILY. Well, I know, of course, how important it is not to
keep a business engagement, if one wants to retain any
sense of the beauty of life, but still I think you had better

wait till Uncle Jack arrives. I know he wants to speak to you about your emigrating.

ALGERNON. About my what?

CECILY. Your emigrating. He has gone up to buy your outfit.

ALGERNON. I certainly wouldn't let Jack buy my outfit. He has no taste in neckties at all.

CECILY. I don't think you will require neckties. Uncle Jack is sending you to Australia.

ALGERNON. Australia! I'd sooner die.

CECILY. Well, he said at dinner on Wednesday night, that you would have to choose between this world, the next world, and Australia.

ALGERNON. Oh, well! The accounts I have received of Australia and the next world are not particularly encouraging. This world is good enough for me, cousin Cecily.

CECILY. Yes, but are you good enough for it?

ALGERNON. I'm afraid I'm not that. That is why I want you to reform me. You might make that your mission, if you don't mind, cousin Cecily.

CECILY. I'm afraid I've not time, this afternoon.

ALGERNON. Well, would you mind my reforming myself this afternoon?

CECILY. That is rather Quixotic of you. But I think you should try.

ALGERNON. I will. I feel better already.

CECILY. You are looking a little worse.

ALGERNON. That is because I am hungry.

CECILY. How thoughtless of me. I should have remembered that when one is going to lead an entirely new life, one requires regular and wholesome meals. Won't you come in?

ALGERNON. Thank you. Might I have a button-hole first? I never have any appetite unless I have a button-hole first.

CECILY. A Maréchal Niel? [*Picks up scissors.*]

ALGERNON. No, I'd sooner have a pink rose.

CECILY. Why? [*Cuts a flower.*]

ALGERNON. Because you are like a pink rose, cousin Cecily.

CECILY. I don't think it can be right for you to talk to me like that. Miss Prism never says such things to me.

ALGERNON. Then Miss Prism is a short-sighted old lady. [CECILY *puts the rose in his button-hole.*] You are the prettiest girl I ever saw.

CECILY. Miss Prism says that all good looks are a snare.

ALGERNON. They are a snare that every sensible man would like to be caught in.

CECILY. Oh! I don't think I would care to catch a sensible man. I shouldn't know what to talk to him about.

[*They pass into the house.* MISS PRISM *and* DR. CHASUBLE *return.*]

MISS PRISM. You are too much alone, dear Dr. Chasuble. You should get married. A misanthrope I can understand—a womanthrope, never!

CHASUBLE [*with a scholar's shudder*]. Believe me, I do not deserve so neologistic a phrase. The precept as well as the practice of the Primitive Church was distinctly against matrimony.

MISS PRISM [*sententiously*]. That is obviously the reason why the Primitive Church has not lasted up to the present day. And you do not seem to realize, dear Doctor, that by persistently remaining single, a man converts himself into a permanent public temptation. Men should be careful; this very celibacy leads weaker vessels astray.

CHASUBLE. But is a man not equally attractive when married?

MISS PRISM. No married man is ever attractive except to his wife.

CHASUBLE. And often, I've been told, not even to her.

MISS PRISM. That depends on the intellectual sympathies of the woman. Maturity can always be depended on. Ripeness can be trusted. Young women are green. [DR. CHASUBLE *starts*]. I spoke horticulturally. My metaphor was drawn from fruits. But where is Cecily?

CHASUBLE. Perhaps she followed us to the school.

[*Enter* JACK *slowly from the back of the garden. He is dressed in the deepest mourning, with crepe hatband and black gloves.*]

MISS PRISM. Mr. Worthing!

CHASUBLE. Mr. Worthing?

MISS PRISM. This is indeed a surprise. We did not look for you till Monday afternoon.

JACK [*shakes* MISS PRISM'S *hand in a tragic manner*]. I have returned sooner than I expected. Dr. Chasuble, I hope you are well?

CHASUBLE. Dear Mr. Worthing, I trust this garb of woe does not betoken some terrible calamity?

JACK. My brother.

MISS PRISM. More shameful debts and extravagance?

CHASUBLE. Still leading his life of pleasure?

JACK [*shaking his head*]. Dead!

CHASUBLE. Your brother Ernest dead?

JACK. Quite dead.

MISS PRISM. What a lesson for him! I trust he will profit by it.

CHASUBLE. Mr. Worthing, I offer you my sincere condolence. You have at least the consolation of knowing that you were always the most generous and forgiving of brothers.

JACK. Poor Ernest! He had many faults, but it is a sad, sad blow.

CHASUBLE. Very sad indeed. Were you with him at the end?

JACK. No. He died abroad; in Paris, in fact. I had a telegram last night from the manager of the Grand Hotel.

CHASUBLE. Was the cause of death mentioned?

JACK. A severe chill, it seems.

MISS PRISM. As a man sows, so shall he reap.

CHASUBLE [raising his hand]. Charity, dear Miss Prism, charity! None of us are perfect. I myself am peculiarly susceptible to draughts. Will the interment take place here?

JACK. No. He seems to have expressed a desire to be buried in Paris.

CHASUBLE. In Paris! [Shakes his head.] I fear that hardly points to any very serious state of mind at the last. You would no doubt wish me to make some slight allusion to this tragic domestic affliction next Sunday. [JACK presses his hand convulsively.] My sermon on the meaning of the manna in the wilderness can be adapted to almost any occasion, joyful, or, as in the present case, distressing. [All sigh.] I have preached it at harvest celebrations, christenings, confirmations, on days of humiliation and festal days. The last time I delivered it was in the Cathedral, as a charity sermon on behalf of the Society for the Prevention of Discontentment among the Upper Orders. The Bishop, who was present, was much struck by some of the analogies I drew.

JACK. Ah, that reminds me, you mentioned christenings I think, Dr. Chasuble? I suppose you know how to christen all right? [DR. CHASUBLE looks astounded.] I mean, of course, you are continually christening, aren't you?

MISS PRISM. It is, I regret to say, one of the Rector's most constant duties in this parish. I have often spoken to the poorer classes on the subject. But they don't seem to know what thrift is.

CHASUBLE. But is there any particular infant in whom you are interested, Mr. Worthing? Your brother was, I believe, unmarried, was he not?

JACK. Oh, yes.

MISS PRISM [*bitterly*]. People who live entirely for pleasure usually are.

JACK. But it is not for any child, dear Doctor. I am very fond of children. No! the fact is, I would like to be christened myself, this afternoon, if you have nothing better to do.

CHASUBLE. But surely, Mr. Worthing, you have been christened already?

JACK. I don't remember anything about it.

CHASUBLE. But have you any grave doubts on the subject?

JACK. I certainly intend to have. Of course, I don't know if the thing would bother you in any way, or if you think I am a little too old now.

CHASUBLE. Not at all. The sprinkling, and, indeed, the immersion of adults is a perfectly canonical practice.

JACK. Immersion!

CHASUBLE. You need have no apprehensions. Sprinkling is all that is necessary, or indeed I think advisable. Our weather is so changeable. At what hour would you wish the ceremony performed?

JACK. Oh, I might trot around about five if that would suit you.

CHASUBLE. Perfectly, perfectly! In fact I have two similar ceremonies to perform at that time. A case of twins that occurred recently in one of the outlying cottages on your own estate. Poor Jenkins the carter, a most hard-working man.

JACK. Oh! I don't see much fun in being christened along with other babies. It would be childish. Would half-past five do?

CHASUBLE. Admirably! Admirably! [*Takes out watch.*] And now, dear Mr. Worthing, I will not intrude any longer into a house of sorrow. I would merely beg you not to be too much bowed down by grief. What seem to us bitter trials at the moment are often blessings in disguise.

MISS PRISM. This seems to me a blessing of an extremely obvious kind.

[*Enter* CECILY *from the house.*]

CECILY. Uncle Jack! Oh, I am pleased to see you back. But what horrid clothes you have on! Do go and change them.

MISS PRISM. Cecily!

CHASUBLE. My child! my child! [CECILY *goes towards* JACK; *he kisses her brow in a melancholy manner.*]

CECILY. What is the matter, Uncle Jack? Do look happy! You look as if you had a toothache and I have such a surprise for you. Who do you think is in the dining-room? Your brother!

JACK. Who!

CECILY. Your brother Ernest. He arrived about half an hour ago.

JACK. What nonsense! I haven't got a brother.

CECILY. Oh, don't say that. However badly he may have behaved to you in the past he is still your brother. You couldn't be so heartless as to disown him. I'll tell him to come out. And you will shake hands with him, won't you, Uncle Jack? [*Runs back into the house.*]

CHASUBLE. These are very joyful tidings.

MISS PRISM. After we had all been resigned to his loss, his sudden return seems to me peculiarly distressing.

JACK. My brother is in the dining-room? I don't know what it all means. I think it is perfectly absurd.

[*Enter* ALGERNON *and* CECILY *hand in hand. They come slowly up to* JACK.]

JACK. Good heavens! [*Motions* ALGERNON *away*.]

ALGERNON. Brother John, I have come down from town to tell you that I am very sorry for all the trouble I have given you, and that I intend to lead a better life in the future. [JACK *glares at him and does not take his hand.*]

CECILY. Uncle Jack, you are not going to refuse your own brother's hand?

JACK. Nothing will induce me to take his hand. I think his coming down here disgraceful. He knows perfectly well why.

CECILY. Uncle Jack, do be nice. There is some good in everyone. Ernest has just been telling me about his poor invalid friend, Mr. Bunbury, whom he goes to visit so often. And surely there must be much good in one who is kind to an invalid, and leaves the pleasures of London to sit by a bed of pain.

JACK. Oh, he has been talking about Bunbury, has he?

CECILY. Yes, he has told me all about poor Mr. Bunbury, and his terrible state of health.

JACK. Bunbury! Well, I won't have him talk to you about Bunbury or about anything else. It is enough to drive one perfectly frantic.

ALGERNON. Of course I admit that the faults were all on my side. But I must say that I think that Brother John's coldness to me is peculiarly painful. I expected a more en-

thusiastic welcome, especially considering it is the first time
I have come here.

CECILY. Uncle Jack, if you don't shake hands with Ernest I
will never forgive you.

JACK. Never forgive me?

CECILY. Never, never, never!

JACK. Well, this is the last time I shall ever do it. [*Shakes
hands with* ALGERNON *and glares.*]

CHASUBLE. It's pleasant, is it not, to see so perfect a reconciliation? I think we might leave the two brothers together.

MISS PRISM. Cecily, you will come with us.

CECILY. Certainly, Miss Prism. My little task of reconciliation
is over.

CHASUBLE. You have done a beautiful action to-day, dear
child.

MISS PRISM. We must not be premature in our judgments.

CECILY. I feel very happy. [*They all go off.*]

JACK. You young scoundrel, Algy, you must get out of this
place as soon as possible. I don't allow any Bunburying
here.

[*Enter* MERRIMAN.]

MERRIMAN. I have put Mr. Ernest's things in the room next
to yours, sir. I suppose that is all right?

JACK. What?

MERRIMAN. Mr. Ernest's luggage, sir. I have unpacked it and
put it in the room next to your own.

JACK. His luggage?

MERRIMAN. Yes, sir. Three portmanteaus, a dressing-case, two
hat-boxes, and a large luncheon-basket.

ALGERNON. I am afraid I can't stay more than a week this
time.

JACK. Merriman, order the dog-cart at once. Mr. Ernest has
been suddenly called back to town.

MERRIMAN. Yes, sir. [*Goes back into the house.*]

ALGEGNON. What a fearful liar you are, Jack. I have not been
called back to town at all.

JACK. Yes, you have.

ALGERNON. I haven't heard anyone call me.

JACK. Your duty as a gentleman calls you back.

ALGERNON. My duty as a gentleman has never interfered with
my pleasures in the smallest degree.

JACK. I can quite understand that.

ALGERNON. Well, Cecily is a darling.

JACK. You are not to talk of Miss Cardew like that. I don't like it.

ALGERNON. Well, I don't like your clothes. You look perfectly ridiculous in them. Why on earth don't you go up and change? It is perfectly childish to be in deep mourning for a man who is actually staying for a whole week with you in your house as a guest. I call it grotesque.

JACK. You are certainly not staying with me for a whole week as a guest or anything else. You have got to leave . . . by the four-five train.

ALGERNON. I certainly won't leave you so long as you are in mourning. It would be most unfriendly. If I were in mourning you would stay with me, I suppose. I should think it very unkind if you didn't.

JACK. Well, will you go if I change my clothes?

ALGERNON. Yes, if you are not too long. I never saw anybody take so long to dress, and with such little result.

JACK. Well, at any rate, that is better than being always over-dressed as you are.

ALGERNON. If I am occasionally a little over-dressed, I make up for it by being always immensely over-educated.

JACK. Your vanity is ridiculous, your conduct an outrage, and your presence in my garden utterly absurd. However, you have got to catch the four-five, and I hope you will have a pleasant journey back to town. This Bunburying, as you call it, has not been a great success for you. [*Goes into the house.*]

ALGERNON. I think it has been a great success. I'm in love with Cecily, and that is everything. [*Enter* CECILY *at the back of the garden. She picks up the can and begins to water the flowers.*] But I must see her before I go, and make arrangements for another Bunbury. Ah, there she is.

CECILY. Oh, I merely came back to water the roses. I thought you were with Uncle Jack.

ALGERNON. He's gone to order the dog-cart for me.

CECILY. Oh, is he going to take you for a nice drive?

ALGERNON. He's going to send me away.

CECILY. Then have we got to part?

ALGERNON. I am afraid so. It's a very painful parting.

CECILY. It is always painful to part from people whom one has known for a very brief space of time. The absence of old friends one can endure with equanimity. But even a momentary separation from anyone to whom one has just been introduced is almost unbearable.

ALGERNON. Thank you.

[*Enter* MERRIMAN.]

MERRIMAN. The dog-cart is at the door, sir. [ALGERNON *looks appealingly at* CECILY.]

CECILY. It can wait, Merriman . . . for . . . five minutes.

MERRIMAN. Yes, miss. [*Exits.*]

ALGERNON. I hope, Cecily, I shall not offend you if I state quite frankly and openly that you seem to me to be in every way the visible personification of absolute perfection.

CECILY. I think your frankness does you great credit, Ernest. If you will allow me I will copy your remarks into my diary. [*Goes over to table and begins writing in diary.*]

ALGERNON. Do you really keep a diary? I'd give anything to look at it. May I?

CECILY. Oh, no. [*Puts her hand over it.*] You see, it is simply a very young girl's record of her own thoughts and impressions, and consequently meant for publication. When it appears in volume form I hope you will order a copy. But pray, Ernest, don't stop. I delight in taking down from dictation. I have reached "absolute perfection." You can go on. I am quite ready for more.

ALGERNON [*somewhat taken aback*]. Ahem! Ahem!

CECILY. Oh, don't cough, Ernest. When one is dictating one should speak fluently and not cough. Besides, I don't know how to spell a cough. [*Writes as* ALGERNON *speaks.*]

ALGERNON [*speaking very rapidly*]. Cecily, ever since I first looked upon your wonderful and incomparable beauty, I have dared to love you wildly, passionately, devotedly, hopelessly.

CECILY. I don't think that you should tell me that you love me wildly, passionately, devotedly, hopelessly. Hopelessly doesn't seem to make much sense, does it?

ALGERNON. Cecily!

[*Enter* MERRIMAN.]

MERRIMAN. The dog cart is waiting, sir.

ALGERNON. Tell it to come round next week, at the same hour.

MERRIMAN [*looks at* CECILY, *who makes no sign*]. Yes, sir.

[MERRIMAN *retires.*]

CECILY. Uncle Jack would be very much annoyed if he knew you were staying on till next week, at the same hour.

ALGERNON. Oh, I don't care about Jack. I don't care for anybody in the whole world but you. I love you, Cecily. You will marry me, won't you?

CECILY. You silly you! Of course. Why, we have been engaged for the last three months.

ALGERNON. For the last three months.

CECILY. Yes, it will be exactly three months on Thursday.

ALGERNON. But how did we become engaged?

CECILY. Well, ever since dear Uncle Jack first confessed to us that he had a younger brother who was very wicked and bad, you of course have formed the chief topic of conversation between myself and Miss Prism. And of course a man who is much talked about is always very attractive. One feels there must be something in him after all. I daresay it was foolish of me, but I fell in love with you, Ernest.

ALGERNON. Darling! And when was the engagement actually settled?

CECILY. On the 14th of February last. Worn out by your entire ignorance of my existence, I determined to end the matter one way or the other, and after a long struggle with myself I accepted you under this dear old tree here. The next day I bought this little ring in your name, and this is the little bangle with the true lovers' knot I promised you always to wear.

ALGERNON. Did I give you this? It's very pretty, isn't it?

CECILY. Yes, you've wonderfully good taste, Ernest. It's the excuse I've always given for your leading such a bad life. And this is the box in which I keep all your dear letters. [Kneels at table, opens box, and produces letters tied up with blue ribbon.]

ALGERNON. My letters! But my own sweet Cecily, I have never written you any letters.

CECILY. You need hardly remind me of that, Ernest. I remember only too well that I was forced to write your letters for you. I wrote always three times a week, and sometimes oftener.

ALGERNON. Oh, do let me read them, Cecily?

CECILY. Oh, I couldn't possibly. They would make you far too conceited. [Replaces box.] The three you wrote me after I had broken off the engagement are so beautiful, and so badly spelled, that even now I can hardly read them without crying a little.

ALGERNON. But was our engagement ever broken off?

CECILY. Of course it was. On the 22nd of last March. You can see the entry if you like. [*Shows diary.*] "Today I broke off my engagement with Ernest. I feel it is better to do so. The weather still continues charming."

ALGERNON. But why on earth did you break it off? What had I done? I had done nothing at all. Cecily, I am very much hurt indeed to hear you broke it off. Particularly when the weather was so charming.

CECILY. It would hardly have been a really serious engagement if it hadn't been broken off at least once. But I forgave you before the week was out.

ALGERNON [*crossing to her, and kneeling*]. What a perfect angel you are, Cecily.

CECILY. You dear romantic boy. [*He kisses her, she puts her fingers through his hair.*] I hope your hair curls naturally, does it?

ALGERNON. Yes, darling, with a little help from others.

CECILY. I am so glad.

ALGERNON. You'll never break off our engagement again, Cecily?

CECILY. I don't think I could break it off now that I have actually met you. Besides, of course, there is the question of your name.

ALGERNON. Yes, of course. [*Nervously.*]

CECILY. You must not laugh at me, darling, but it had always been a girlish dream of mine to love some one whose name was Ernest. [ALGERNON *rises,* CECILY *also.*] There is something in that name that seems to inspire absolute confidence. I pity any poor married woman whose husband is not called Ernest.

ALGERNON. But, my dear child, do you mean to say you could not love me if I had some other name?

CECILY. But what name?

ALGERNON. Oh, any name you like—Algernon, for instance. . . .

CECILY. But I don't like the name of Algernon.

ALGERNON. Well, my own dear, sweet, loving little darling, I really can't see why you should object to the name of Algernon. It is not at all a bad name. In fact, it is rather an aristocratic name. Half of the chaps who get into the Bankruptcy Court are called Algernon. But seriously, Cecily . . . [*Moving to her*] . . . if my name was Algy, couldn't you love me?

CECILY [*rising*]. I might respect you, Ernest, I might admire
your character, but I fear that I should not be able to give
you my undivided attention.

ALGERNON. Ahem! Cecily! [*Picking up hat.*] Your Rector
here is, I suppose, thoroughly experienced in the practice
of all the rites and ceremonials of the church?

CECILY. Oh, yes. Dr. Chasuble is a most learned man. He has
never written a single book, so you can imagine how much
he knows.

ALGERNON. I must see him at once on a most important christening—I mean on most important business.

CECILY. Oh!

ALGERNON. I sha'n't be away more than half an hour.

CECILY. Considering that we have been engaged since February
the 14th, and that I only met you to-day for the first time,
I think it is rather hard that you should leave me for so
long a period as half an hour. Couldn't you make it twenty
minutes?

ALGERNON. I'll be back in no time. [*Kisses her and rushes
down the garden.*]

CECILY. What an impetuous boy he is. I like his hair so much.
I must enter his proposal in my diary.

[*Enter* MERRIMAN.]

MERRIMAN. A Miss Fairfax has just called to see Mr. Worthing. On very important business, Miss Fairfax states.

CECILY. Isn't Mr. Worthing in his library?

MERRIMAN. Mr. Worthing went over in the direction of the
Rectory some time ago.

CECILY. Pray ask the lady to come out here; Mr. Worthing is
sure to be back soon. And you can bring tea.

MERRIMAN. Yes, miss. [*Goes out.*]

CECILY. Miss Fairfax! I suppose one of the many good elderly
women who are associated with Uncle Jack in some of his
philanthropic work in London. I don't quite like women
who are interested in philanthropic work. I think it is so
forward of them.

[*Enter* MERRIMAN.]

MERRIMAN. Miss Fairfax.

[*Enter* GWENDOLEN. *Exit* MERRIMAN.]

CECILY [*advancing to meet her*]. Pray let me introduce myself
to you. My name is Cecily Cardew.

GWENDOLEN. Cecily Cardew? [*Moving to her and shaking hands.*] What a very sweet name! Something tells me that we are going to be great friends. I like you already more than I can say. My first impressions of people are never wrong.

CECILY. How nice of you to like me so much after we have known each other such a comparatively short time. Pray sit down.

GWENDOLEN [*still standing up*]. I may call you Cecily, may I not?

CECILY. With pleasure!

GWENDOLEN. And you will always call me Gwendolen, won't you?

CECILY. If you wish.

GWENDOLEN. Then that is all quite settled, is it not?

CECILY. I hope so. [*A pause. They both sit down together.*]

GWENDOLEN. Perhaps this might be a favorable opportunity for my mentioning who I am. My father is Lord Bracknell. You have never heard of papa, I suppose?

CECILY. I don't think so.

GWENDOLEN. Outside the family circle, papa, I'm glad to say, is entirely unknown. I think that is quite as it should be. The home seems to me to be the proper sphere for the man. And certainly once a man begins to neglect his domestic duties he becomes painfully effeminate, does he not? And I don't like that. It makes men so very attractive. Cecily, mamma, whose views on education are remarkably strict, has brought me up to be extremely short-sighted; it is part of her system; so do you mind my looking at you through my glasses?

CECILY. Oh, not at all, Gwendolen. I am very fond of being looked at.

GWENDOLEN [*after examining* CECILY *carefully through a lorgnette*]. You are here on a short visit, I suppose.

CECILY. Oh, no, I live here.

GWENDOLEN [*severely*]. Really? Your mother, no doubt, or some female relative of advanced years, resides here also?

CECILY. Oh, no. I have no mother, nor, in fact, any relations.

GWENDOLEN. Indeed?

CECILY. My dear guardian, with the assistance of Miss Prism, has the arduous task of looking after me.

GWENDOLEN. Your guardian?

CECILY. Yes, I am Mr. Worthing's ward.

GWENDOLEN. Oh! It is strange he never mentioned to me that

he had a ward. How secretive of him! He grows more interesting hourly. I am not sure, however, that the news inspires me with feelings of unmixed delight. [*Rising and going to her.*] I am very fond of you, Cecily; I have liked you ever since I met you. But I am bound to state that now that I know that you are Mr. Worthing's ward, I cannot help expressing a wish you were—well, just a little older than you seem to be—and not quite so very alluring in appearance. In fact, if I may speak candidly—

CECILY. Pray do! I think that whenever one has anything unpleasant to say, one should always be quite candid.

GWENDOLEN. Well, to speak with perfect candour, Cecily, I wish that you were fully forty-two, and more than usually plain for your age. Ernest has a strong upright nature. He is the very soul of truth and honour. Disloyalty would be as impossible to him as deception. But even men of the noblest possible moral character are extremely susceptible to the influence of the physical charms of others. Modern, no less than Ancient History, supplies us with many most painful examples of what I refer to. If it were not so, indeed, History would be quite unreadable.

CECILY. I beg your pardon, Gwendolen, did you say Ernest?

GWENDOLEN. Yes.

CECILY. Oh, but it is not Mr. Ernest Worthing who is my guardian. It is his brother—his elder brother.

GWENDOLEN [*sitting down again*]. Ernest never mentioned to me that he had a brother.

CECILY. I am sorry to say they have not been on good terms for a long time.

GWENDOLEN. Ah! that accounts for it. And now that I think of it I have never heard any man mention his brother. The subject seems distasteful to most men. Cecily, you have lifted a load from my mind. I was growing almost anxious. It would have been terrible if any cloud had come across a friendship like ours, would it not? Of course you are quite, quite sure that it is not Mr. Ernest Worthing who is your guardian.

CECILY. Quite sure. [*A pause.*] In fact, I am going to be his.

GWENDOLEN [*enquiringly*]. I beg your pardon?

CECILY [*rather shy and confidingly*]. Dearest Gwendolen, there is no reason why I should make a secret of it to you. Our little county newspaper is sure to chronicle the fact next week. Mr. Ernest Worthing and I are engaged to be married.

GWENDOLEN [*quite politely, rising*]. My darling Cecily, I think there must be some slight error. Mr. Ernest Worthing is engaged to me. The announcement will appear in the *Morning Post* on Saturday at the latest.

CECILY [*very politely, rising*]. I am afraid you must be under some misconception. Ernest proposed to me exactly ten minutes ago. [*Shows diary.*]

GWENDOLEN [*examines diary through her lorgnette carefully*]. It is certainly very curious, for he asked me to be his wife yesterday afternoon at 5.30. If you would care to verify the incident, pray do so. [*Produces diary of her own.*] I never travel without my diary. One should always have something sensational to read in the train. I am so sorry, dear Cecily, if it is any disappointment to you, but I am afraid *I* have the prior claim.

CECILY. It would distress me more than I can tell you, dear Gwendolen, if it caused you any mental or physical anguish, but I feel bound to point out that since Ernest proposed to you he clearly has changed his mind.

GWENDOLEN [*meditatively*]. If the poor fellow has been entrapped into any foolish promise I shall consider it my duty to rescue him at once, and with a firm hand.

CECILY [*thoughtfully and sadly*]. Whatever unfortunate entanglement my dear boy may have got into, I will never reproach him with it after we are married.

GWENDOLEN. Do you allude to me, Miss Cardew, as an entanglement? You are presumptuous. On an occasion of this kind it becomes more than a moral duty to speak one's mind. It becomes a pleasure.

CECILY. Do you suggest, Miss Fairfax, that I entrapped Ernest into an engagement? How dare you? This is no time for wearing the shallow mask of manners. When I see a spade I call it a spade.

GWENDOLEN [*satirically*]. I am glad to say that I have never seen a spade. It is obvious that our social spheres have been widely different.

[*Enter* MERRIMAN, *followed by the footman. He carries a salver, tablecloth, and plate-stand.* CECILY *is about to retort. The presence of the servants exercises a restraining influence, under which both girls chafe.*]

MERRIMAN. Shall I lay tea here as usual, miss?

CECILY [*sternly, in a calm voice*]. Yes, as usual. [MERRIMAN

begins to clear and lay cloth. A long pause. CECILY *and*
GWENDOLEN *glare at each other.*]

GWENDOLEN. Are there many interesting walks in the vicinity,
Miss Cardew?

CECILY. Oh, yes, a great many. From the top of one of the
hills quite close one can see five counties.

GWENDOLEN. Five counties! I don't think I should like that,
I hate crowds.

CECILY [*sweetly*]. I suppose that is why you live in town?
[GWENDOLEN *bites her lip, and beats her foot nervously
with her parasol.*]

GWENDOLEN [*looking round*]. Quite a well-kept garden this is,
Miss Cardew.

CECILY. So glad you like it, Miss Fairfax.

GWENDOLEN. I had no idea there were any flowers in the
country.

CECILY. Oh, flowers are as common here, Miss Fairfax, as
people are in London.

GWENDOLEN. Personally I cannot understand how anybody
manages to exist in the country, if anybody who is anybody
does. The country always bores me to death.

CECILY. Ah! This is what the newspapers call agricultural de-
pression, is it not? I believe the aristocracy are suffering
very much from it just at present. It is almost an epidemic
amongst them, I have been told. May I offer you some tea,
Miss Fairfax?

GWENDOLEN [*with elaborate politeness*]. Thank you. [*Aside.*]
Detestable girl! But I require tea!

CECILY [*sweetly*]. Sugar?

GWENDOLEN [*superciliously*]. No, thank you. Sugar is not
fashionable any more. [CECILY *looks angrily at her, takes
up the tongs and puts four lumps of sugar into the cup.*]

CECILY [*severely*]. Cake or bread and butter?

GWENDOLEN [*in a bored manner*]. Bread and butter, please.
Cake is rarely seen at the best houses nowadays.

CECILY [*cuts a very large slice of cake, and puts it on the
tray*]. Hand that to Miss Fairfax. [MERRIMAN *does so, and
goes out with footman.* GWENDOLEN *drinks the tea and
makes a grimace. Puts down cup at once, reaches out her
hand to the bread and butter, looks at it, and finds it is
cake. Rises in indignation.*]

GWENDOLEN. You have filled my tea with lumps of sugar, and
though I asked most distinctly for bread and butter, you
have given me cake. I am known for the gentleness of my

disposition, and the extraordinary sweetness of my nature, but I warn you, Miss Cardew, you may go too far.

CECILY [*rising*]. To save my poor, innocent, trusting boy from the machinations of any other girl there are no lengths to which I would not go.

GWENDOLEN. From the moment I saw you I distrusted you. I felt that you were false and deceitful I am never deceived in such matters. My first impressions of people are invariably right.

CECILY. It seems to me, Miss Fairfax, that I am trespassing on your valuable time. No doubt you have many other calls of a similar character to make in the neighbourhood.

[*Enter* JACK.]

GWENDOLEN [*catching sight of him*]. Ernest! My own Ernest!

JACK. Gwendolen! Darling! [*Offers to kiss her.*]

GWENDOLEN [*drawing back*]. A moment! May I ask if you are engaged to be married to this young lady? [*Points to* CECILY.]

JACK [*laughing*]. To dear little Cecily! Of course not! What could have put such an idea into your pretty little head?

GWENDOLEN. Thank you. You may. [*Offers her cheek.*]

CECILY [*very sweetly*]. I knew there must be some misunderstanding, Miss Fairfax. The gentleman whose arm is at present around your waist is my dear guardian, Mr. John Worthing.

GWENDOLEN. I beg your pardon?

CECILY. This is Uncle Jack.

GWENDOLEN [*receding*]. Jack! Oh!

[*Enter* ALGERNON.]

CECILY. Here is Ernest.

ALGERNON [*goes straight over to* CECILY *without noticing anyone else.*] My own love! [*Offers to kiss her.*]

CECILY [*drawing back*]. A moment, Ernest! May I ask you— are you engaged to be married to this young lady?

ALGERNON [*looking round*]. To what young lady? Good heavens! Gwendolen!

CECILY. Yes, to good heavens, Gwendolen, I mean to Gwendolen.

ALGERNON [*laughing*]. Of course not! What could have put such an idea into your pretty little head?

CECILY. Thank you. [*Presenting her cheek to be kissed.*] You may. [ALGERNON *kisses her.*]

GWENDOLEN. I felt there was some slight error, Miss Cardew. The gentleman who is now embracing you is my cousin, Mr. Algernon Moncrieff.

CECILY [*breaking away from* ALGERNON]. Algernon Moncrieff! Oh! [*The two girls move towards each other and put their arms round each other's waists as if for protection.*]

CECILY. Are you called Algernon?

ALGERNON. I cannot deny it.

CECILY. Oh!

GWENDOLEN. Is your name really John?

JACK [*standing rather proudly*]. I could deny it if I liked. I could deny anything if I liked. But my name certainly is John. It has been John for years.

CECILY [*to* GWENDOLEN]. A gross deception has been practised on both of us.

GWENDOLEN. My poor wounded Cecily!

CECILY. My sweet, wronged Gwendolen!

GWENDOLEN [*slowing and seriously*]. You will call me sister, will you not? [*They embrace.* JACK *and* ALGERNON *groan and walk up and down.*]

CECILY [*rather brightly*]. There is just one question I would like to be allowed to ask my guardian.

GWENDOLEN. An admirable idea! Mr. Worthing, there is just one question I would like to be permitted to put to you. Where is your brother Ernest? We are both engaged to be married to your brother Ernest, so it is a matter of some importance to us to know where your brother Ernest is at present.

JACK [*slowly and hesitatingly*]. Gwendolen—Cecily—it is very painful for me to be forced to speak the truth. It is the first time in my life that I have ever been reduced to such a painful position, and I am really quite inexperienced in doing anything of the kind. However I will tell you quite frankly that I have no brother Ernest. I have no brother at all. I never had a brother in my life, and I certainly have not the smallest intention of ever having one in the future.

CECILY [*surprised*]. No brother at all?

JACK [*cheerily*]. None!

GWENDOLEN [*severely*]. Had you never a brother of any kind?

JACK [*pleasantly*]. Never. Not even of any kind.

GWENDOLEN. I am afraid it is quite clear, Cecily, that neither of us is engaged to be married to anyone.

CECILY. It is not a very pleasant position for a young girl suddenly to find herself in. Is it?

GWENDOLEN. Let us go into the house. They will hardly venture to come after us there.

CECILY. No, men are so cowardly, aren't they? [*They retire into the house with scornful looks.*]

JACK. This ghastly state of things is what you call Bunburying, I suppose?

ALGERNON. Yes, and a perfectly wonderful Bunbury it is. The most wonderful Bunbury I have ever had in my life.

JACK. Well, you've no right whatsoever to Bunbury here.

ALGERNON. That is absurd. One has a right to Bunbury anywhere one chooses. Every serious Bunburyist knows that.

JACK. Serious Bunburyist! Good heavens!

ALGERNON. Well, one must be serious about something, if one wants to have any amusement in life. I happen to be serious about Bunburying. What on earth you are serious about I haven't got the remotest idea. About everything, I should fancy. You have such an absolutely trivial nature.

JACK. Well, the only small satisfaction I have in the whole of this wretched business is that your friend Bunbury is quite exploded. You won't be able to run down to the country quite so often as you used to do, dear Algy. And a very good thing, too.

ALGERNON. Your brother is a little off colour, isn't he, dear Jack? You won't be able to disappear to London quite so frequently as your wicked custom was. And not a bad thing, either.

JACK. As for your conduct towards Miss Cardew, I must say that your taking in a sweet, simple, innocent girl like that is quite inexcusable. To say nothing of the fact that she is my ward.

ALGERNON. I can see no possible defence at all for your deceiving a brilliant, clever, thoroughly experienced young lady like Miss Fairfax. To say nothing of the fact that she is my cousin.

JACK. I wanted to be engaged to Gwendolen, that is all. I love her.

ALGERNON. Well, I simply wanted to be engaged to Cecily. I adore her.

JACK. There is certainly no chance of your marrying Miss Cardew.

ALGERNON. I don't think there is much likelihood, Jack, of you and Miss Fairfax being united.

JACK. Well, that is no business of yours.

ALGERNON. If it was my business, I wouldn't talk about it.

[*Begins to eat muffins.*] It is very vulgar to talk about one's business. Only people like stock-brokers do that, and then merely at dinner parties.

JACK. How you can sit there, calmly eating muffins, when we are in this horrible trouble, I can't make out. You seem to me to be perfectly heartless.

ALGERNON. Well, I can't eat muffins in an agitated manner. The butter would probably get on my cuffs. One should always eat muffins quite calmly. It is the only way to eat them.

JACK. I say it's perfectly heartless your eating muffins at all, under the circumstances.

ALGERNON. When I am in trouble, eating is the only thing that consoles me. Indeed, when I am in really great trouble, as anyone who knows me intimately will tell you, I refuse everything except food and drink. At the present moment I am eating muffins because I am unhappy. Besides, I am particularly fond of muffins. [*Rising.*]

JACK [*rising*]. Well, that is no reason why you should eat them all in that greedy way. [*Takes muffin from* ALGERNON.]

ALGERNON [*offering tea-cake*]. I wish you would have tea-cake instead. I don't like tea-cake.

JACK. Good heavens! I suppose a man may eat his own muffins in his own garden.

ALGERNON. But you have just said it was perfectly heartless to eat muffins.

JACK. I said it was perfectly heartless of you, under the circumstances. That is a very different thing.

ALGERNON. That may be. But the muffins are the same. [*He seizes the muffin dish from* JACK.]

JACK. Algy, I wish to goodness you would go.

ALGERNON. You can't possibly ask me to go without having some dinner. It's absurd. I never go without my dinner. No one ever does, except vegetarians and people like that. Besides I have just made arrangements with Dr. Chasuble to be christened at a quarter to six under the name of Ernest.

JACK. My dear fellow, the sooner you give up that nonsense the better. I made arrangements this morning with Dr. Chasuble to be christened myself at 5.30, and I naturally will take the name of Ernest. Gwendolen would wish it. We can't both be christened Ernest. It's absurd. Besides, I have a perfect right to be christened if I like. There is no evidence at all that I ever have been christened by anybody. I should think it extremely probable I never was, and so does Dr. Chasuble. It is entirely different in your case. You have been christened already.

ALGERNON. Yes, but I have not been christened for years.

JACK. Yes, but you have been christened. That is the important thing.

ALGERNON. Quite so. So I know my constitution can stand it. If you are not quite sure about your ever having been christened, I must say I think it rather dangerous your venturing on it now. It might make you very unwell. You can hardly have forgotten that someone very closely connected with you was very nearly carried off this week in Paris by a severe chill.

JACK. Yes, but you said yourself that a severe chill was not hereditary.

ALGERNON. It usedn't to be, I know—but I daresay it is now. Science is always making wonderful improvements in things.

JACK [picking up the muffin-dish]. Oh, that is nonsense; you are always talking nonsense.

ALGERNON. Jack, you are at the muffins again! I wish you wouldn't. There are only two left. [Takes them.] I told you I was particularly fond of muffins.

JACK. But I hate tea-cake.

ALGERNON. Why on earth then do you allow tea-cake to be served up for your guests? What ideas you have of hospitality!

JACK. Algernon! I have already told you to go. I don't want you here. Why don't you go?

ALGERNON. I haven't quite finished my tea yet, and there is still one muffin left. [JACK groans, and sinks into a chair. ALGERNON still continues eating.]

CURTAIN

ACT THREE

Morning-room at the Manor House. GWENDOLEN *and* CECILY *are at the window, looking out into the garden.*

GWENDOLEN. The fact that they did not follow us at once into the house, as anyone else would have done, seems to me to show that they have some sense of shame left.

CECILY. They have been eating muffins. That looks like repentance.

GWENDOLEN [*after a pause*]. They don't seem to notice us at all. Couldn't you cough?

CECILY. But I haven't got a cough.

GWENDOLEN. They're looking at us. What effrontery!

CECILY. They're approaching. That's very forward of them.

GWENDOLEN. Let us preserve a dignified silence.

CECILY. Certainly. It's the only thing to do now.

[*Enter* JACK, *followed by* ALGERNON. *They whistle some dreadful popular air from a British opera.*]

GWENDOLEN. This dignified silence seems to produce an unpleasant effect.

CECILY. A most distasteful one.

GWENDOLEN. But we will not be the first to speak.

CECILY. Certainly not.

GWENDOLEN. Mr. Worthing, I have something very particular to ask you. Much depends on your reply.

CECILY. Gwendolen, your common sense is invaluable. Mr. Moncrieff, kindly answer me the following question. Why did you pretend to be my guardian's brother?

ALGERNON. In order that I might have an opportunity of meeting you.

CECILY [*to* GWENDOLEN]. That certainly seems a satisfactory explanation, does it not?

GWENDOLEN. Yes, dear, if you can believe him.

CECILY. I don't. But that does not affect the wonderful beauty of his answer.

GWENDOLEN. True. In matters of grave importance, style, not sincerity, is the vital thing. Mr. Worthing, what explanation can you offer to me for pretending to have a brother? Was it in order that you might have an opportunity of coming up to town to see me as often as possible?

JACK. Can you doubt it, Miss Fairfax?

GWENDOLEN. I have the gravest doubts upon the subject. But I intend to crush them. This is not the moment for German scepticism. [*Moving to* CECILY.] Their explanations appear to be quite satisfactory, especially Mr. Worthing's. That seems to me to have the stamp of truth upon it.

CECILY. I am more than content with what Mr. Moncrieff said. His voice alone inspires one with absolute credulity.

GWENDOLEN. Then you think we should forgive them?

CECILY. Yes. I mean no.

GWENDOLEN. True! I had forgotten. There are principles at stake that one cannot surrender. Which of us should tell them? The task is not a pleasant one.

CECILY. Could we not both speak at the same time?

GWENDOLEN. An excellent idea! I nearly always speak at the same time as other people. Will you take the time from me?

CECILY. Certainly. [GWENDOLEN *beats time with uplifted finger.*]

GWENDOLEN *and* CECILY [*speaking together*]. Your Christian names are still an insuperable barrier. That is all!

JACK *and* ALGERNON [*speaking together*]. Our Christian names! Is that all? But we are going to be christened this afternoon.

GWENDOLEN [*to* JACK]. For my sake you are prepared to do this terrible thing?

JACK. I am.

CECILY [*to* ALGERNON]. To please me you are ready to face this fearful ordeal?

ALGERNON. I am!

GWENDOLEN. How absurd to talk of the equality of the sexes! Where questions of self-sacrifice are concerned, men are infinitely beyond us.

JACK. We are. [*Clasps hands with* ALGERNON.]

CECILY. They have moments of physical courage of which we women know absolutely nothing.

GWENDOLEN [*to* JACK]. Darling!

ALGERNON [*to* CECILY]. Darling! [*They fall into each other's arms.*]

[*Enter* MERRIMAN. *When he enters he coughs loudly, seeing the situation.*]

MERRIMAN. Ahem! Ahem! Lady Bracknell!

JACK. Good heavens!

[*Enter* LADY BRACKNELL. *The couples separate in alarm.*

Exit MERRIMAN.]

LADY BRACKNELL. Gwendolen! What does this mean?

GWENDOLEN. Merely that I am engaged to be married to Mr. Worthing, Mamma.

LADY BRACKNELL. Come here. Sit down. Sit down immediately. Hesitation of any kind is a sign of mental decay in the young, of physical weakness in the old. [*Turns to* JACK.] Apprised, sir, of my daughter's sudden flight by her trusty maid, whose confidence I purchased by means of a small coin, I followed her at once by a luggage train. Her unhappy father is, I am glad to say, under the impression that she is attending a more than usually lengthy lecture by the University Extension Scheme on the Influence of a Permanent Income on Thought. I do not propose to undeceive him. Indeed I have never undeceived him on any question. I would consider it wrong. But of course, you will clearly understand that all communication between yourself and my daughter must cease immediately from this moment. On this point, as indeed on all points, I am firm.

JACK. I am engaged to be married to Gwendolen, Lady Bracknell!

LADY BRACKNELL. You are nothing of the kind, sir. And now, as regards Algernon! . . . Algernon!

ALGERNON. Yes, Aunt Augusta.

LADY BRACKNELL. May I ask if it is in this house that your invalid friend Mr. Bunbury resides?

ALGERNON [*stammering*]. Oh, no! Bunbury doesn't live here. Bunbury is somewhere else at present. In fact, Bunbury is dead.

LADY BRACKNELL. Dead! When did Mr. Bunbury die? His death must have been extremely sudden.

ALGERNON [*airily*]. Oh, I killed Bunbury this afternoon. I mean poor Bunbury died this afternoon.

LADY BRACKNELL. What did he die of?

ALGERNON. Bunbury? Oh, he was quite exploded.

LADY BRACKNELL. Exploded! Was he the victim of a revolutionary outrage? I was not aware that Mr. Bunbury was interested in social legislation. If so, he is well punished for his morbidity.

ALGERNON. My dear Aunt Augusta, I mean he was found out! The doctors found out that Bunbury could not live, that is what I mean—so Bunbury died.

LADY BRACKNELL. He seems to have had great confidence in the opinion of his physicians. I am glad, however, that he made up his mind at the last to some definite course of action, and acted under proper medical advice. And now that we have finally got rid of this Mr. Bunbury, may I ask, Mr. Worthing, who is that young person whose hand my nephew Algernon is now holding in what seems to me a peculiarly unnecessary manner?

JACK. That lady is Miss Cecily Cardew, my ward. [LADY BRACKNELL *bows coldly to* CECILY.]

ALGERNON. I am engaged to be married to Cecily, Aunt Augusta.

LADY BRACKNELL. I beg your pardon?

CECILY. Mr. Moncrieff and I are engaged to be married, Lady Bracknell.

LADY BRACKNELL [*with a shiver, crossing to the sofa and sitting down*]. I do not know whether there is anything peculiarly exciting in the air of this particular part of Hertfordshire, but the number of engagements that go on seems to me considerably above the proper average that statistics have laid down for our guidance. I think some preliminary enquiry on my part would not be out of place. Mr. Worthing, is Miss Cardew at all connected with any of the larger railway stations in London? I merely desire information. Until yesterday I had no idea that there were any families or persons whose origin was a Terminus. [JACK *looks perfectly furious, but restrains himself.*]

JACK [*in a clear, cold voice*]. Miss Cardew is the granddaughter of the late Mr. Thomas Cardew of 149, Belgrave Square, S.W.; Gervase Park, Dorking, Surrey; and the Sporran, Fifeshire, N.B.

LADY BRACKNELL. That sounds not unsatisfactory. Three addresses always inspire confidence, even in tradesmen. But what proof have I of their authenticity?

JACK. I have carefully preserved the Court Guide of the period. They are open to your inspection, Lady Bracknell.

LADY BRACKNELL [*grimly*]. I have known strange errors in that publication.

JACK. Miss Cardew's family solicitors are Messrs. Markby, Markby, and Markby.

LADY BRACKNELL. Markby, Markby, and Markby? A firm of

the very highest position in their profession. Indeed I am told that one of the Mr. Markbys is occasionally to be seen at dinner parties. So far I am satisfied.

JACK [*very irritably*]. How extremely kind of you, Lady Bracknell! I have also in my possession, you will be pleased to hear, certificates of Miss Cardew's birth, baptism, whooping cough, registration, vaccination, confirmation, and the measles; both the German and the English variety.

LADY BRACKNELL. Ah! A life crowded with incident, I see; though perhaps somewhat too exciting for a young girl. I am not myself in favour of premature experiences. [*Rises, looks at her watch.*] Gwendolen! the time approaches for our departure. We have not a moment to lose. As a matter of form, Mr. Worthing, I had better ask you if Miss Cardew has any little fortune?

JACK. Oh, about a hundred and thirty thousand pounds in the Funds. That is all. Good-bye, Lady Bracknell. So pleased to have seen you.

LADY BRACKNELL [*sitting down again*]. A moment, Mr. Worthing. A hundred and thirty thousand pounds! And in the Funds! Miss Cardew seems to me a most attractive young lady, now that I look at her. Few girls of the present day have any really solid qualities, any of the qualities that last, and improve with time. We live, I regret to say, in an age of surfaces. [*To* CECILY.] Come over here, dear. [CECILY *goes across.*] Pretty child! your dress is sadly simple, and your hair seems almost as Nature might have left it. But we can soon alter all that. A thoroughly experienced French maid produces a really marvellous result in a very brief space of time. I remember recommending one to young Lady Lancing, and after three months her own husband did not know her.

JACK [*aside*]. And after six months nobody knew her.

LADY BRACKNELL [*glares at* JACK *for a few moments. Then bends, with a practised smile, to* CECILY]. Kindly turn round, sweet child. [CECILY *turns completely round.*] No, the side view is what I want. [CECILY *presents her profile.*] Yes, quite as I expected. There are distinct social possibilities in your profile. The two weak points in our age are its want of principle and its want of profile. The chin a little higher, dear. Style largely depends on the way the chin is worn. They are worn very high, just at present. Algernon!

ALGERNON. Yes, Aunt Augusta!

LADY BRACKNELL. There are distinct social possibilities in Miss Cardew's profile.

ALGERNON. Cecily is the sweetest, dearest, prettiest girl in the whole world. And I don't care twopence about social possibilities.

LADY BRACKNELL. Never speak disrespectfully of society, Algernon. Only people who can't get into it do that. [*To* CECILY.] Dear child, of course you know that Algernon has nothing but his debts to depend upon. But I do not approve of mercenary marriages. When I married Lord Bracknell I had no fortune of any kind. But I never dreamed for a moment of allowing that to stand in my way. Well, I suppose I must give my consent.

ALGERNON. Thank you, Aunt Augusta.

LADY BRACKNELL. Cecily, you may kiss me!

CECILY [*kisses her*]. Thank you, Lady Bracknell.

LADY BRACKNELL. You may also address me as Aunt Augusta for the future.

CECILY. Thank you, Aunt Augusta.

LADY BRACKNELL. The marriage, I think, had better take place quite soon.

ALGERNON. Thank you, Aunt Augusta.

CECILY. Thank you, Aunt Augusta.

LADY BRACKNELL. To speak frankly, I am not in favour of long engagements. They give people the opportunity of finding out each other's character before marriage, which I think is never advisable.

JACK. I beg your pardon for interrupting you, Lady Bracknell, but this engagement is quite out of the question. I am Miss Cardew's guardian, and she cannot marry without my consent until she comes of age. That consent I absolutely decline to give.

LADY BRACKNELL. Upon what grounds, may I ask? Algernon is an extremely, I may almost say an ostentatiously, eligible young man. He has nothing, but he looks everything. What more can one desire?

JACK. It pains me very much to have to speak frankly to you, Lady Bracknell, about your nephew, but the fact is that I do not approve at all of his moral character. I suspect him of being untruthful. [ALGERNON *and* CECILY *look at him in indignant amazement.*]

LADY BRACKNELL. Untruthful! My nephew Algernon? Impossible! He is an Oxonian.

JACK. I fear there can be no possible doubt about the matter.

This afternoon, during my temporary absence in London on an important question of romance, he obtained admission to my house by means of the false pretence of being my brother. Under an assumed name he drank, I've just been informed by my butler, an entire pint bottle of my Perrier-Jouet, Brut, '89; a wine I was specially reserving for myself. Continuing his disgraceful deception, he succeeded in the course of the afternoon in alienating the affections of my only ward. He subsequently stayed to tea, and devoured every single muffin. And what makes his conduct all the more heartless is, that he was perfectly well aware from the first that I have no brother, that I never had a brother, and that I don't intend to have a brother, not even of any kind. I distinctly told him so myself yesterday afternoon.

LADY BRACKNELL. Ahem! Mr. Worthing, after careful consideration I have decided entirely to overlook my nephew's conduct to you.

JACK. That is very generous of you, Lady Bracknell. My own decision, however, is unalterable. I decline to give my consent.

LADY BRACKNELL [to CECILY]. Come here, sweet child. [CECILY goes over.] How old are you, dear?

CECILY. Well, I am really only eighteen, but I always admit to twenty when I go to evening parties.

LADY BRACKNELL. You are perfectly right in making some slight alteration. Indeed, no woman should ever be quite accurate about her age. It looks so calculating. . . . [In meditative manner.] Eighteen, but admitting to twenty at evening parties. Well, it will not be very long before you are of age and free from the restraints of tutelage. So I don't think your guardian's consent is, after all, a matter of any importance.

JACK. Pray excuse me, Lady Bracknell, for interrupting you again, but it is only fair to tell you that according to the terms of her grandfather's will Miss Cardew does not come legally of age till she is thirty-five.

LADY BRACKNELL. That does not seem to me to be a grave objection. Thirty-five is a very attractive age. London society is full of women of the very highest birth who have of their own free choice, remained thirty-five for years. Lady Dumbleton is an instance in point. To my own knowledge she has been thirty-five ever since she arrived at the age of forty, which was many years ago now. I see no reason why our dear Cecily should not be even still more attractive at the age you mention than she is at present. There will be a large accumulation of property.

CECILY. Algy, could you wait for me till I was thirty-five?

ALGERNON. Of course I could, Cecily. You know I could.

CECILY. Yes, I felt it instinctively, but I couldn't wait all that time. I hate waiting even five minutes for anybody. It always makes me rather cross. I am not punctual myself, I know, but I do like punctuality in others, and waiting, even to be married, is quite out of the question.

ALGERNON. Then what is to be done, Cecily?

CECILY. I don't know, Mr. Moncrieff.

LADY BRACKNELL. My dear Mr. Worthing, as Miss Cardew states positively that she cannot wait till she is thirty-five—a remark which I am bound to say seems to me to show a somewhat impatient nature—I would beg of you to reconsider your decision.

JACK. But my dear Lady Bracknell, the matter is entirely in your own hands. The moment you consent to my marriage with Gwendolen, I will most gladly allow your nephew to form an alliance with my ward.

LADY BRACKNELL [rising and drawing herself up]. You must be quite aware that what you propose is out of the question.

JACK. Then a passionate celibacy is all that any of us can look forward to.

LADY BRACKNELL. That is not the destiny I propose for Gwendolen. Algernon, of course, can choose for himself. [Pulls out her watch.] Come, dear, [GWENDOLEN rises] we have already missed five, if not six, trains. To miss any more might expose us to comment on the platform.

[Enter DR. CHASUBLE.]

CHASUBLE. Everything is quite ready for the christenings.

LADY BRACKNELL. The christenings, sir! Is not that somewhat premature?

CHASUBLE [looking rather puzzled, and pointing to JACK and ALGERNON]. Both these gentlemen have expressed a desire for immediate baptism.

LADY BRACKNELL. At their age? The idea is grotesque and irreligious! Algernon, I forbid you to be baptised. I will not hear of such excesses. Lord Bracknell would be highly displeased if he learned that that was the way in which you wasted your time and money.

CHASUBLE. Am I to understand then that there are to be no christenings at all this afternoon?

JACK. I don't think that, as things are now, it would be of much practical value to either of us, Dr. Chasuble.

CHASUBLE. I am grieved to hear such sentiments from you, Mr. Worthing. They savour of the heretical views of the Anabaptists, views that I have completely refuted in four of my unpublished sermons. However, as your present mood seems to be one peculiarly secular, I will return to the church at once. Indeed, I have just been informed by the pew-opener that for the last hour and a half Miss Prism has been waiting for me in the vestry.

LADY BRACKNELL [*starting*]. Miss Prism! Did I hear you mention a Miss Prism?

CHASUBLE. Yes, Lady Bracknell. I am on my way to join her.

LADY BRACKNELL. Pray allow me to detain you for a moment. This matter may prove to be one of vital importance to Lord Bracknell and myself. Is this Miss Prism a female of repellent aspect, remotely connected with education?

CHASUBLE [*somewhat indignantly*]. She is the most cultivated of ladies, and the very picture of respectability.

LADY BRACKNELL. It is obviously the same person. May I ask what position she holds in your household?

CHASUBLE [*severely*]. I am a celibate, madam.

JACK [*interposing*]. Miss Prism, Lady Bracknell, has been for the last three years Miss Cardew's esteemed governess and valued companion.

LADY BRACKNELL. In spite of what I hear of her, I must see her at once. Let her be sent for.

CHASUBLE [*looking off*]. She approaches; she is nigh.

[*Enter* MISS PRISM *hurriedly*.]

MISS PRISM. I was told you expected me in the vestry, dear Canon. I have been waiting for you there for an hour and three-quarters. [*Catches sight of* LADY BRACKNELL, *who has fixed her with a stony glare.* MISS PRISM *grows pale and quails. She looks anxiously round as if desirous to escape.*]

LADY BRACKNELL [*in a severe, judicial voice*]. Prism! [MISS PRISM *bows her head in shame.*] Come here, Prism! [MISS PRISM *approaches in a humble manner.*] Prism! Where is that baby? [*General consternation. The Canon starts back in horror.* ALGERNON *and* JACK *pretend to be anxious to shield* CECILY *and* GWENDOLEN *from hearing the details of a*

terrible public scandal.] Twenty-eight years ago, Prism, you
left Lord Bracknell's house, Number 104, Upper Grosvenor
Street, in charge of a perambulator that contained a baby,
of the male sex. You never returned. A few weeks later,
through the elaborate investigations of the Metropolitan
police, the perambulator was discovered at midnight, standing by itself in a remote corner of Bayswater. It contained
the manuscript of a three-volume novel of more than usually revolting sentimentality. [MISS PRISM *starts in in-
voluntary indigation.*] But the baby was not there! [*Everyone looks at* MISS PRISM.] Prism, where is that baby? [*A
pause.*]

MISS PRISM. Lady Bracknell, I admit with shame that I do
not know. I only wish I did. The plain facts of the case are
these. On the morning of the day you mention, a day that
is forever branded on my memory, I prepared as usual to
take the baby out in its perambulator. I had also with me a
somewhat old but capacious hand-bag in which I had intended to place the manuscript of a work of fiction that I
had written during my few unoccupied hours. In a moment
of mental abstraction, for which I never can forgive myself,
I deposited the manuscript in the bassinette, and placed the
baby in the hand-bag.

JACK [*who has been listening attentively*]. But where did you
deposit the hand-bag?

MISS PRISM. Do not ask me, Mr. Worthing.

JACK. Miss Prism, this is a matter of no small importance to
me. I insist on knowing where you deposited the hand-bag
that contained that infant.

MISS PRISM. I left it in the cloak-room of one of the larger
railway stations in London.

JACK. What railway station?

MISS PRISM [*quite crushed*]. Victoria. The Brighton line. [*Sinks
into a chair.*]

JACK. I must retire to my room for a moment. Gwendolen,
wait here for me.

GWENDOLEN. If you are not too long, I will wait here for you
all my life.

[*Exit* JACK *in great excitement.*]

CHASUBLE. What do you think this means, Lady Bracknell?

LADY BRACKNELL. I dare not even suspect, Dr. Chasuble. I
need hardly tell you that in families of high position strange

coincidences are not supposed to occur. They are hardly considered the thing. [*Noises heard overhead as if someone was throwing trunks about. Everybody looks up.*]

CECILY. Uncle Jack seems strangely agitated.

CHASUBLE. Your guardian has a very emotional nature.

LADY BRACKNELL. This noise is extremely unpleasant. It sounds as if he was having an argument. I dislike arguments of any kind. They are always vulgar, and often convincing.

CHASUBLE [*looking up*]. It has stopped now. [*The noise is redoubled.*]

LADY BRACKNELL. I wish he would arrive at some conclusion.

GWENDOLEN. The suspense is terrible. I hope it will last.

[*Enter* JACK *with a hand-bag of black leather in his hand.*]

JACK [*rushing over to* MISS PRISM]. Is this the handbag, Miss Prism? Examine it carefully before you speak. The happiness of more than one life depends on your answer.

MISS PRISM [*calmly*]. It seems to be mine. Yes, here is the injury it received through the upsetting of a Gower Street omnibus in younger and happier days. Here is the stain on the lining caused by the explosion of a temperance beverage, an incident that occurred at Leamington. And here, on the lock, are my initials. I had forgotten that in an extravagant mood I had had them placed there. The bag is undoubtedly mine. I am delighted to have it so unexpectedly restored to me. It has been a great inconvenience being without it all these years.

JACK [*in a pathetic voice*]. Miss Prism, more is restored to you than this hand-bag. I was the baby you placed in it.

MISS PRISM [*amazed*]. You?

JACK [*embracing her*]. Yes . . . mother!

MISS PRISM [*recoiling in indignant astonishment*]. Mr. Worthing! I am unmarried!

JACK. Unmarried! I do not deny that is a serious blow. But after all, who has the right to cast a stone against one who has suffered? Cannot repentance wipe out an act of folly? Why should there be one law for men and another for women? Mother, I forgive you. [*Tries to embrace her again.*]

MISS PRISM [*still more indignant*]. Mr. Worthing, there is some error. [*Pointing to* LADY BRACKNELL.] There is the lady who can tell you who you really are.

JACK [*after a pause*]. Lady Bracknell, I hate to seem inquisitive, but would you kindly inform me who I am?

LADY BRACKNELL. I am afraid that the news I have to give you will not altogether please you. You are the son of my poor sister, Mrs. Moncrieff, and consequently Algernon's elder brother.

JACK. Algy's elder brother! Then I have a brother after all. I knew I had a brother! I always said I had a brother! Cecily, —how could you have ever doubted that I had a brother? [*Seizes hold of* ALGERNON.] Dr. Chasuble, my unfortunate brother. Miss Prism, my unfortunate brother. Gwendolen, my unfortunate brother. Algy, you young scoundrel, you will have to treat me with more respect in the future. You have never behaved to me like a brother in all your life.

ALGERNON. Well, not till to-day, old boy, I admit. I did my best, however, though I was out of practice. [*Shakes hands.*]

GWENDOLEN [*to* JACK]. My own! But what own are you? What is your Christian name, now that you have become someone else?

JACK. Good heavens! . . . I had quite forgotten that point. Your decision on the subject of my name is irrevocable, I suppose?

GWENDOLEN. I never change, except in my affections.

CECILY. What a noble nature you have, Gwendolen!

JACK. Then the question had better be cleared up at once. Aunt Augusta, a moment. At the time when Miss Prism left me in the hand-bag, had I been christened already?

LADY BRACKNELL. Every luxury that money could buy, including christening, had been lavished on you by your fond and doting parents.

JACK. Then I was christened! That is settled. Now, what name was I given? Let me know the worst.

LADY BRACKNELL. Being the eldest son you were naturally christened after your father.

JACK [*irritably*]. Yes, but what was my father's Christian name?

LADY BRACKNELL [*meditatively*]. I cannot at the present moment recall what the General's Christian name was. But I have no doubt he had one. He was eccentric, I admit. But only in later years. And that was the result of the Indian climate, and marriage, and indigestion, and other things of that kind.

JACK. Algy! Can't you recollect what our father's Christian name was?

ALGERNON. My dear boy, we were never even on speaking terms. He died before I was a year old.

JACK. His name would appear in the Army Lists of the period, I suppose, Aunt Augusta?

LADY BRACKNELL. The General was essentially a man of peace, except in his domestic life. But I have no doubt his name would appear in any military directory.

JACK. The Army Lists of the last forty years are here. These delightful records should have been my constant study. [*Rushes to bookcase and tears the books out.*] M. Generals . . . Mallam, Maxbohm, Magley, what ghastly names they have—Markby, Migsby, Mobbs, Moncrieff! Lieutenant 1840, Captain, Lieutenant-Colonel, Colonel, General 1869, Christian names, Ernest John. [*Puts book very quietly down and speaks quite calmly.*] I always told you, Gwendolen, my name was Ernest didn't I? Well, it is Ernest after all. I mean it naturally is Ernest.

LADY BRACKNELL. Yes, I remember the General was called Ernest. I knew I had some particular reason for disliking the name.

GWENDOLEN. Ernest! My own Ernest! I felt from the first that you could have no other name!

JACK. Gwendolen, it is a terrible thing for a man to find out suddenly that all his life he has been speaking nothing but the truth. Can you forgive me?

GWENDOLEN. I can. For I feel sure that you are sure to change.

JACK. My own one!

CHASUBLE [*to* MISS PRISM]. Lætitia! [*Embraces her.*]

MISS PRISM [*enthusiastically*]. Frederick! At last!

ALGERNON. Cecily! [*Embraces her.*] At last!

JACK. Gwendolen! [*Embraces her.*] At last!

LADY BRACKNELL. My nephew, you seem to be displaying signs of triviality.

JACK. On the contrary, Aunt Augusta, I've now realized for the first time in my life the vital Importance of Being Earnest.

TABLEAU
CURTAIN

BOY MEETS GIRL

Bella *and* Samuel Spewack

Boy Meets Girl was first produced at the Cort Theatre, New York, by George Abbott, on November 27, 1935, and closed on June 19, 1937.

THE CAST

ROBERT LAW	SLADE
LARRY TOMS	SUSIE
J. CARLYLE BENSON	A NURSE
ROSETTI	DOCTOR
MR. FRIDAY [C.F.]	CHAUFFEUR
PEGGY	YOUNG MAN
MISS CREWS	STUDIO OFFICER
RODNEY BEVAN	CUTTER
GREEN	ANOTHER NURSE

MAJOR THOMPSON

SCENES

ACT ONE
Mr. Friday's Office, the Royal Studios in Hollywood

ACT TWO
SCENE I
A Neighborhood Theatre. Seven months later

SCENE II
Mr. Friday's office
SCENE III
The same. Several hours later

ACT THREE
SCENE I
A hospital corridor. Three weeks later
SCENE II
In your home
SCENE III
Mr. Friday's office

ACT ONE

The room we see is one of a suite of three, comprising the sanctum of MR. C. ELLIOT FRIDAY, *a supervisor, sometimes called a producer, who is engaged in manufacturing motion pictures in Hollywood, California.*

In its present state the room is a happy combination of the Regency and Russell Wright periods—given over to pale green, mauve and canary yellow, with Rodier-cloth-covered easy chairs and couch. A magnificent, be-French-phoned desk is at one end of the room. On it rests the inter-office dictograph, over which in the course of the play we hear the voice of the great B.K., chief executive of the studio. Beside it, appropriately, stands an amiable photograph of Mrs. C. Elliot Friday, a cultured if fatuous lady; a copy of Swann's Way *[leaves uncut], a bronze nude astride an ash tray, a bottle of Pyramidon and a copy of* Variety. *In the trash basket is a copy of* Hollywood Reporter. *[It was very unkind to* MR. FRIDAY.*] On the wall back of the desk are bookshelves with pots of hanging ivy on the top shelf, the rest given over, curiously enough, to books—and occasional bric-a-brac. There are a few end tables with ash trays and boxes of cigarettes, for it is the unwritten law in Hollywood that supervisors must provide cigarettes for writers during conferences and other times of stress. The two windows, although of the old-fashioned, non-casement kind, are framed by tasteful, expensive drapes and are partially concealed by half-drawn Venetian blinds. [A supervisor would lose caste without Venetian blinds.] The door Left leads to an anteroom where sits* MISS CREWS, *secretary to* MR. FRIDAY. *The door at Right rear leads to a smaller office where* MR. FRIDAY *sometimes thinks in solitude. This room contains* MR. FRIDAY'S *Commencement Day photograph [Harvard '19], snapshots of B.K.'s wedding, at which* MR. FRIDAY *served as an usher, and a huge picture of Pola Negri inscribed "Sincerely yours." There are other photographs with more florid inscriptions upon faces once famous and since vanished in film dust. The room is also memorable for the fact that* MR. FRIDAY—*a bit of a diplomat in his way—sometimes keeps earnest writers here while he submits their scripts to other writers in his inner office. At times as many as fifteen bright* *minds are thus let loose upon a C. Elliot Friday production, with sometimes startling results.*

All this, however, is very much by the by. It is really more important to note that through those Venetian blinds you can feel the sweet sterility of the desert that is so essentially Southern California. The sun is bright of course, and it pours endlessly through the windows. The time is two o'clock, and the boys have been at it since noon.

One of the boys is BENSON—J. CARLYLE BENSON, *whom we discover prone on a couch. He is in his thirties and in his flannels. Years ago, as he will tell you, he worked as a scene painter and a property boy. He became a writer because he learned how bricks were made and laid. He knows every cliché, every formula, and in his heart of hearts he really believes the fairy tale is a credo of life. And he's a damned nice guy; handicapped somewhat by the fact that he married a beautiful but extravagant young woman who obviously doesn't love him. They live in a gorgeous home, have four dogs, two cars and, as* MR. FRIDAY *would put it, "a menage."*

The other member of the writing team is ROBERT LAW *whom you will find listed in O'Brien's* Best Short Stories *of five years ago. He came to Hollywood to make a little money and run right back to Vermont where he could really write. He is rather handsome, a little round-shouldered; smokes incessantly. He's a damned nice guy, too.*

There is a deep and abiding affection between the two men, even though LAW'S *nostalgia for realism and sincerity and substance finds no echoing response in* MR. BENSON. *They have one great thing in common—their mutual love of a great gag, a practical joke to enliven the monotony of the writing factory.*

For we are dealing here with a factory that manufactures entertainment in approved sizes; that puts the seven arts right on the belt. And it is this very quality that makes MR. FRIDAY'S *office as fascinating as a power house and a good deal more entertaining.*

The other inmates of the room are LARRY TOMS—*you know* LARRY TOMS—*a Western star, and one* ROSETTI, *an agent. It is* MR. ROSETTI'S *business to see to it that* MR. TOMS *is profitably employed, for* MR. ROSETTI *collects ten per cent of* MR. TOMS' *weekly salary which, despite the star's fading popularity, is still a respectable sum.* MR. TOMS *is handsome, of course. He is also parsimonious. He leads a completely righteous life, and*

*if you don't like him it isn't our fault; in all respects he is an
extremely admirable character.*

As the curtain goes up we see that LAW *is on his feet and
obviously he has been telling a story to* MR. TOMS—*a story
that* MR. TOMS *is expected to re-enact before the camera.*

LAW. And this bozo comes up to you and you look him
straight in the eye and you say, "Why, damn your soul, I
loved her before you ever married her." And then in walks
the bitch, and she cries, "Larry, I heard everything you
said." And you just look at her, and there's a long pause
—a *long* pause. And then finally you say, "Did you?" That's
all. Just a plain, quiet, simple "Did you?" Boy, what a
moment! [*He lies down on the couch beside* BENSON.]

LARRY. But what's the story about?

BENSON [*rolling over*]. Love!

LAW [*singing*]. "Love is the sweetest thing—"

LARRY. Now, come on, boys—get off the couch. This ain't fair.
I got a lot at stake in this picture. It's the last one in my
contract. If I get a poor story I'm out in the cold.

LAW. Shivering with a million-dollar annuity.

ROSETTI. Now, gentlemen, don't let's get personal.

LARRY [*rises and crosses to couch*]. When they told me I was
getting the star team of writers on the lot, I was all for it.
But you've done nothing but clown around, and the shooting date's only two weeks off. I've got to play this picture.

LAW. Why?

LARRY [*swallowing*]. Tell me your story in a few simple words.

LAW. Mr. Benson, what's our story?

BENSON. How the hell do I know.

LAW [*sits up*]. Didn't you listen?

BENSON. No. We ought to have a stenographer.

LAW. But they won't wear tights. And I can't dictate to a
stenographer who won't wear tights.

LARRY. Now listen, boys—

LAW. Don't speak to me. You don't like our story.

LARRY. I didn't say I didn't like it. I couldn't follow it. [*He
slumps in disgust.*]

BENSON [*indignantly*]. You couldn't follow it? Listen, I've been
writing stories for eleven years. Boy meets girl. Boy loses
girl. Boy gets girl.

LAW. Or—girl meets boy. Girl loses boy. Girl gets boy. Love
will find a way. Love never loses. Put your money on love.

You can't lose. [*Rises and saunters to window.*] I'm getting
hungry.

BENSON. It's a sorry state of affairs when an actor insists on
following a story. Do you think this is a golf tournament?

ROSETTI [*earnestly*]. If I may make a point, I don't think
you're showing the proper respect to one of the biggest stars
in this studio. A man who's not only captivated millions of
people but is going to captivate millions more—

BENSON [*wearily*]. With his little lasso—

LARRY. Just because I don't get Gable's fan mail don't mean I
ain't got his following. A lot of those that want to write
me ain't never learned how.

LAW. Benson, injustice has been done. We've been lacking in
respect for the idol of illiteracy.

BENSON. Do we apologize?

LAW. No!

ROSETTI. Well, let me tell you something. Before I became an
agent I taught diction for years, and Larry Toms is po-
tentially the greatest actor I've ever met. And I can prove
it with X-rays. I was just taking them up to show B.K.
He's got the Barrymore larynx. I'll put his larynx against
John Barrymore's and I defy you to tell me which is which.
[*Takes X-rays from brief case. Gives one to* BENSON, *one to*
LAW.]

LARRY. I couldn't tell it myself and it's my own larynx.

BENSON [*drawling*]. Say—are you sure this is his *larynx?*

ROSETTI [*the diplomat; retrieving X-rays*]. Gentlemen, I
wouldn't be surprised with the proper training if Larry
couldn't sing. That opens up the whole field of musicals.
[*Puts brief case on chair.*]

BENSON [*to* LAW]. What are we waiting for?

LAW. Lunch.

LARRY [*angrily rising*]. I'm getting fed up with this. I got
writers who are just plain crazy—a producer who can't
concentrate—and ain't even here—and—[*Throws hat on
floor and starts for* BENSON *and* LAW. LAW *moves to back
of couch and* BENSON *goes up to door.*]

ROSETTI [*crossing down on* LARRY'S *left*]. Now . . . now . . .
Larry . . . don't lose your temper.

LARRY [*righteously*]. The idea of writers getting fifteen hundred a week for acting like hoodlums.

LAW. I agree with you.

LARRY. Huh?

LAW. We're not writers. We're hacks. If we weren't, would I be sitting here listening to your inarticulate grunts?

LARRY. Huh?

LAW. That's exactly what I mean. For two cents, Benson, I'd take the next train back to Vermont.

LARRY. That's all right with me.

BENSON. Will you forget Vermont?

LAW. At least I wouldn't have to sit around with *that* in Vermont. I'd write—really write. My God, I wrote once. I wrote a book. A darn good book. I was a promising young novelist. O'Brien reprinted three of my stories. 1928–1929–1930. And in 1935 I'm writing dialogue for a horse!

LARRY [*enraged*]. Now, listen—

ROSETTI [*pleading*]. Larry—Larry, take a deep breath. The boys mean no harm. . . . Exhale!

LAW [*sniffing*]. I smell carbon monoxide.

LARRY. One more crack, that's all—just one more crack! [*Phone rings.*]

ROSETTI [*at phone*]. Hello . . . oh, yes . . . just a minute. For you, Benson.

BENSON [*taking up phone*]. Yes, speaking. Who? Of course, Mrs. Benson's check is good. How much is it for? Thirty-five hundred? Oh! I hope it was real ermine. . . . Certainly it's all right. You put the check through tomorrow. [*Hangs up; dials phone.*]

ROSETTI [*with a feline purr*]. Ermine is a nice fur.

[MISS CREWS *enters regally; puts letters on desk.*]

LARRY [*grumbling*]. Miss Crews, what's keeping C.F.?

MISS CREWS. He's still up with B.K. [*She exits regally.*]

BENSON [*into phone*]. Jim? Benson. Listen, sell three of my Municipal Fives this afternoon, will you? And put it in my joint account in the Security. I've got a check to meet. Never mind about that. I'll talk to her. Right. [*Hangs up.*]

LAW. Pearl is certainly spreading prosperity.

BENSON. What the hell? She's only a kid. She's having a good time. What's money for?

[C.F. *enters.* C.F. *is, of course,* C. ELLIOTT FRIDAY.]

C.F. [*briskly*]. Good morning.

ROSETTI [*rises*]. Good morning, C.F.

LARRY [*rises and sits*]. Hello, C.F. [BENSON *lies on sofa.* LAW *rises and salaams Hindu fashion, as popularized by Mr. De Mille.*]

C.F. Boys, no antics, please. We've got a heavy day ahead of us. [*Sits at desk; picks up phone. Into phone.*] I don't want to be disturbed by anybody—understand? And order some lunch. A plate of raw carrots, and a bottle of certified raw milk. See that it's *raw*. Bring enough for everybody. [*About to hang up.*]

LAW [*rises*]. Just a moment. [*Takes phone.*] Mr. Benson and Mr. Law want two cups of chicken broth—some ham hocks —cabbage—lemon meringue pie—and some bicarbonate of soda. [*Hangs up; returns to couch.*]

C.F. You're slaughtering yourselves, boys. You won't be able to think with that poison in your stomachs, and we've got to think. I've just seen the front office. Boys, we're facing a crisis.

ROSETTI [*eagerly*]. Any truth in the report, C.F., that Gaumont British wants to buy the studio?

C.F. You know as much about it as I do, Rosetti.

LAW. Why sell? I thought we were sitting pretty. We're in receivership.

ROSETTI. Well, I'm going up to see B.K. I hope you boys get a good story for Larry.

C.F. [*ignoring him; C.F can ignore beautifully*]. As a matter of fact, you may as well know it. There may be a reorganization.

BENSON. Again?

C.F. And you know my position. I'm the only college-bred man in the studio. They resent me.

LAW. The big snobs.

C.F. Just because I've always tried to do something fine, something dignified, something worth while, I'm being hammered on all sides. Boys, if my next picture fails, I'm out. And you're out, Larry. And it won't do you boys any good either. Of course you can always write plays.

LAW. I don't see why not. We never wrote any.

C.F. I have an idea for a play I want to discuss with you sometime. You'll be wild about it. Just one set, too—simple to produce, and practically anybody can play it. Katharine Cornell would be marvelous for the girl. She dies in the first act.

LARRY. Listen here, C.F., I ain't in the theatre. What about my picture?

C.F. Boys, we need a big picture. Not just a good story. I want to do something fine—with sweep, with scope—stark, honest, gripping, adult, but with plenty of laughs and a little hokum.

LARRY [*bitterly*]. And no "Did you?" scenes.

C.F. Something we'll be proud of. Not just another picture, but the picture of the year. A sort of Bengal Lancer, but as Kipling would have done it. Maybe we could wire Kipling and get him to write a few scenes. It would be darned good publicity. [PEGGY *enters*; PEGGY *is the manicurist on the lot*.] Oh, come in ... come in, Peggy. [PEGGY *puts tray of manicurist's paraphernalia on desk; moves small chair at* C.F.'S *side; takes bowl and exits for water*.]

BENSON [*in astonishment*.] He doesn't think we're as good as Kipling.

C.F. [*quickly*]. Mind you, not that I think Kipling is a great writer. A storyteller, yes. But greatness? Give me Proust anytime. Now, boys, how about a story?

LAW. Nestling on your desk for two weeks there's a script we wrote for Larry Toms.

BENSON. A beautiful script. That one with my fingerprints on the cover.

C.F. [*picking up script, holding it in his hands as if weighing it*]. This? This won't do.

LAW. That's where you're wrong. I had it weighed at the A. & P. and the manager went wild over it.

[C.F. *puts script on top of dictograph.* MISS CREWS *enters*.]

MISS CREWS. Excuse me, Mr. Friday, but Casting wants to know how many midgets you'll need.

C.F. [*irritably*]. Midgets? I don't need any midgets.

MISS CREWS. Casting says you ordered midgets and they've got them.

C.F. They're crazy. I'm not doing a horror story. [*Phone rings; at phone*.] Hello. ... It's for you, Benson.

BENSON. For me?

C.F. I think it's Mrs. Benson. Listen, Miss Crews, we're in conference. Please don't disturb us again.

MISS CREWS. Yes, Mr. Friday. [*She exits*.]

BENSON [*into telephone*]. Oh, hello, darling. ... Yes, I know you've been shopping. ... Why don't you try Woolworth's? ... No, I'm not mad. ... Oh, you're taking the dogs for a walk? That's good. ... Oh, no, I can't take you to lunch. I'm in a story conference. ... But look, darling, I'm in a story conference. ... Hello ... [*He mops his brow and tries to shake off his gloom*.]

C.F. How is Mrs. Benson?

BENSON. Swell.

C.F. I must get Mrs. Friday to invite her over to her French class. All the wives are taking it up very seriously. Gives them something to do, and as I said to Mrs. Friday: I'm a linguist—why shouldn't you be? That's the great thing in marriage—mutual interests. [BENSON *crosses to couch*.] Of course, Mrs. Benson isn't the studious type, is she? Beautiful girl, though. . . . Where were we? What was I saying?

BENSON [*crosses back to desk; sighs; indicates script*]. You were saying that this is one of the greatest picture scripts ever written.

C.F. [*with a superior smile*]. Now, just a minute—

LAW [*quickly*]. And do you know why? Because it's the same story Larry Toms has been doing for years.

BENSON. We *know* it's good.

LAW. Griffith used it. Lubitsch used it. And Eisenstein's coming around to it.

BENSON. Boy meets girl. Boy loses girl. Boy gets girl.

LAW. The great American fairy tale. Sends the audience back to the relief rolls in a happy frame of mind.

BENSON. And why not?

LAW. The greatest escape formula ever worked out in the history of civilization . . .

C.F. Of course, if you put it that way . . . but, boys, its hackneyed.

LAW. You mean classic.

C.F. [*triumphantly*]. *Hamlet* is a classic—but it isn't hackneyed!

LAW. *Hamlet* isn't hackneyed? Why, I'd be ashamed to use that poison gag. He lifted that right out of the Italians. [PEGGY *enters and crosses to her chair and sits*.] Ask Peggy. [PEGGY *puts the bowl now half filled with water down on the desk*.]

BENSON. Yes, let's ask Peggy . . . if she wants to see Larry Toms in a different story. She's your audience.

PEGGY. Don't ask me anything, Mr. Benson. I've got the damnedest toothache. [*She takes* C.F.*'s hand and looks up at him suddenly*.] Relax! [*She begins filing*.]

BENSON [*wheedling*]. But, Peggy, you go to pictures, don't you?

PEGGY. No.

BENSON. But you've seen Larry's pictures and enjoyed them?

PEGGY. No.

BENSON. . . . As millions of others have . . .

LAW. Why, one man sent him a rope all the way from Manila
—with instructions.

C.F. Boys, this isn't getting us anywhere.

BENSON [*assuming the manner of a district attorney; barking
at* PEGGY]. Peggy, do you mean to sit there and tell me you
haven't seen *one* Larry Toms picture?

PEGGY. I saw one.

BENSON. Ah!

PEGGY. *Night in Death Valley.*

BENSON. This isn't getting us anywhere, eh? How would you
like to see *Night in Death Valley* again—with a new title?

PEGGY. I wouldn't.

BENSON. That's all. Step down. [*Crosses to couch; slaps* LAW
on shoulder.] May I point out to this court that the body
was found only two feet away, in an open field, with every
door and window shut? [*To* LAW.] Your witness. [*He exits.*]

LAW [*rises*]. I've got to see a man about a woman. [*He exits.
Our writers have vanished. They love to vanish from story
conferences.*]

C.F. [*rises*]. Come back here! [*Picks up phone.*]

LARRY. That's what I mean—clowning.

C.F. [*at phone*]. Miss Crews, leave word at the gate Benson
and Law are not to be allowed off the lot. They're to come
right back to my office. [*Hangs up.*]

LARRY. Why do you stand for it?

C.F. Larry, those boys are crazy, but they've got something.

LARRY. They've been fired off every other lot.

C.F. I'll fire them off this one, after they've produced a story
I've made up my mind to that. Meanwhile, patience.

LARRY. That's easy to say.

C.F. You can't quibble with the artistic temperament when
produces.

LARRY [*grumbling*]. They've been producing nothing but trou
ble around here.

[YOUNG ACTOR *enters in the resplendent uniform of the Col
stream Guards. His name is* RODNEY. *Both uniform and act
explain themselves as the play proceeds.*]

MISS CREWS. Right in here.

RODNEY. How do you do?

C.F. What do *you* want?

RODNEY. Why, Wardrobe sent me. Do you approve the un
form?

C.F. Uniform for what?

RODNEY. *Young England.*

C.F. You see, Larry—three pictures in production—all going on at the same time—I'm standing on my head—and then they wonder what's wrong with the industry. [*Rises; barks at* RODNEY.] Stand over there. [MISS CREWS *exits.* C.F. *surveys the actor judicially.*] I can't say I like the hat. [*He is referring, of course, to the awe-inspiring busby.*]

RODNEY [*mildly*]. The hat is authentic, sir.

C.F. I still don't like it. You can't photograph it. [*Phone rings.*] Yes?—What midgets? I didn't send out any call for midgets. Get rid of them. [*Hangs up. He jiggles the phone.*] Get me Wardrobe. [*Hubbub is heard outside window.*] Who's making all that noise? [PEGGY *goes to the window.*] This is C.F. —I don't like the hat.—I don't care if it's authentic or not —Who's making all that noise?

PEGGY [*at window*]. Midgets.

C.F. [*into phone*]. Change the hat. . . . You can't photograph it. . . . We want to see faces, not hats. [*Hangs up. Stone crashes through the window left.*] Good God! Somebody's thrown a rock through my window. [*To* RODNEY.] Here, you—pull down those blinds.

RODNEY [*always the little gentleman*]. Yes, sir.

C.F. [*in phone*]. Get me Casting. . . . This is C.F. . . . Somebody's thrown a rock through my window. One of the midgets. Of course they're indignant! Sour grapes! I'm telling you to get rid of them. [*Hangs up.*]

RODNEY. What shall I tell Wardrobe, sir?

C.F. Tell them I don't like the hat.

RODNEY [*smiles diffidently*]. Well, it's very peculiar that you should take umbrage at the hat as it happens to be the only correct item in the entire outfit.

C.F. What's that?

RODNEY. This coat doesn't hang properly—these buttons are far too large. These shoulder straps are absurd, of course. And the boots . . . if I may say so . . . are too utterly fantastic. Any Guardsman would swoon away at the sight of them.

C.F. So!

RODNEY. The hat, however *is* authentic.

C.F. It is, eh? What's your salary.

RODNEY. As I understand it, I'm to receive seven dollars a day Monday and Tuesday, when I speak no lines, and fifteen dollars a day Thursday, Friday and Saturday, when I propose a toast.

C.F. And you're telling a fifty-thousand-dollar-a-year man how to run his picture. Look here—I spent two weeks in London, my man, at the Savoy, and I watched them change the Guards, personally.

RODNEY. At the Savoy?

C.F. Young man, we have a technical adviser on this picture. And it doesn't happen to be you.

RODNEY. Quite. He's a splendid fellow, but he's a third-generation Canadian. He's never even been to London.

C.F. So you don't like the uniform and you don't like the technical expert. [*Smoothly*.] What's your name?

RODNEY. Rodney Bevan. Of course, it's a sort of *nom de plume,* or *nom de guerre*—

C.F. Rodney Bevan. [*Picks up phone*.] Give me Casting. . . . This is C.F. Extra here by the name of Rodney Bevan doesn't like his uniform. Fire him.

RODNEY [*aghast*]. Fire? Have you given me the sack?

C.F. I've enough trouble without extras telling me how to make pictures. That's the trouble with this business. A man spends his life at it, and anybody can walk in and tell him how to run it.

RODNEY. But I merely suggested—

[MISS CREWS *enters*.]

MISS CREWS. Mr. Green and Mr. Slade are outside, Mr. Friday. They want you to hear the song.

RODNEY. I've waited a long time for this opening—

C.F. Get out! [*To* MISS CREWS.] I'm in no mood for *music.*

[GREEN *and* SLADE *enter*.]

GREEN. We've got it, and you're going to listen. If you don't like it, Schulberg's nuts about it. [SLADE *crosses to piano and starts playing the song.*] We wrote it for *Young England,* but its flexible—Flexible as hell.

[MISS CREWS *exits*. RODNEY *turns forlornly and fades out through the door. What else can he do?*]

C.F. Boys, I'm in no mood for—

GREEN. It's a touching little thing, but, boy, what power! "There's a Pain in My Heart, and My Heart's on My Sleeve." Like the title? [SLADE *is one of those who glues himself to a piano. He's all pasted together now, and his*

fingers fly. GREEN *sings with all the fervid sincerity of
Georgie Jessel with a cold.*]

> You promised love undying,
> And begged me to believe;
> Then you left, and left me crying
> With a pain in my heart, and my
>   heart on my sleeve.
>
> It isn't right to show it,
> To flaunt the way I grieve;
> But the world will quickly know it,
> For the pain's in my heart, and my
>   heart on my sleeve.
>
> I confess that I'm a mess—
> The way I lived my life,
> But what does it matter?
> Yes, I guess that happiness
> Is only for a wife;
> Sorrow isn't served on a silver platter.
>
> I really shouldn't blame you
> Because you chose to leave;
> But one thing forever will shame
>   you—
> It's the pain in my heart, and my
>   heart on my sleeve.

[*During the song* MISS CREWS *enters with glass of orange juice.
She crosses around desk, puts glass in front of* C.F., *gets book
from lower drawer.*]

C.F. [*as* GREEN *finishes song*]. Miss Crews, get hold of Benson
and Law! [MISS CREWS *exits.*]

LARRY [*as the din grows*]. I've worked for Biograph. . . . I've
worked for Monogram. . . . I've worked for Columbia.
. . . I've worked for Warners. . . . I've worked for Metro
. . . but a screwier outfit I never did see!

[BENSON *and* LAW *enter in costume of beefeaters. They, too,
wear busbies.*]

C.F. [*whose nails are being buffed*]. What do you want? [*At
the musicians.*] Quiet! [*At the busbies, for* C.F. *doesn't deign
to look at actors' faces.*] I told Wardrobe I don't like the
hats.

BENSON. He doesn't like the hats.

LAW. Call Jock Whitney. We want to be in color.

C.F. [*exasperated*]. For God's sake! This is a fine time to be masquerading.

BENSON [*leaping into character; picking up stone*]. Wait! What a pretty stone! I wonder where that came from.

LAW [*in his own big scene*]. I wonder.

BENSON [*transporting himself to the desert*]. I think we've found gold, partner.

LAW [*grabbing for it*]. Gold!

BENSON. Stand back—you desert rat!

LAW. Gold—after all these years! I'm going mad . . . mad . . . mad. . . .

C.F. Oh, stop it, boys.

LARRY [*suddenly inspired. To* C.F.]. I wouldn't be surprised if they threw that there rock through the window.

BENSON. What an innuendo!

C.F. You didn't do that, did you, boys? Smash my Vita-glass?

LAW. To think—after all these years of loyal, faithful service —Larry Toms, you ought to be ashamed!

BENSON. The man with the poison-pen mind. We're going to tell Louella Parsons on you.

C.F. [*impatiently*]. *Very* well . . . *very* well. . . . But I still have my suspicions. [*Snaps.*] Now what about our story?

BENSON. Right here. [*Indicating script on desk.*]

LAW [*takes a statuette from top of desk*]. Mr. Benson, for the most brilliant script of the year, the Academy takes great pleasure in presenting to you this little gargoyle—

BENSON. Wrap it up, please.

[LAW *drops it in* LARRY's *hat and stands back of couch. Music plays.*]

LARRY [*rising in a dither*]. Now, listen—

[C.F. *crosses below desk, retrieves statue, places it back on desk.*]

GREEN [*to* SLADE *at piano*]. What do you say to this, Otto, for the second chorus:

> Yes, I've been kissed,
> But like Oliver Twist,
> I'm still crying for more.

[*Without waiting for an answer, to* C.F.] How did you like the song, C.F.?

LAW. Darn good. Can you play *Over the Waves?*

C.F. Boys, can't you be sensible for a moment? You're trying my patience. What about our story?

LAW. What about it? It's a rich, protean part for Larry.

LARRY. It just don't make sense.

LAW. I resent that as a gentleman and a grammarian.

C.F. Now really, boys, I'm tolerant, but I've got to see results. I'm not one to put the creative urge in a strait jacket. But you've been fired off every other lot in this industry for your pranks. Perhaps you've forgotten, Benson, but when I hired you for this job you promised me to behave in no uncertain terms. And you promised me Law would toe the line. Now, I'm warning you, boys. Let's get to work. Let's concentrate. [*Crosses above desk to chair back of desk.*] Do you realize you boys are making more than the President of the United States.

LAW. But look at the fun he's having!

LARRY [*angrily*]. Now looka here—

GREEN. How do you like the song, C.F.?

C.F. It lacks body.

LAW. No breasts.

C.F. That's exactly it—Pallid.

GREEN. Come on, Otto.

SLADE [*starts for door*]. This isn't my idea of a fair audition.

GREEN. Wait'll they hear it at the Cocoanut Grove. They'll be sorry.

[GREEN *and* SLADE *exit.* PEGGY *enters and* LAW, *humming "Merry Widow," intercepts her, dances a few measures with her.*]

C.F. Listen, boys—we've had enough of this.

[SUSIE *enters carrying a tray.* SUSIE *is a waitress. We worship* SUSIE. *Why describe her? We'll tell you what she wears— the full-blown costume of a Hollywood waitress. Of her blonde fragility, her intricate but blameless sex life, and the ineffable charm of her touching naïveté we won't say a word.*]

LAW. *Lunch!*

BENSON. Grub! Susie, I love you.

[PEGGY *exits. She never comes back. Why should she?*]

C.F. Wait a minute—wait a minute—

[LAW *gets end table and places it in front of couch.* BENSON *takes tray from* SUSIE.]

SUSIE [*weakly*]. Please, Mr. Benson, be careful.

LAW. Put that tray right down here.

SUSIE [*quavering*]. Thanks. . . . It's not very heavy . . . [*She then collapses neatly on the floor.*]

C.F. Good Lord!

LAW [*bending over her*]. Susie—Susie—

BENSON [*grabbing phone*]. Get the doctor over here—right away—

LAW. Somebody give me water. [BENSON *takes glass from tray on table.*]

C.F. [*disapprovingly*]. This is a nice thing to happen in my office. . . . Who is this girl, anyway?

LAW [*putting water to her as he kneels beside her*]. Come on, Susie. [*Lifting her head up to glass.*]

LARRY [*whose father wrote letters to the papers.*] That commissary shouldn't employ people with epilepsy.

C.F. [*bitter, still*]. I had an actor who did that to me once. Held up my shooting schedule fourteen days.

LAW. She's all right. Here.

SUSIE. Did you all get napkins? [*Opens her eyes for the first time.*]

BENSON. Now, Susie—get into this chair.

SUSIE. Thanks. [*She sits.*]

C.F. [*sharply*]. What's wrong with you, young woman?

SUSIE [*still quavering*]. Nothing. . . . I'm much better now. . . . Thanks.

C.F. Where's that doctor?

SUSIE. Did you call for a doctor? You didn't have to.

C.F. Do you get these epileptic fits often?

SUSIE. I didn't have an epileptic fit.

C.F. Then what's wrong with you?

SUSIE. There's nothing wrong . . . it's only natural.

C.F. Only natural for you to come into my office and collapse on the floor.

SUSIE. Oh, no, sir . . . it's only natural for you to feel sick when you're going to have a baby.

LAW. A baby!

BENSON. Susie, you're not going to have a baby!

SUSIE. That's what they told me. . . .

BENSON. Susie's going to have a baby!

LAW. Let's get drunk!

C.F. [*into phone*]. Tell that doctor not to come. You heard me. I don't want him. [*He hangs up.*] I won't have my office converted into a maternity ward! [*He turns on* SUSIE.] I don't think much of your husband—letting you work at a time like this!

SUSIE. Oh, but I haven't got a husband.

C.F. Huh?

SUSIE [*rises*]. You'd better eat your lunch before it gets cold. Have you all got napkins?

LAW [*humbly*]. The new generation! Faces the facts of nature without squeamishness, without subterfuge. "I haven't got a husband," she says. "It's only natural," she says. "I'm going to have a baby." . . . Susie, you're magnificent.

SUSIE. I'm quitting at the end of the week so I thought I'd tell everybody why. I wouldn't want them to think I was discontented.

LAW. Our little mother!

SUSIE. Oh, don't make fun of me.

LAW [*rises*]. Fun? I've never been so touched in my life. Susie, I feel purified.

BENSON. Susie—can we be godfather?

SUSIE. Do you mean it?

BENSON. Do we mean it? We haven't got a baby. And we've been collaborating for years.

SUSIE. Oh, I think that would be wonderful for Happy to have writers for a godfather.

BENSON. Happy?

SUSIE. I'm going to call him Happy—even if he's a girl. Because I want him to be happy—even if he's a girl.

BENSON. Beautiful! A beautiful thought! Where are you going to have this baby, Susie?

SUSIE. In the County Hospital. It's all fixed. I was very lucky because I've only lived in the county three months and I'm not eligible.

C.F. Now, listen, boys—enough of this.

LAW [*into phone*]. Give me the Cedars of Lebanon Hospital—and make it snappy.

BENSON [*jubilant*]. We've got a baby!

C.F. Just a minute. Hang up that phone. [BENSON *good-naturedly brushes his arm down.*]

LAW. Dr. Marx, please. . . . Willy, this is Law of Benson and Law. Reserve the best suite in the house for us. I'm serious. Dead serious. A little friend of ours is going to have a baby and we want the goddamnedest confinement you've got in stock. . . .

BENSON. Day and night nurse.

LAW [*to* BENSON]. And not the one with the buck teeth either.

She's dynamite. [*Into phone.*] We want everything that Gloria Swanson had—only double. What's that? Bill? Bill the studio, of course. [*He hangs up.*]

C.F. You'll do no such thing! What kind of a gag is this?

[MISS CREWS *enters.*]

MISS CREWS. Do you want to hear the trumpet call? The men are here. Music Department wants your O.K.

C.F. Trumpets?

MISS CREWS. For *Young England.*

C.F. Look here—I haven't time to listen to them now. Come back here at two o'clock. And give it to me from out there. I don't want them blasting in my ear.

[*Meanwhile,* BENSON *and* LAW *have been in whispered conference.*]

MISS CREWS. Yes, Mr. Friday. [*Exits.*]

C.F. Now, boys—let's get together on this. [*Turns on* SUSIE *from below desk.*] And you—what are you sitting here for? Get out! [SUSIE *tries to rise.*]

LAW. Sit right where you are. [*Crosses to front of desk.*] Don't you bark at our inspiration! We've got it!

C.F. What?

LAW [*with mounting excitement*]. A baby!

C.F. Boys, I'm a patient man, but you're trying me.

BENSON [*awed*]. *Larry Toms and a baby!*

LAW [*to* C.F.]. Do you see it?

LARRY [*bellowing*]. Wait a minute—wait a minute!

LAW [*quickly*]. He finds a baby—in the Rockies—

BENSON [*inspired; quickly to* C.F.]. Girl with a no-good gambler—out of Las Vegas—has a baby . . . gambler is killed. Girl leaves baby on the ranger's door step. Larry is the ranger.

LAW [*dramatizing it all*]. My God, he says—a baby!

BENSON [*awed*]. A baby!

LAW. The most precious thing in life. The cutest, God-damn little bastard you ever saw.

BENSON. Tugging at every mother's heart. And every potential mother.

LAW. And who isn't?

BENSON. A love story between Larry and the baby—

LAW. The two outcasts! Get it?

BENSON. And then he meets the mother!

LAW. She wants her baby back.

BENSON. She's been through the fires of hell.

LAW. The man she loved . . . let her down. . . .

BENSON. She hates men . . . all men. . . .

LAW. She won't look at Larry.

BENSON [to LARRY]. No. There she sits . . . bitter, brooding, cynical, but underneath—a mother's heart.

LAW. Out on the Rockies—

BENSON. The hell with the Rockies—back to the Foreign Legion!

LAW. Right! Larry's joined to forget. He's out on the march. We can use all that stock stuff—and he finds a baby!

BENSON. He's gone off to fight the Riffs.

LAW. The hell with the Riffs! Ethiopians!

BENSON. Stick to the Riffs. We don't want any race problem.

LAW. Right! She doesn't know if he's coming back.

BENSON. She's waiting—waiting!

LAW. We cut to the Riffs—

BENSON. Cut back—

LAW [to BENSON]. Right into the battle.

BENSON [really inspired now]. His father's the Colonel!

LAW. Talk about Kipling—

BENSON. Talk about scope—sweep—what a set-up!

LAW. A love story!

BENSON. A great love story!

LAW. Mary Magdalen of the Foreign Legion and the West Point man who wanted to forget!

BENSON [rises]. The baby brings them together, splits them apart, brings them together—

LAW. Boy meets girl—

BENSON. Boy loses girl—

LAW. Boy gets girl!

C.F. [rising in excitement]. Boys, I think you've got something! Let's go up and try it on B.K. while it's hot.

LAW. Let's go! [They move forward.]

LARRY [crosses to behind couch]. Wait a minute—you can't act with a baby. They steal every scene— Look what happened to Chevalier.

LAW. Are you selling motherhood short? [LAW, BENSON and C.F. exit through next speech.]

LARRY. They'll be looking at the baby when they should be looking at me. I tell you—I won't play it. [Follows off. SUSIE tries to rise, now she is left alone. She sits down again. RODNEY, in the Coldstream Guards uniform, enters. SUSIE turns.]

RODNEY. Oh, I'm sorry. I hope I didn't startle you.

SUSIE. Oh, no. [*Then, as he looks at* C.F.'s *desk.*] They all stepped out and they didn't even touch their lunch.

RODNEY [*licking his lips involuntarily*]. Lunch?—You don't happen to know when Mr. Friday is coming back?

SUSIE. No, I don't.

RODNEY. I did want to see him. It's rather urgent. Do you mind if I wait here?

SUSIE. No, of course not. [*He seats himself on couch, near a tray. There is an awkward silence.* SUSIE *stares straight ahead.* RODNEY *plays with a cracker. Finally* SUSIE *breaks the silence.*] What are you supposed to be?

RODNEY. Eh? Oh! That's just it. . . . I'm supposed to be a Buckingham Palace Guard, sergeant major—[*He pops the cracker into his mouth and swallows it.* SUSIE *looks at him rather intently.*] Good Lord! What am I doing?

SUSIE. You're eating Mr. Friday's cracker.

RODNEY. I'm awfully sorry. I don't understand how I—

SUSIE. You must be very hungry.

RODNEY. Not a bit. Not at all.

SUSIE. You *look* hungry.

RODNEY. Do I?

SUSIE. Why don't you have something? They'll never eat it. They're always sending things back they order—never even touched.

RODNEY. Really?

SUSIE. You'll only be doing me a favor.

RODNEY. Oh?

SUSIE. I won't have so much to carry back to the commissary. Sometimes I think I carry back more than I bring.

RODNEY. You're pulling my leg, of course.

SUSIE. What did you say?

RODNEY. You're not really a waitress.

SUSIE. Sure I am.

RODNEY [*triumphantly*]. Waitresses don't usually sit in producers' offices.

SUSIE. They do when they don't feel well.

RODNEY. You don't feel well? Oh, I'm sorry. Is there anything I can do?

SUSIE. No, thanks.

RODNEY. But what's wrong?

SUSIE. Oh, there's no use telling you. I told Mr. Friday and he made such a fuss about it I guess I better keep it to myself.

RODNEY. I'm afraid I don't quite understand.

SUSIE. Try the chicken soup. It's very good.

RODNEY. Are you seriously suggesting that I filch some of this broth?

SUSIE. We make it special for B.K. with nine chickens.

RODNEY. Well, dash it, I will eat it. Just to make the joke good! [*He laughs weakly and picks up the bowl and puts it to his lips, and sips it.*]

SUSIE [*warningly*]. It's hot!

RODNEY [*now quite gay*]. So I've learned.

SUSIE. When did you eat last?

RODNEY [*lying, of course*]. I had my lunch an hour ago.

SUSIE. Have some crackers with it.

RODNEY. Thanks.

SUSIE. You're English, aren't you?

RODNEY. Yes, of course.

SUSIE. So is Ronald Colman.

RODNEY [*bolting his food*]. So he is.

SUSIE. I like the way the English talk.

RODNEY. Do you?

SUSIE. It's very soothing.

RODNEY. What an idea!

SUSIE. Of course, that's only *my* idea. I'm very ignorant.

RODNEY. Oh, please don't say that. I think you're very intelligent.

SUSIE. Oh, I'm intelligent. But I don't know anything.

RODNEY. You're an extraordinary girl.

SUSIE. I've never been to high school.

RODNEY [*gallantly*]. May I say that's the high school's loss?

SUSIE. But some day I'll go to high school. That's my secret ambition. Try the ham hocks. The cook eats them himself. He comes from Czechoslovakia.

RODNEY. Does he really? Look here—I feel an awful swine guzzling by myself. Won't you join me?

SUSIE. Well, I'm not very hungry, but I can eat.

RODNEY. Good! [*He rises and adjusts a chair for her.*]

SUSIE. It's funny how I keep on eating.

RODNEY. Some ham hocks?

SUSIE. No. Happy doesn't like ham. He likes milk.

RODNEY [*mystified*]. I beg your pardon? [*But he doesn't press the point.*] Did you say milk?

SUSIE. Yes. Milk.

RODNEY [*as he pours*]. There you are.

SUSIE. Thanks.

RODNEY. Cozy, this—what?

SUSIE. It's good milk. Have some.

RODNEY. Do you know, I think you're the most extraordinary girl I ever met.

SUSIE. Why?

RODNEY. You're so kind. You're so direct, so sincere. Most girls one meets play about with words so. They're so infernally smart. They make one feel like a worm.

SUSIE. Of course, I'm different on account of my condition. Most girls aren't in my condition.

RODNEY. Your condition?

SUSIE. The minute I found out about Happy I said to myself: I'm going to be very good and very sincere, because then Happy will be very good and very sincere.

RODNEY. I'm afraid I don't quite follow.

SUSIE [*sighing*]. Nobody does.

RODNEY. Eh? Oh, yes. . . . As I was saying— What was I saying?

SUSIE [*looking into his eyes and feeling strangely stirred*]. Have some mustard.

RODNEY. Do you know, I must confess I was hungry. As a matter of fact, I was close to wiring home for funds today. But I didn't. [*Looks very determined, righteous.*]

SUSIE. You mean you need money, and you can get it—and you won't wire for it?

RODNEY. I can't—and keep my pride. I told *them* I was on my own. You see, my family didn't want me to act. Not that they've any prejudices against the stage—or the films. Not at all. In fact, one of my aunts was a Gaiety girl. Quite all right. But they don't think I *can* act. That's what hurts.

SUSIE. Can you act?

RODNEY. No.

SUSIE. Not at all?

RODNEY. Not at all: I'm awful!

SUSIE. Oh, that's too bad.

RODNEY. But I only realized it in the stock company . . . out in Pasadena. I was the worst member of the company. At first I thought it was because they were always giving me character parts—American gangsters—and that sort of thing. And then one week I played a Cambridge undergraduate. And, mind you, I've been a Cambridge undergraduate. And do you know that I was utterly unconvincing?

SUSIE. Then why don't you give it up?

RODNEY. Pride.

SUSIE. I can understand that—Pride.

RODNEY. Can you really?

SUSIE. Sure I can.

RODNEY. That's why I simply must see Mr. Friday. [*Suddenly.*] Look here— [*He takes a book from couch and opens it.*] Look at this color plate. Does this uniform remotely resemble the one I'm wearing? [*He crosses down right.*]

SUSIE [*looks at book; then at* RODNEY]. Yes, I think so.

RODNEY [*crosses to her left*]. But, my dear girl, look at the coat and the buttons—and note the heels—and look at mine. [*Steps back.*]

SUSIE. Well, come to think of it, I guess it is different.

RODNEY. Of course. And I've taken this book right out of their own research department. When I show this to Mr. Friday he's bound to be sporting enough to admit an error.

SUSIE. Oh, sure.

RODNEY [*leaning over her*]. You see, all I want is to appear in *one* picture—and then I can tell the family: "I've done it. But it's not good enough. I'm chucking it." But I'll have my pride.

SUSIE [*gazing at him*]. I see.

RODNEY. Oh . . . I say . . . I'm not boring you?

SUSIE. Oh, no. Finish your ham.

RODNEY. Eh! Oh! Don't mind if I do. A bit of pie for you? [*He extends plate with fork.*]

SUSIE [*brightly; almost flirting*]. Well, I'll try. [*She smiles at him and he at her, fork poised in mid-air.*]

RODNEY. Do you know, I've never enjoyed a lunch quite as much as this one—thanks to you. [*Suddenly.*] Would it bore you if I tried out my lines—in *Young England*, you know?

SUSIE. Oh, no.

RODNEY. Very well. [*He rises, holding glass of milk.*] Gentlemen, the Queen— [*He waits.*]

SUSIE. Is that all?

RODNEY. That's all. But of course I could say: "Gentlemen, I give you the Queen." Fatten up the part a bit, what? . . . Gentlemen, I give you the Queen! . . . Sounds rather better, doesn't it? [*Then with profound bass.*] Gentlemen, I give you the Queen!

[LARRY *enters followed by* C.F. C.F. *stares.*]

LARRY. I don't cotton to the whole idea, and if B.K.'s got any sense, he won't listen to those maniacs.

C.F. What's going on here?

RODNEY. How'd you do. . . . I . . . I . . . [*Puts glass of milk back on tray.*]

C.F. What is this? A tête-à-tête in my office! Good Gad! You've been drinking my milk!

SUSIE It's all right, Mr. Friday. I told him he could have it.

C.F. *You* told him?

RODNEY. I'm awfully sorry. I owe you an apology, and money, of course. Will you accept my I.O.U.? And I have the book —from Research. I can show you the really authentic uniform. I'm sure if you study this—[SUSIE *finds the page and hands book to* RODNEY.]

C.F. I've a good mind to call the studio police.

SUSIE [*rises*]. Oh, please don't do that, Mr. Friday.

LARRY. That's what you get for having foreign actors around. Take the food right out of your mouth!

RODNEY. I'm terribly sorry, of course.

C.F. Get out!

RODNEY. I realize there's nothing I can say—[*He turns to* SUSIE.] except—my eternal gratitude. [*He grabs her by the hand and shakes it. Exits.*]

SUSIE. Oh, you shouldn't have done that. He's been having a terrible time.

C.F. [*glaring at* SUSIE]. Get these dishes out of here.

SUSIE [*meekly*]. Yes, sir. [*She begins piling up dishes on tray.*]

LARRY. The idea of a baby! The more I think of it, the less I like it.

C.F. [*crosses to chair at desk*]. Larry, you're driving me into a nervous breakdown. I had to take you out of B.K.'s office so you'd stop arguing before he could make a decision.

LARRY. There's nothing to decision. I won't play it.

C.F. If B.K. likes the idea, you'll play it.

LARRY. Maybe—and maybe not. I'm willing to bet ten to one right now B.K. kicks the whole story in the ash can. He's no fool.

[BENSON *and* LAW *enter in shirt sleeves. They've obviously had a hot session with* B.K.]

BENSON. Sold! Lock, stock and baby! B.K. says it's the best mother-love story he's heard in years.

LARRY. What? What's that?

LAW [*magnificently*]. Susie, put that tray down!

SUSIE. Please, Mr. Law, I've got to get back to the commissary.

LARRY. You sold him that story, huh?

BENSON. Lie down, actor!

LARRY. I'll see about this. [*He exits.*]

BENSON. Now listen, Susie—and listen carefully.

LAW. Let me tell her, will you? [*He faces her.*] Susie, nature meant you for a sucker. You were designed to get the short end of the stick. The girl who gets slapped.

BENSON [*quickly*]. But we're changing all that.

LAW. Susie, in real life, you'd have your baby in the County Hospital . . . get yourself a job, if lucky, with a philanthropic Iowa family of fourteen adults and twelve minors for twenty bucks a month. And when your grateful son grew up he'd squirt tobacco juice in your eye and join the Navy.

BENSON. There you go with your God-damn realism. [*Turns to* SUSIE *with paper and pencil.*] Sign, please—

SUSIE. Here? [*She signs; and then turns, brightly.*] What is it?

BENSON. Just a power of attorney authorizing us to deal for you in all matters with this studio.

C.F. What power of attorney? What are you boys up to?

LAW. We said to ourselves upstairs—why shouldn't Susie have the good things of life?

BENSON. After all, we're godfathers.

SUSIE. I—I don't feel very good.

LAW. Get this, Susie. We've just sold a story about a baby.

BENSON. Sweetest story ever told!

LAW. A new-born baby.

BENSON. Brand new.

LAW. We're going to watch that baby—the first hair—the first tooth—the first smile—

BENSON. The same baby. No switching—first time in the history of pictures. That baby's going to grow up before your eyes.

LAW. Open up like a flower. . . . Just like the Dionne quintuplets.

BENSON. Minute he's born we set the cameras on him. We stay with him—

LAW. That baby's going to gurgle and google and drool his way to stardom!

SUSIE. But—

LAW. And that baby, Susie, is Happy. Upstairs in B.K.'s office we put your unborn child into pictures!

SUSIE [*transported*]. Happy—in pictures! Oh—that's wonderful—[*Then, with a sudden gasp*] Oh!

LAW [*quickly*] Susie! What's the matter?

SUSIE. I don't know . . . I . . . I . . . I don't feel so good

. . . I think . . . I . . . [*In these broken words,* SUSIE *tells all.* BENSON *helps* SUSIE *to lie on couch.* LAW *looks over* SUSIE'S *shoulder; whistles; runs to phone.*]

LAW [*into phone*]. Emergency! Get the ambulance over to Mr. Friday's office right away—get the doctor—get the nurse. . . .

C.F. [*staring*]. What is it? In *my* office. Good Gad! Miss Crews!

[*Door opens.*]

MISS CREWS [*at door*]. The trumpets are here!

[*Trumpets sound their triumphant clarion call.*]

LAW [*through the Wagnerian brass, to* BENSON, *awed*]. Happy's on his way!

CURTAIN

ACT TWO

Scene I

We are in your neighborhood theatre, seven months later.

As the curtain rises we face a motion-picture screen, and to the sound-track accompaniment of "Home on the Range," these glaring titles pop out at us:

> IF YOU LIKED HAPPY
> IN
> "WANDERING HEARTS"
> YOU'LL ADORE HIM
> IN
> "GOLDEN NUGGET"

This is what is known as a trailer, in technical terms. It is shown at neighborhood theatres prior to the release of the picture so that the customers will be teased into returning the following week.

There are, of course, beautifully composed shots of horses, men and open spaces, and finally we come upon a series of close-ups of HAPPY, over which these titles dance:

> HAPPY!
> HAPPY!
> *HAPPY!*

The sound track blares forth "Ride of the Valkyries."

> CROWN PRINCE OF COMEDY!
> KING OF TRAGEDY!
> EMPEROR OF EMOTION!

Just prior to these titles we have seen a Chinese, who has emerged from God knows where, but what is a ranch without a Chinese? The general idea is that the Chinese finds HAPPY on the doorstep and communicates his discovery to LARRY TOMS. There follows a title which explains all:

> THE DESERT WAIF WHO MADE
> A SOFTIE OF A BAD MAN

The picture is further described as:

[271]

The Big Gold Strike
of Mother Love

We see horses galloping, men falling, revolvers barking, and nice, big, wavy

THRILLS
CHILLS

The credit card is as follows:

FROM A STORY BY H. G. WELLS
ADAPTED BY J. CARLYLE BENSON AND ROBERT LAW
DIRECTED BY SERGE BORODOKOV

and, appropriately enough, in solitary grandeur:

PRODUCED BY C. ELLIOT FRIDAY

Scene II

The screen lifts, and once more we are in MR. FRIDAY'S *office.* C.F. *is at his desk,* MISS CREWS *is seated upstage and at desk;* BENSON *is on the couch beside* LARRY. ROSETTI *is seated on the piano bench.*

BENSON. Read those figures, Miss Crews.

MISS CREWS. Eighty-two thousand at the Music Hall. Forty-eight thousand five hundred and thirty-eight in Des Moines.

BENSON. Without a stage show.

LARRY. I always went big in Des Moines.

MISS CREWS. Twenty-eight thousand in Newark.

LARRY. That's one of my big towns.

MISS CREWS. Forty-two thousand three hundred and eighty-four in San Francisco.

LARRY. I'm big there, too.

MISS CREWS. Twenty-six thousand eight hundred and seventy-five in Detroit.

BENSON [*to* C.F.]. And you sit there and tell me Happy isn't worth thirty-five hundred a week?

C.F. But, Benson, be reasonable. I can't go to B.K. with any such fantastic figure.

BENSON [*sighing*]. Read that list again, Miss Crews.

C.F. Never mind, Miss Crews.

LARRY. What about me? *Wandering Hearts* was my picture, wasn't it? Folks came to see me. They didn't come to see Happy.

BENSON [*taking Variety from his pocket*]. Let me read *Variety* to the assembled multitude. *Wandering Hearts* socko in Minneapolis despite Larry Toms . . .

LARRY. Huh?

BENSON. Mexico nuts about Happy but no like Larry Toms—

LARRY. Where? Where does it say that? [*He takes paper.* ROSETTI *rises and looks over* LARRY'S *shoulder*.]

BENSON. This is an accidental business in an accidental world. Happy is going to get it while it's hot.

C.F. Benson, you owe me something.

BENSON. What?

C.F. Gratitude. . . . After all, the idea of a baby was mine—more or less.

BENSON. More or less.

C. F. I made that baby act.

BENSON. All right, Svengali.

C.F. Shall we say three hundred a week for Happy?

BENSON. Shall we say thirty-five hundred a week for Happy?

C.F. I've a good mind to have you thrown out of this studio.

BENSON. All right. Happy goes with us. We've still got that power of attorney.

C.F. Of course, I didn't mean that literally.

BENSON. I did. [*Telephone rings*.]

C.F. Hello. . . . Yes, Miss Goodwin. . . . What? You can't write about Brussels because you've never been there? My dear girl, why do you think we have a research department? After all, Bernard Shaw wrote *Don Juan* and he never went to Bulgaria. Imagination, my dear girl—imagination. [*Hangs up*.] Look here, Benson, I knew I couldn't deal with Law. I thought I could with you. After all, you're in no position to antagonize this studio. Some day you may need my friendship.

BENSON. I'm supposed to be working with our Mr. Law on a story. To wit: *Tiger Tamer*. Do you mind if I join my partner in a little English composition?

C.F. Some day you may be very sorry for this, Benson.

BENSON. What do you think, Miss Crews?

MISS CREWS. I think Happy ought to get it while it's hot.

C.F. Get back to your desk.

MISS CREWS. Yes, Mr. Friday. [*She exits*.]

LARRY [*waving Variety*]. I said that baby'd ruin me! Well, he ain't going to steal no more pictures! I won't play that new scene.

C.F. [*irritably*]. What new scene?

LARRY. I'm supposed to wash Happy.

C.F. That's a cute scene. I read it.

LARRY. Am I the type that washes babies?

C.F. Why not?

LARRY. 'Tain't manly!

BENSON. No. You want the baby to wash you!

LARRY. Listen!

BENSON. Any further business before the house? [*Turns to* LARRY.] By the way, I saw you with Susie at the Trocadero last night. We don't approve of you as an escort. Remind me to speak to her about that.

C.F. Benson, I'm asking you once more. Be fair—be reasonable.

BENSON. I am. We're asking thirty-five hundred a week. We'll consider three thousand and settle for twenty-five hundred. But not a penny less. Incidentally, Fox'll pay twenty-five hundred for Happy. We promised to let them know by Saturday. No hurry, of course. [*Exits.*]

C.F. Have you ever seen anything more damnably unfair? Imagine *writers* holding up this studio at the point of a gun. It's nothing but blackmail.

ROSETTI [*rises*]. I've got a hunch, C.F. When did you sign Happy? Do you remember?

C.F. Of course I remember . . . July fourteenth . . . Fall of the Bastille. I remember my wife pointing out the coincidence at the time. Why?

ROSETTI [*crosses to desk*]. I've got a hunch that power of attorney expires pretty soon. I want to be prepared.

C.F. Rosetti, I'm not interested in the future. I'm interested in signing Happy right now—before we lose him to Fox.

[*Phone rings.*]

ROSETTI. You've got to have vision in this business, C.F. [*He reaches for other phone, changes his mind, and then exits.*]

C.F. [*into phone*]. Hello. . . . Yes, listen, Gregg. . . . I ran the sound track on *Young England* last night. I don't like the trumpets. They're sour. They spoil the whole mood. . . . What? . . . What's that? You can't walk out on a picture like that. What kind of a director are you if you can't take constructive criticism . . . hello . . . hello . . . [*Hangs up.*] Gregg is walking out on *Young England,* I can't sign Happy—

LARRY. What about me?

C.F. Ten thousand feet of film sick—and he walks out. I'll

have to run the picture all the afternoon and sit up all night cutting it.

[MISS CREWS *enters.*]

MISS CREWS. Happy's through for the day.

NURSE [*wheeling in a streamlined baby carriage*]. Through for the day.

DOCTOR [*as he enters*]. Through for the day. Is his mother here?

MISS CREWS. No, Doctor, but she should be here very soon.

NURSE. [*backing carriage in front of desk.*] Say da-da to Mr. Friday.

C.F. [*waving obediently*]. Da-da, Happy.

DOCTOR. Nurse, take the little trouper out into the garden and keep him in the sunshine.

LARRY. He's through for the day and I'm working until eight. He's sure got it soft.

[NURSE *exits with* HAPPY. ROSETTI *enters.*]

DOCTOR. They've been overworking you, have they?

LARRY. I ain't feeling so hearty, doc. I wish you'd look me over.

C.F. [*rises and goes below desk*]. Just your imagination. I wish I had your constitution. I've got to see B.K. [*He exits.*]

DOCTOR. All you picture people are hypochondriacs. However, come up to my office and I'll look you over. [*He exits.*]

LARRY. I'm a star. I've been a star for ten years. I've worked hard to get where I'm at— [*He rises. Phone rings.*]

ROSETTI [*at phone*]. Hello.... Yes ... speaking—

LARRY. I don't drink. I don't smoke. I don't swear. I don't get into no scandal. And the girls I passed up!

ROSETTI [*into phone*]. Oh, you've got that, Mr. Williams? Fine. When does it expire? ... It *did* expire? Last week? ... No, don't do that. I'll tell the boys. ... You see, I may be handling Happy's new contract. Right. [*He hangs up.*]

LARRY. They ain't making pictures here no more. They're shooting nothing but close-ups of babies. Happy laughing! Happy crying! Happy! ... Happy! ...

ROSETTI. Larry, I've just checked with the Legal Department. The boys' power of attorney expired last week. And they don't even know it.

LARRY. What's that got to do with me?

ROSETTI. Larry, there's been something developing in the

back of my mind for some weeks. Why do you think I asked you to take Susie to the Trocadero?

LARRY. She talked me deaf, dumb, and blind about going to high school. Set me back fourteen bucks. Lucky she don't drink.

ROSETTI [*the dreamer*]. I wanted you to get friendly with her because I visualized a way for you and me to get Happy—for life.

LARRY. Huh?

ROSETTI [*with Napoleonic intensity*]. Larry, here's the tactical move. You marry Susie.

LARRY. Marry her?

ROSETTI. That's what I said.

LARRY. I won't do it.

ROSETTI [*who knows his client*]. All right, suit yourself.

LARRY. We got community property in California. If there's a bust-up the woman gets half.

ROSETTI. Larry, I don't want to hurt your feelings, but I can't get you a new contract the way things are now. B.K. is dickering to borrow Clark Gable or Gary Cooper for Happy's next picture.

LARRY [*touched to the quick*]. What?

ROSETTI. I'd marry her myself if I was free. Show me a girl with a better heart—with more culture—

LARRY. You don't expect me to believe what the studio hands out—her husband was a prominent portrait painter who went down on the *Morro Castle*?

ROSETTI [*indignantly*]. Who are you to cast the first stone?

LARRY. I don't want to marry nobody. Anyways, there's no sense to it.

ROSETTI [*patiently*]. If you marry her, you're Happy's legal guardian and we control the situation. A father and son team off the screen as well as on! Is that practical or am I just an idealist? Look at Guy Lathrop! He argued with me when I told him to marry Betty Bird. But he finally had the sense to play along with me and we've been drawing top money ever since.

LARRY. I don't want to marry nobody.

ROSETTI. Larry, you're at the crossroads right now. One road leads to stardom and big pictures, with Happy and me. The other leads to Poverty Row and cheap Westerns. Will you put your hand in mine and let me guide you?

[MISS CREWS *enters.*]

MISS CREWS. Mr. Toms, you're wanted on the set.

LARRY [*growling*]. All right.

MISS CREWS. Oh, hello, Mrs. Seabrook . . . how nice you look.

[*SUSIE enters. She wears a white middy blouse and a navy blue, pleated skirt.*]

SUSIE. We had gym today. . . . Hello, Larry. . . . Hello, Mr. Rosetti. I hope I didn't interrupt anything important.

ROSETTI. Not at all. . . . [*Significantly.*] I'll be in the Legal Department, Larry. [*He exits.*]

SUSIE. Where's Happy?

MISS CREWS. Happy's in the garden with his nurse. He's all through for the day.

SUSIE. Oh, that's wonderful. I don't get to see him very much. He's working and I'm going to high school.

[*CHAUFFEUR enters.*]

CHAUFFEUR. Excuse me, Miss.

SUSIE. What is it, Simpson?

CHAUFFEUR. You forgot your algebra book, Miss.

SUSIE. Oh, thank you, Simpson. That was very thoughtful.

[*CHAUFFEUR exits.*]

MISS CREWS. And I have a new batch of fan mail for you and Happy. [*Exits.*]

SUSIE. It's wonderful to get mail. Nobody used to write me before. Now I even get letters from Japan. [*MISS CREWS enters with letters.*] All those letters? Thank you, Miss Crews.

LARRY [*sighs*]. Miss Crews, call the set and tell 'em I may be a little late.

MISS CREWS. Very well. [*She exits.*]

SUSIE [*sitting on desk, poring over her hand-written, moronic literature*]. Here's one from North Carolina. Oh, the poor thing! There's so much sadness in this world. [*LARRY sighs; she looks up at him.*] You look sad, too, Larry. What's the matter?

LARRY. Well—[*He rises and crosses to* SUSIE.]—uh—I been waiting a long time to talk to you, Susie. I couldn't go to the high school. All those girls would mob me for autographs, especially when I tell them who I am.

SUSIE. All the girls are crazy about Clark Gable.

LARRY [*clears his throat*]. Susie—I can get two tickets for the opening at the Chinese—the de Mille picture.

SUSIE. Can you?

LARRY. I knew that'd knock you over.

SUSIE. Oh, it'll be wonderful.

LARRY. I'm always thinkin' of little things to make life wonderful—for you.

SUSIE [*nods*]. Everybody is.

LARRY [*bridling*]. What do you mean—everybody?

SUSIE. Only the other day Mr. Benson said something very true. He said: "Susie, you're Cinderella." And that's just what I feel like. And you know what else he said? He said: "All you need now is a Prince Charming."

LARRY. He did, huh? Who did he have in mind?

SUSIE. Oh, nobody.

LARRY. He didn't mention me, did he?

SUSIE. Oh, no. [LARRY *grunts*.] Of course, I've never met a Prince Charming. I wouldn't know what he looks like. Although, one day an awful nice boy came in here.

LARRY. Who?

SUSIE. I don't even know his name. He was in uniform and I was in my condition—I've never seen him since.

LARRY. You shouldn't be thinking of him. You should be thinking of Happy.

SUSIE. But I do . . . only sometimes it gets lonesome for me, especially at night. And of course, Mr. Benson and Mr. Law are busy all the time. Happy used to say good night to them on the telephone. Not really good night—just goo-n'—just like that. But they're so busy they won't come to the telephone any more.

LARRY. Happy needs a father.

SUSIE. Do you think so?

LARRY. Well, you want him to be able to look the whole world in the face, don't you?

SUSIE [*twinkling*]. He does!

LARRY. I mean when he grows up. He's gonna be ashamed when he finds out he never had a father.

SUSIE. Of course he had a father.

LARRY. I mean—a married father.

SUSIE. He was married—but I didn't know it.

[LARRY *winces*.]

LARRY. Uh—listen, Susie—I'm mighty fond of you and Happy. [*He tries playing the bashful Western hero*] Mighty fond.

SUSIE. Are you really, Larry?

LARRY. Mighty fond.

SUSIE. Who would have thought six months ago that I'd be sitting in the same room with Larry Toms and he'd be saying to me he was—

LARRY. Mighty fond.

SUSIE. Do you know something very odd? When I first came to California, it was raining very hard—oh, it rained for three weeks—it was very unusual—and I was looking for a job, and I couldn't find one—and I had fifteen cents— and I just had to get out of the rain—and I went into a theatre and there you were—on the screen—

LARRY. Mighty fond—

SUSIE [awed]. That's just what you were saying to Mary Brian —and now you're saying it to me.

LARRY. What was the picture?

SUSIE. *Thunder over Arizona.* It was a beautiful picture. I don't remember what it was about, but I saw it four times. Until I got dry.

LARRY. Susie, soon's this picture's over, how'd you like to come up to my ranch? You and Happy—

SUSIE [rises]. Ranch? Oh, that would be lovely! Maybe Mr. Benson and Mr. Law could come, too?

LARRY. Maybe they could, but they won't.

SUSIE. But I couldn't go alone—without a chaperon.

LARRY. Susie—you and Happy'll love that ranch. I got a mighty nice house, big and rambling. I got plenty of barns and a corral and plenty of livestock. But no baby.

SUSIE. I know Happy'll just love it.

LARRY. Susie—I know you don't expect this, and I don't want you to get too excited—but, Susie, I been thinkin' about you and Happy—thinkin' a lot. Ever since the day you come into this office and fell on that there floor, I said to myself: Larry, there's your leadin' lady—for life.

SUSIE. Me?

LARRY. Nobody else.

SUSIE. But I don't—you won't get mad?—but I'm not in love with you.

LARRY. You shouldn't be thinking of yourself—I'm not thinking of myself—you should be thinking of Happy.

SUSIE. I guess you're right. I don't know what to say. [Pause.] I'll ask Mr. Benson and Mr. Law—

LARRY. Huh?

SUSIE. They've been so good to me.

LARRY. I'm not proposing to them!

SUSIE. I know, but—

LARRY. You don't mean nothing to them. Before you came along they had a Spanish snake charmer until they got tired of her. And before that they had a broken-down pug who wiggled his ears. They was groomin' him for my place. There ain't nothin' holy to them!

SUSIE. But they've done everything for me.

LARRY [crosses to SUSIE]. I'm offering you my ranch—my name—and a father Happy'll be proud of!

SUSIE. I know, but—

LARRY. Don't give me your answer now. Think it over. [Pats her arm.] Only don't think too long. I'll be waiting for your answer in the Legal Department. You know where that is?

SUSIE. Oh, yes.

[MISS CREWS opens the door.]

LARRY. I'll be there. [He exits. SUSIE looks a little dazed.]

MISS CREWS. Oh, Mrs. Seabrook—I've located that young man you were looking for. He's outside.

SUSIE. Oh, you have? Really?

MISS CREWS [at door]. Come in.

[SUSIE tenses herself. A strange YOUNG MAN enters and stops.]

SUSIE [staring at him.] Oh! Oh, no, that's not him—I mean— he.

YOUNG MAN [earnestly]. Won't I do? I've just finished a short for Hal Roach—I'm making a test for Metro tomorrow, and—

MISS CREWS [firmly escorting him out]. Thank you for coming!

[YOUNG MAN shrugs and exits, and MISS CREWS closes the door.]

SUSIE. He's not English.

MISS CREWS. English? We didn't have any English actors in Young England.

SUSIE. This boy was an extra.

MISS CREWS. Does he owe you a lot of money?

SUSIE. Oh, no. It was nothing like that.

MISS CREWS [as it dawns on her]. Oh, I see! A personal matter! Well, I'll try again. [Brightly.]

SUSIE. I guess it's no use, Miss Crews. [Sighs.] He probably swallowed his pride and went back to England.

[BENSON *and* LAW *enter.* BENSON *carries paper and pencil.* BENSON *sits upstage end of desk.* LAW *crosses to front of couch.*]

LAW. Hi, Susie! How's the little mother? Clear out. We're trying to work and a hundred chorus boys are practicing fencing underneath our windows. [*Turns to* MISS CREWS.] Miss Crews, leave a note for C.F. He's got to change our office. We can't work with fencing fairies! [*Sits on couch.*]

MISS CREWS. Yes, Mr. Law. [*She exits.*]

SUSIE. Are you very busy?

BENSON. We still need an opening.

LAW. Fade-in. . . . A zoo!

SUSIE [*crossing to* BENSON]. I just wanted to thank you, Mr. Benson, for the beautiful white teddy bear.

BENSON. What teddy bear?

SUSIE. Mrs. Benson brought it herself.

BENSON [*looking up from typewriter*]. Oh, she did?

SUSIE. She played with Happy, too. And even after he went for his nap, she stayed and looked at him.

BENSON [*to* LAW—*covering*]. Where were we?

SUSIE. When she left, she was crying. I think she ought to have a baby of her own.

BENSON [*angered*]. Come on, Law—come on—fade-in on the zoo.

LAW. I've got it! Larry's carrying a hunk of meat for his pet tiger. He's crossing the road. Bang! The dame comes tearing down ninety miles an hour.

BENSON. Give her a little character.

LAW. She's a high-handed rich bitch. Bang! She almost runs the bastard down. . . . Where the hell do you think you're going? . . . She burns. . . . Society girl. . . . She's never been talked to like that before. . . . Why, you lousy bum, she snarls. . . . Listen, here's a cute piece of business. She bawls the hell out of him and he throws the hunk of meat right in her puss!

BENSON [*enthusiastically*]. That's charming!

LAW. Listen, Susie, what are you standing there for? Go home and write in your diary.

SUSIE. Boys, I wanted to ask you something . . .

BENSON. Fade-out!

LAW. Fade-in!

SUSIE. . . . and then I'll go.

LAW [*wearily*]. What is it?

SUSIE. Do you think I should marry Larry Toms?

LAW. Who?

SUSIE. Larry Toms.

LAW [*rises, crosses below couch*]. No. . . . Fade-in. . . .

BENSON. Better get a different background. We've been stay-ing in the zoo too long.

LAW. Right! Girl's home—a Pan shot—fifteen hundred butlers with white socks. . . . [*Turns to* SUSIE.] Did he ask you to marry him?

SUSIE. Yes.

LAW. Did you spit in his face?

SUSIE. He's taking me to the opening tonight. He says he's mighty fond of Happy and me.

LAW [*crosses to back of couch*]. Why shouldn't he be? His contract depends on it. Even Wilkes Barre doesn't want him and they're still calling for Theda Bara—

SUSIE. Don't you think he'd be good for Happy? He's an out-door man.

LAW. So is the fellow who collects my garbage.

BENSON. Listen, let's get on with this. Introducing the fiancé. A pale anemic louse. A business man!

LAW. Right! The minute the audience sees him they yell: Don't marry that heel.

SUSIE. I know you're very busy. . . .

LAW. Go away, Susie.

SUSIE. You boys were so sweet to me. I felt I had somebody. But lately I've been awfully alone. . . .

LAW. Sure! Everybody's alone. What do you think life is? Why do you have crowds? Because everybody's alone. [*Stops; crosses above couch to front.*] That's a thought. That's what I should be writing instead of this titivating drivel. Life as it is. People as they are.

SUSIE. But that would be terrible. You don't know, Mr. Law; you don't know how awful life can be.

BENSON. When you philosophers are through I'd like to get on with this story.

SUSIE [*eagerly, to* BENSON]. You wouldn't come out and say hello to Happy? He's in the garden. [LAW *waves her away; crosses and sits on couch.* SUSIE *is quite defeated now.*]

BENSON [*ignoring her*]. I've got it. [*To* SUSIE.] Don't bother me! [SUSIE *crosses to desk, gets mail, and fades from the scene.*] I've got it! Introducing Happy! Back to the zoo—Larry gets up in the morning and there, curled up with his pet tiger cub, is a baby! Happy!

LAW. Not bad!

BENSON. Larry looks at him. "How'd you get here?" [*He mimics* LARRY'S *voice.*]

LAW. The baby can't answer. The tiger begins to growl. Happy cries. Larry takes the baby to his hut.

BENSON. We meet Larry's drunken pal, the comic [*Rises and crosses to* LAW.] That's where we have swell business. Two clumsy men pinning up his diapers—

LAW [*his enthusiasm gone*]. Formula 284 . . . Diapers gag.

BENSON [*exulting*]. Ah, yes, but the tiger runs away with the diapers! Fade-out! Now we need excitement. The tigers are loose—

LAW. How did they get loose?

BENSON [*crosses to* LAW]. The comic's drunk. He opens the cages by accident. Christ! I see it! The city in uproar— National Guard —the girl's come down to the zoo—she's trapped with Larry—and the baby. Fifty tigers snapping at Happy's throat.

LAW. And where does my priceless dialogue come in? [*Rises and crosses to chair back of desk.*] That's the worst of hack writing. It's hard work.

BENSON. Suppose—Larry—thinks—it's the girl's baby?

LAW. Society girls go around leaving foundlings in the zoo? [*Drinking.*] Prostitution of a God-given talent! [*Sits.*] Pasteboard pictures of pasteboard people.

BENSON. Will you shut up? I've got to get this line-up today. Pearl expects me to take her to the opening.

LAW [*fiddling with the dictograph*]. Eenie . . . Meenie . . . Mina . . . Mo . . . [*Dictograph buzzes.*] Music Department?

GREEN'S VOICE. Yes, this is the Music Department. This is Mr. Green.

LAW [*mimics* C.F.'S *voice*]. Not Mr. Green! This is C.F. . . . can you write me a roundelay with a symphonic undertone in about fifteen minutes? . . . Do it! [*Dictograph buzzes.*] Yes?

GREEN'S VOICE. Look, Mr. Friday, did you say a lullaby?

LAW. No. I didn't say a lullaby. I said a roundelay. The sort of thing Beethoven dashes off. [*He clicks the dictograph off.* ROSETTI *enters.*]

ROSETTI [*genially*]. Hello, boys . . . have a cigar.

LAW. Hello, buzzard. What's the occasion?

BENSON. Fade-out, stooge, we're busy.

ROSETTI. Same old boys! Anything for a gag! Well, I'm feeling pretty good myself. I've just set Larry to a long-term contract. And he didn't have to take a cut, either. I got him a nice little set-up. A joint contract with Happy!

BENSON. With Happy?

LAW [*rises*]. Huh? You're crazy!

ROSETTI. Well, the mother came to me just now and said you two were tired of her. And I happened to look up your power of attorney, and it seems you didn't even care to get a new one when it expired.

BENSON. Is this on the level?

LAW. Where's that power of attorney?

BENSON. I thought you had it.

LAW [*aghast*]. What'd you get for Happy?

ROSETTI. Three hundred!

LAW. Why, we turned down fifteen hundred from Fox!

ROSETTI. You should have taken it. But three hundred's a lot of money. Anyway, what's the difference? It's all in the family—now.

LAW. Where's Susie?

ROSETTI. She went out with Larry. They're going to the opening tonight. They're celebrating.

LAW. Who thought this up—you?

ROSETTI. Sure.

LAW. Why, you scavenging son of a—

ROSETTI. You better be careful how you talk to me. And you'd better be careful how you talk to Larry from now on. He's fed up with your gags and insults. You got away with a lot of stuff around here because you had Happy. Well, Larry's got him now, and he's going to have plenty to say around here. I'm warning you. He'd like to see you boys off this lot. And he's in a position to do it—now. So be careful. If you want to keep your jobs. [*Turns away to door.*] And if I had a wife who was throwing my money away before I even made it, I'd be plenty careful.

BENSON. Why, you—[ROSETTI *exits quickly.* BENSON *crosses to door, then turns to* LAW.] Why the hell didn't you keep track of that power of attorney?

LAW. Why didn't *I?*

BENSON. Why the hell didn't you talk to Susie? She was in here.

LAW. Yeah.

BENSON. I see it—I see it now. Larry—Rosetti—and we let her walk right into it. Do you realize what this means? We're on our way out. [*Crosses to piano.*]

LAW. That's fine.

BENSON. Fine?

LAW. Now I'll have to go back to Vermont. Now I'll have to write.

BENSON. Pearl doesn't like Vermont.

LAW. The whims of your wife don't interest me. I've got a book—all planned.

BENSON. Listen—I want to stay in pictures. I love pictures. I'm knee-deep in debts. We've got to bust this Larry thing wide open. We've got to get Happy back.

LAW. But it's closed.

BENSON. Well, what of it? We'll open it. We've got to get Happy back.

LAW. How?

BENSON. Suppose we get Larry Toms to break that joint contract.

LAW. All right—but how?

BENSON. He's scared green of scandal. Suppose we show up at the opening tonight with a drunken dame. *Larry's deserted wife!*

LAW. Has he got one?

BENSON. We'll get one of your tarts.

LAW. That's too damned obvious.

BENSON. Can you top it?

LAW. Let me think.

BENSON. How about a poor deserted mother? I'll bet he's got one.

LAW [*rises, carried away*]. I know! *Happy's father!*

BENSON. Huh?

LAW. We're going to produce Happy's father on the air—tonight. [*Crosses to phone.*]

BENSON. Happy's father! That's swell! That's marvelous. . . . [*Pause*] But where'll we get a father?

LAW [*into phone*]. Central Casting, please. . . . Hello. I want a handsome young extra, a gentleman, a little down at the heel, not too well fed, neat business suit—shiny but well pressed; quiet manner . . .

[*Door opens and* RODNEY *enters.*]

BENSON. What do you want?

RODNEY. I received a message from Miss Crews but apparently she's stepped out. Is Mr. Friday here? I assume I've been called for a part.

LAW [*into phone, as his eyes refuse to leave* RODNEY]. Never mind—cancel it. [*Hangs up.*]

BENSON. Will you shut the door, please? [RODNEY *complies.*] So you're an actor, my boy? [*Paternally.*]

RODNEY. Of course, I haven't had much experience. As a matter of fact, I never appeared in a picture. I almost did. Since then I've been out of the profession, so to speak. Odd jobs—barbecue stand, and when that closed I offered to show tourists homes of the movie stars. Unfortunately I haven't a motor car and they won't walk. . . . I don't mind saying this call was an extremely pleasant surprise.

LAW. He's perfect!

RODNEY. Do you really think I'll do?

LAW [*inspired*]. Benson, take these lines. . . .

[BENSON *goes to chair.*]

RODNEY. Oh, are there lines? Then the fee will be fifteen dollars, I assume?

LAW. Fifteen? One hundred for you.

RODNEY. I'm afraid I'm not worth that.

LAW. This is a trailer we're making tonight. We pay more for trailers.

RODNEY. Oh, I say!

BENSON [*at desk, with paper and pencil*]. We're going to shoot this at Grauman's Chinese in the lobby. There'll be a girl at the microphone. Her name is Susie. You come running up . . . you say . . .

LAW [*at downstage end of desk*]. "Susie, why did you leave me?" . . . Say it.

RODNEY. Susie, why did you leave me?

BENSON. With feeling.

RODNEY [*with feeling*]. Susie, why did you leave me?

LAW. I'm Happy's father.

RODNEY. I'm Happy's father.

BENSON. Louder.

RODNEY. *I'm Happy's father.*

LAW. I did not go down on the *Morro Castle.* . . . Susie, I've searched for you in the four corners of the earth. . . . *Susie, why did you leave me?*

RODNEY [*who has been repeating the ends of the phrases in* LAW'S *speech*]. *Susie, why did you leave me?*

BENSON [*jubilant*]. Right!

BLACKOUT AND CURTAIN

Scene III

A radio voice is heard in the theatre before the rise of the curtain. We're right in Grauman's Chinese Theatre in Hollywood.

RADIO ANNOUNCER. Folks, this is the première of Cecil B. de Mille's super-spectacle of Egyptian life—*King Saul*— at Grauman's Chinese. Your favorite stars, folks, in person —and the *crowds*. They're pushing and shoving and yelling for autographs, but it's all in good-natured fun. Only two hurt and they've refused medical treatment. There's Constance Bennett, folks, with her husband, the Marquis de la Falaise. No, I'm wrong. Sorry. It's not the Marquis . . . it's not Constance Bennett. It's Mary Pickford. By the way, I've been reading our Mary's book, folks. She's selling God, folks, and that's something we all ought to be in the market for. Give a thought to God and He'll give a thought to you. That's the big lesson in *King Saul*, folks. Oh, there's Leotta Marvin. . . .

As the curtain rises, the booming voice softens to the normal tone of a radio.

Again we are in MR. FRIDAY'S *office, later in the evening. At the rise of the curtain.* C.F. *is seated with a* CUTTER, *and* BENSON *sits a little apart from him, in chair back of the couch, near the radio, which is on.*

RADIO ANNOUNCER. . . . And if you've seen her on the screen, I don't have to tell you she's blonde, beautiful and gorgeous. Folks, I want to tell you that this is the most thrilling première it's been my privilege to cover. *King Saul*, de Mille's super-spectacle of Egyptian life at Grauman's Chinese—

C.F. Benson, turn down that radio. We've got to get three thousand feet out of *Young England*. It's a sick picture, Benson. Where's Law? I left word at his hotel.

BENSON. He'll be here. I'm inside man tonight. He's outside.

C.F. [*to* CUTTER]. Cut the coronation scene—it drags. And give me an underlying something that means something. I want a stirring Britannic quality.

[BENSON *turns up the radio.*]

RADIO ANNOUNCER. . . . And that, folks was Mr. Stanley Oswald, veteran of old silent films. . . . This is the première of *King Saul*, Cecil B. de Mille's super-spectacle at Grauman's Chinese . . .

C.F. Benson, turn to page 94 and read that scene. I want to lap-dissolve through Queen Victoria. Simmons, you're supposed to be a cutter. Give me some ideas.

RADIO ANNOUNCER. . . . And now, folks, I'm told that none other than Larry Toms is with us tonight. And he's not altogether by his lonesome for hanging on his manly arm is none other than Mrs. Susan Seabrook, mother of America's Crown Prince—Happy!

BENSON. Hooray!

CUTTER. I got a way of cutting all that Boer War stuff so you won't even miss it.

RADIO ANNOUNCER. . . . And now I have the honor to present Mrs. Seabrook, the mother of Happy . . .

C.F. Will you turn that infernal thing off? [*To* CUTTER.] I can't cut the Boer War. It's historically valuable.

RADIO ANNOUNCER. . . . And now I have the honor to present Mrs. Seabrook, the mother of Happy—

SUSIE'S VOICE. But I don't know what to say!

BENSON. Susie's on the air.

RADIO ANNOUNCER. Is it true, Mrs. Seabrook, that you and Larry have been window shopping?

SUSIE'S VOICE [*and it's very nervous indeed*]. Well—

RADIO ANNOUNCER. The microphone is yours.

SUSIE'S VOICE. I would like to thank all of you for the thousands of letters and gifts that you've sent my baby Happy. I read all your letters and some of them make me cry—they're so pathetic. I would like to send all of you money only I haven't got that much and the studio won't let me. I'd like to say a few words about the letters asking about Happy's diet. You read a lot of advertisements of what he eats but if Happy ate everything they said he ate I guess he'd be a giant, and he's really got a very little stomach.

BENSON. Good for Susie! Truth in advertising!

C.F. [*struck by appalling thought*]. Benson, was Queen Victoria alive during the Boer War?

BENSON. If she's alive in the picture, she was.

RADIO ANNOUNCER [*through this*]. Folks, this is the première of Cecil B. de Mille's super-spectacle of Egyptian life, *King Saul*, at Grauman's Chinese—

SUSIE'S VOICE. Can I say hello to all my girl friends at the Julia Marshall High School? . . . *Hello!*

C.F. Benson—

BENSON. Ssssh . . . Susie's talking.

SUSIE'S VOICE. A lot of you wonder in your letters how a grown woman can go to high school. Well, it's not easy. I'm a mother, and the other girls aren't . . .

BENSON. Let's hope not.

SUSIE'S VOICE [*brightly*]. . . . although some of the girls are very developed.

RADIO ANNOUNCER [*quickly*]. Folks, this is the première of *King Saul,* Cecil B. de Mille's super-spectacle of Egyptian life. . . .

C.F. Shut that infernal thing off.

[BENSON *lifts hand like traffic signal "Stop."*]

SUSIE'S VOICE. I didn't finish. I wanted to explain that I'm going to high school so I can keep up with Happy when he goes to college. Because I'm the only one Happy can go to. He hasn't got a father, and—

RADIO ANNOUNCER [*very, very firmly*]. That was Happy's mother, folks. . . . She was wearing a white evening gown. And folks, meet Larry Toms, the lucky man.

C.F. Benson, can we lap-dissolve through, do you think, on page 94?

LARRY'S VOICE. I know this is going to be a wonderful picture.

RADIO ANNOUNCER. A little bird has whispered to me that you and Mrs. Seabrook are contemplating marriage, Larry.

BENSON. Well, what do you know about that?

C.F. Will you come here, Benson, with that script?

LARRY'S VOICE. Well, to tell you the truth—

BENSON. He's blushing.

LARRY'S VOICE. I kinda missed the little fella after the day's work was done. So I guess pretty soon I'll be Happy's father off the screen as well as on—

BENSON. Who wrote his speech? You or Rosetti?

RODNEY'S VOICE. Stop! I'm Happy's father.

C.F. [*rises*]. What's that?

RODNEY'S VOICE. I did not go down on the *Morro Castle.* I've searched for you in the four corners of the earth. Susie, why did you leave me?

C.F. [*excitedly*]. Did you hear that?

BENSON [*softly*]. I wonder what that was . . .

[*Cries are heard of "Here, Officer"—inarticulate shouts—a siren.*]

RADIO ANNOUNCER. Folks, there was a slight interruption. That voice you heard was a young man . . . he . . . well, he threw his arms about Mrs. Seabrook and kissed her. There's some confusion—a police officer is making his way through —they've got the young man . . . no, they haven't got him . . . Folks, this is the opening of Cecil B. de Mille's super-spectacle of Egyptian life, *King Saul*, at Grauman's Chinese . . .

[BENSON *turns it off.*]

C.F. [*stunned*]. Good Gad! [*Phone rings. He moves to it.*]

BENSON [*shakes his head*]. Strangest thing I ever heard.

C.F. Oh, hello, B.K. . . . Yes, I've just heard it over the radio . . . [*Miserable.*] I'm sitting here trying to cut *Young England* . . . what? . . . But, B.K., . . . yes, of course, it's a serious situation . . . I agree with you . . . yes, . . . yes . . . of course . . . I'll get hold of the mother immediately. [*He rises; hangs up, still dazed. To* BENSON.] B.K.'s coming down to the studio! [*Phone rings.*] Yes . . . Look here, I've nothing to say to the press. It's a canard. [*He hangs up. Phone rings again.*] I won't answer it.

[MISS CREWS *enters.*]

MISS CREWS. Doctor Tompkins is calling you, Mr. Friday. He says it's important.

C.F. What's he want? I'm not in. Call Mrs. Seabrook's house and have her ring me the minute she comes in.

MISS CREWS. Yes, Mr. Friday. [*She exits.*]

C.F. Benson, do you think that young man was genuine?

BENSON [*rises, crosses around downstage end of couch*]. Search me.

C.F. Well, we'll soon find out. B.K.'s set the police after him

BENSON [*a little disturbed*]. Why do that? Best thing the studio can do is ignore it.

C.F. We can't ignore it. This has brought up the whole paternity issue.

BENSON. What of it?

C.F. Suppose Happy has a skeleton in his closet?

BENSON [*lies on couch*]. I don't even know if he's got a closet

C.F. Save your gags for your pictures. They need them. I've never heard B.K. so excited. [*Crosses to window.*] What do you think the reaction will be in the sticks—in the provinces? An illegitimate baby!

BENSON. This is 1935.

C.F. To me, yes. But how many intellectuals have we in America?

BENSON. One.

C.F. You don't seem to realize—

BENSON. Why, this is going to send Happy's stock up one hundred per cent. From now on he's not only cute he's romantic.

C.F. He's illegitimate! I know America!

CUTTER [*studying the script*]. What about Prince Albert? I can cut him out of the picture and you won't even miss him.

C.F. [*crossing below desk*]. Yes, yes, Simmons. You go to the cutting room and do the best you know how. [SIMMONS *rises and puts chair up against wall.*] I've something more urgent right now. [*Crosses to* SIMMONS.] And, for God's sake, Simmons, get me some trumpets that sound like trumpets.

CUTTER [*not gruffly, but politely*]. You sure you don't mean trombones, C.F.?

C.F. No. I mean trumpets. I'm not a musician but I know what I mean. Trumpets—that slide. [*He pantomimes a trombone, of course.*]

BENSON [*to* CUTTER]. He wants a slide trumpet.

[CUTTER *exits. Simultaneously through other door* GREEN *and* SLADE *appear.*]

GREEN. Well, we've got that roundelay.

C.F. What do you want? What roundelay?

[*Phone rings.*]

GREEN. Park it, Otto. [*Both go to piano.*]

C.F. [*at phone*]. Yes—yes—no, Mr. Friday is not here. He has nothing to say to the press. [*He hangs up.*]

GREEN. You're going to be enthusiastic about this. We've been up all night working on it. [SLADE *starts playing Beethoven's Turkish March. As* C.F. *starts toward the piano, the phone rings.*] Smooth, ain't it?

C.F. [*at phone*]. Miss Crews? Where's Mrs. Seabrook? Why haven't you got her? [*To* GREEN.] I will not listen to any more music.

GREEN. Get a load of this. It's the real McCoy.

C.F. [*at phone*]. Yes—I'm holding the line—all right, never mind. Call me. [*Hangs up. To* SLADE *and* GREEN.] I'll call the studio guards if you don't stop that infernal din. I'll report you to B.K. for insubordination. I'll have your contracts torn up!

GREEN. Are you kidding, or is this on the level?

C.F. Get out!

GREEN. O.K. Don't get tough! Come on, Otto. [*Crosses back of couch to door.*] But it's a fine how-do-you-do when you call up a couple of artists late at night and put 'em to work going through Beethoven's symphonies for a little inspiration and then give them the bum's rush just because you ain't in the mood. [GREEN *and* SLADE *exit.*]

[LARRY *and* ROSETTI *enter, both in tails and toppers.*]

ROSETTI. Now calm down, Larry, calm down—

LARRY. I'm not saying a word.

C.F. Where's Mrs. Seabrook? What did you do with her?

LARRY. I don't know, and I don't care.

BENSON [*mockingly*]. "I kinda missed the little fella after the day's work was done—"

C.F. [*quickly*]. Look here, Larry, I want to know what Susie said. Did she know the young man? What did she say?

LARRY. You listen to what *I* gotta say. I ain't goin' to go through with no contract to play with no unbaptized baby!

ROSETTI [*placatingly*]. Just a moment, Larry—

LARRY. I'm through! [*Overwhelmed with the memory.*] On the air—with all my fans listening in! I'm serving you notice now. I ain't marrying her. I ain't doing no more pictures with Happy.

ROSETTI. Larry, will you listen to reason?

LARRY. There's only one thing you can do for me, Rosetti. Get me a doctor. I'm going up to my dressing room. I need a sedative.

[LAW *enters quietly.*]

BENSON. Don't stand there. Get him a doctor—

LAW. Take me. I'm a qualified veterinary.

[ROSETTI *exits with* LARRY.]

C.F. Law—

[BENSON *sits up.*]

LAW. Hello, C.F. I just got your message at the hotel. *Young England* in trouble? Well, the old salvaging crew will pitch in. [*Takes off his coat.*]

C.F. Were you there?

LAW. Where? At the opening? Yes. Extraordinary, wasn't it

BENSON [*significantly*]. *We* heard it over the radio.

LAW [*casually*]. How'd it come over?

BENSON [*admiringly*]. Clear as a bell!

LAW. It certainly broke Larry up. You should have seen our chivalrous hero running from the rescue. Why, the wind whistled right past me!

C.F. Law, do you think that fellow was a crank, or do you think he was really—

LAW [*judicially*]. Hard to say. He had a sinister underlip.

C.F. [*into phone*]. Miss Crews, did you get Mrs. Seabrook's house? No one answers? Someone *must* answer—she has a ménage! [*Hangs up. Dictograph buzzes.*] Hello?

B.K.'S VOICE. Look here, Friday . . .

C.F. Yes, B.K.

B.K.'S VOICE. Did you get any dope on that young man?

C.F. No. I can't get any information. No one seems to know.

B.K.'S VOICE. Why not? I ask you to do the simplest little thing and, as usual, you fall down on me.

C.F. [*piteously*]. Why blame me? I was sitting here cutting *Young England.*

B.K.'S VOICE. Don't bother me with *Young England.* You come up here—I want to talk with you.

C.F. Yes, B.K. I'll be right up. [*He moves to the door; sighs.*] Sometimes I wonder if this industry is worth the sacrifice. [*He exits.*]

BENSON [*smiles*]. What'd you do with him?

LAW. Put him in an office across the hall.

BENSON [*aghast*]. What? Why here?

LAW. They won't look for him here.

BENSON. Why didn't you dump him somewhere else?

LAW. And leave him free to roam—and blab? Listen Benson, B.K.'s called the Chief personally and the whole damn police department is scouring the town for Rodney. [*Crosses to liquor cabinet; pours a drink.*] And you don't know what I've been up against with Rodney. [*He drinks.*] In his own peculiar English fashion, he's not entirely nitwitted. I had to shove him at the mike, and he's been demanding explanations ever since.

BENSON. One question: What'll we do with him?

LAW [*crossing back to couch; sits*]. Frankly, I planned everything but Rodney's disposal. I don't know. But given a little time we'll work this problem out.

BENSON [*really aghast now*]. Time?

LAW. Rodney's all right. He doesn't know it, but I've locked him in.

BENSON. Listen: I've got a wife to support! I've got a job to keep! I haven't got Vermont on my mind! I *like* writing pictures! I'm no god-damn realist!

LAW [*soothingly*]. Easy, there, easy—

BENSON. If B.K. even dreamed we had anything to do with this we'd be blacklisted in the industry.

LAW [*rising*]. Give me a chance to think, will you? Why the panic? I'll admit I've overlooked a few details.

BENSON. Get that guy out of the studio. Put him on a plane to Mexico. Strangle him! I don't care what you do.

LAW. No—no. Murder leads to theft and theft leads to deceit. Haven't you read De Quincey?

BENSON. C.F. may breeze in here any minute. Will you get going?

LAW. Very well, my sweet—I go. [*He starts for door, remembers that he had a coat, looks around room and finally locates it on couch. Gets it and exits. Phone rings.*]

BENSON [*into phone*]. Hello . . . Yes, right here. Oh, hello, darling. How are you feeling? [*Tenderly.*] Of course I recognized your voice . . . Pearl, I'll be home in half an hour. . . . Less . . . Well, what are you crying about? . . . But I told you I couldn't take you to the opening. Well, if Louise was going why didn't you go with them? They'd be tickled to have you . . . Listen, darling . . . I know . . . I know . . . Yes, I'm listening. . . . [LAW *re-enters—a changed* LAW. *He goes right to the second telephone.*]

LAW [*picking up the second telephone*]. Give me the front gate!

BENSON [*into phone*]. Yes, darling . . . yes . . . [*Sincerely.*] Darling, please—please don't say that.

LAW. Smitty, this is Mr. Law. Any stranger go through the gate in the last ten minutes? . . . No?

BENSON [*sighs*]. Yes, darling. . . .

LAW. Well, listen. The fellow that was on the air tonight—Happy's father—yes! He's loose in the studio . . . Yeah. . . .

BENSON [*turns to* LAW, *still holding the phone*]. What?

LAW. Grab him and hold him. Don't let anyone come near him. Report to me personally . . . yeah . . .

BENSON. Darling, I'll call you back. [*Slams down the phone.*]

LAW [*hangs up*]. The damn cleaning woman let him out!

BENSON [*apoplectic*]. I told you, didn't I? I told you you shouldn't have brought him here!

[SUSIE *enters. She has been magnificently decked out for the opening, but despite her splendor she seems extremely unhappy.*]

SUSIE. Oh, Mr. Benson . . . I tried to get you at your house but Mrs. Benson said you were here. I tried to get you, too, Mr. Law, at the hotel.

LAW. Now, now, Susie—I know—I know.

SUSIE. Oh, I should never have gone to that opening. I didn't want to go. When I was dressing I put my slip on the wrong side. I knew something terrible was going to happen. And then in the nursery when I went to say good night to Happy, he wouldn't eat his formula. And he wouldn't say good night to me. He was so cross. I told Larry I didn't want to leave Happy—but he insisted—and then the way Larry ran out on me—

LAW [*consolingly*]. Now, now—

SUSIE. Why should he do that? Oh, I was so ashamed . . . I didn't even see the picture. And then when I got home—I knew I shouldn't have gone—I should never have left Happy. When I went to the hospital. . . .

LAW. Hospital?

BENSON. Hospital?

SUSIE. They won't let me in . . . not for two weeks.

BENSON [*crosses to* SUSIE]. Happy's in the hospital?

SUSIE [*puzzled*]. Happy's got the measles.

LAW. What?

SUSIE. And they won't let me come near him.

BENSON. Measles!

LAW. He certainly picked the right time for it!

SUSIE. That's why he wouldn't eat his formula.

C.F.'S VOICE [*offstage grimly*]. Well, we'll see— [*As he opens the door.*] I brought you some visitors, boys. Come in. [RODNEY *enters with* STUDIO OFFICER. *To* RODNEY.] Are these the men?

RODNEY. They most certainly are.

SUSIE [*crosses to* RODNEY]. You know you're not Happy's father.

RODNEY. Of course not, but—

SUSIE. You couldn't be!

RODNEY. Of course not! My dear, I'm very sorry. Look here, we always seem to meet under extraordinary circumstances . . . I never dreamt . . . I'd no idea . . . It was all so spectacular . . . And to do this to you—You were so kind to me

... They said it was a trailer ... I didn't realize until I was in the midst of it ... And then I found myself in a car ... with him ... [*Indicates* LAW.] I asked him to bring me to you at once. Instead, he locked me in a dusty office.

C.F. So you boys put him up to it!

LAW. Before you say anything you'll be sorry for, C.F. .... [*Turns to* OFFICER.] Smitty, who called you tonight to tell you this unfortunate young man was loose in the studio?

OFFICER. *You* did, Mr. Law.

LAW [*grandly*]. That's all.

BENSON. Take him away.

LAW. It's an obvious psychiatric case, C.F.

BENSON [*to* C.F.]. I wouldn't be surprised if he's the boy that's been springing out of bushes.

LAW. Certainly. Look at the way he kissed Susie!

RODNEY [*appalled*]. But you coached me for hours. Both of you. Wait—here are my lines. [*He fumbles in his pocket.*] I know I have them—unless I've lost them.

LAW. So you're an author, too! And I thought it was extemporaneous.

RODNEY. Here—here they are! My dear, will you please read these lines? [*He hands the paper to* SUSIE.] They're the very words I spoke over the radio.

SUSIE [*reads and backs away from* RODNEY]. You never said *these* lines. You *must* be a crank. Maybe you do spring out of bushes.

RODNEY [*stares*]. Oh, I beg your pardon. My lines are on the other side.

LAW [*grabs for paper*]. I'll take that! Susie—

C.F. [*taking paper out of* SUSIE'S *hand, brushes* LAW *aside*]. Just a minute. [*Reads.*] "She's a high-handed rich bitch."— *Tiger Tamer!*—There it is in the corner. *Tiger Tamer* by J. Carlyle Benson and Robert Law!

LAW [*hurt to the quick*]. It's a forgery. Benson, we've been framed!

C.F. [*grimly*]. This is the last prank you'll ever play. [*Clicks the dictograph.*]

MISS CREWS [*enters*]. The new trumpets are here. [*For once, C.F. is not interested. The trumpets blare out.*]

C.F. [*into dictograph*]. B.K.? I just found out—Benson and Law put that young man on the radio.

B.K.'S VOICE. Are you sure of that?

C.F. I have the proof. The young man is in my office.

B.K.'s VOICE. All right, fire them. I don't want them on this lot. If they think they can get away with that—
C.F. Fire them? Of course I'll fire them.

[LARRY's *voice is heard as he enters.*]

LARRY. Don't tell me nothing—let go of me. [DOCTOR *and* ROSETTI *enter, following* LARRY *and struggling with him.*]
C.F. Quiet there—
LARRY. Let go of me!
C.F. Larry, I have neither the time nor the patience to pander to actors!
LARRY [*bellowing with the hurt roar of a wounded bull*]. No? Babies, huh . . . [*Turns on* SUSIE.] You—you—
SUSIE [*frightened; runs to* BENSON]. What do you want?
LARRY. What do I want? That god-damn baby of yours has given me the measles!

CURTAIN

ACT THREE
Scene I

A hospital corridor. Several weeks later. Facing us are several doors, punctuated by the little white cards identifying the patients within.

As the curtain rises, a white-clad NURSE *is walking down the corridor bearing a covered tray. Before she disappears,* BENSON *enters. He knocks on the door of the room where* HAPPY *is ensconced.* SUSIE *opens the door.*

SUSIE. Oh, hello, Mr. Benson. I'd ask you to come in but Happy's still sleeping. The doctor says he can be discharged tomorrow or the day after, he's getting along so fine. Where's Mr. Law?

BENSON. I don't know. We haven't been patronizing the same barrooms.

SUSIE. You look as if you didn't get much sleep.

BENSON [*slumping into a wheel chair*]. I didn't.

SUSIE [*pityingly*]. Why don't you go home?

BENSON. Home?

SUSIE. Is there anything wrong?

BENSON. Not a thing! Everything's fine.

SUSIE. How's Mrs. Benson?

BENSON. She's fine.

SUSIE. That's good. I called your house to thank her for the radio for Happy but they said you moved.

BENSON. We *were* moved.

SUSIE. You mean you were thrown out?

BENSON. If you want to be technical about it, yes.

SUSIE. Oh, I'm sorry.

BENSON [*broodingly*]. What hurts is Aggrafino Jesus.

SUSIE. Who?

BENSON. My favorite Filipino butler. He slapped a lien on my brand-new Packard.

SUSIE. Oh!

BENSON. That's what the missionaries taught *him!*

SUSIE. You boys shouldn't have played that joke on me. You only hurt yourselves. Please don't drink any more, Mr. Benson.

BENSON. So it's come to that! You're going to reform me.

SUSIE. Well, I feel just like a sister to you boys. That's why

I couldn't stay mad at you. Please, Mr. Benson, if you need money—I can give you some. I mean—when the studio sends Happy's checks. They haven't sent them yet.

BENSON [*looking up*]. They haven't? How many do they owe you?

SUSIE. Two. I called Mr. Friday but he wouldn't talk to me. Do you think they're docking Happy?

BENSON. They can't do that. Measles are an act of God.

[NURSE *enters with a box of flowers.*]

NURSE. Some flowers for you, Mrs. Seabrook.

SUSIE [*extending her hand for it*]. Oh, thank you.

NURSE. And he'd like to know if he can come up to see you. He's downstairs.

SUSIE [*embarrassed*]. Oh . . .

BENSON. Who's downstairs? Who's sending you flowers?

SUSIE [*reluctantly*]. It's Mr. Bevan. You know—

BENSON. You haven't been seeing our Nemesis?

SUSIE. Oh, no. But he's been writing me every day and sending me flowers. I didn't tell you. I didn't want to get you excited.

BENSON [*to NURSE; sweetly*]. Tell him to come up, Nurse. And stand by.

SUSIE [*quickly*]. Oh, no, Nurse. He's not to come up. I don't want to see him. Ever. And give him back his flowers. [*She hands box back to* NURSE.]

NURSE [*taking it*]. Very well. [*She exits.*]

BENSON. Why deprive me of the pleasure of kicking an actor?

SUSIE. It wasn't his fault. After all, you put him up to it.

BENSON [*outraged*]. Are you defending him?

SUSIE. Oh, no, I'm just as disappointed in him as you are. But I'm trying to be fair. [*She pauses.*] He writes very nice letters. [*A faraway look comes into her eyes.*]

BENSON [*suspiciously*]. What kind of letters do you write him?

SUSIE [*hastily*]. Oh, I don't write *any* letters.

BENSON. Good!

SUSIE. I'm afraid of my spelling.

[LAW *enters. There's an air of on-my-way about him.*]

LAW. Hello, Susie. . . . And goodbye, Susie.

SUSIE. Hello, Mr. Law. Are you going away?

LAW. I am.

SUSIE. Where?

LAW. Where I belong. Vermont. Where you can touch life and feel life, and write it! [*Glares at* BENSON.]

BENSON. When does the great exodus begin?

LAW. In exactly thirty-five minutes. I'm flying back to my native hills, like a homing pigeon. No stopping in New York for me! I've chartered a plane—right to Vermont.

BENSON. Chartered a plane! Where'd you get the money?

LAW [*grudgingly*]. Well, there are twelve Rotarians coming along.

BENSON. You'll be back in a week.

SUSIE [*eagerly*]. Will you, Mr. Law?

LAW [*scornfully*]. Back to what? Sunshine and psyllium seed? Listen, I've got me a little shack overlooking the valley . . . I'm going to cook my own food, chop my own wood, and write—

BENSON [*sardonically*]. At twenty below?

LAW [*rapturously*]. Snow! . . . God, how I love snow! [*He raises his eyes to Heaven.*]

> And since to look at things in bloom
> Fifty springs are little room.
> About the woodlands I will go
> To see the cherry—hung with snow!

SUSIE. That's poetry.

LAW. A. E. Housman! *Shropshire Lad.* [*He puts the book in his pocket.*]

BENSON. There's plenty of snow in Arrowhead.

LAW. Yeah; they deliver it in trucks. And even when it's real you think it's cornflakes.

SUSIE. You won't drink too much in Vermont, will you, Mr. Law?

LAW. Only the heady wine air that has no dregs!

SUSIE. Because you're crazy enough without drinking.

LAW [*defensively*]. I drank for escape . . . escape from myself . . . but now I'm free! I've found peace!

SUSIE. You'll say good-bye to Happy before you go? I want him to remember you.

LAW. Right now!

SUSIE. Wait! I'll see if he's awake. [*She enters* HAPPY'S *room.*]

BENSON. Will you send me a copy of the book—autographed?

LAW. You get copy number one—first edition.

BENSON. What's the book about?

LAW. I'm going to bare my soul . . . I'm going to write life in the raw. I've got the opening all planned—two rats in a sewer!

BENSON. Sounds delightful.

LAW [*scornfully*]. You wouldn't appreciate real writing. You've been poisoned. On second thought, I won't send you a book.

BENSON. Tell me more about the rats. What's your story?

LAW [*slightly patronizing*]. This isn't a picture that you paste together, Mr. Benson. I'm going to write Life. Life isn't a story . . . it's a discordant overture to death!

BENSON. Well, if you want people to read it, the boy had better meet the girl.

LAW. There is no girl. There is no boy. These are people— real, live people—listen! I'm not even going to use a typewriter! I'm going to weigh every word—with a pencil!

BENSON. Well, maybe you're on the right track. You've got something to say—and the talent to say it with.

LAW. It's finally penetrated!

BENSON. You're probably doing the right thing.

LAW. The only thing. It's different with you—you've got a wife.

BENSON. I had.

LAW. Huh?

BENSON. Oh—uh—Pearl left last night.

LAW. No! I'm sorry.

BENSON [*shrugs*]. You can't blame her. She wasn't wild about marrying me in the first place. I coaxed her into it. I painted some pretty pictures for her. It just didn't pan out.

LAW. You still want her?

BENSON [*almost to himself*]. I guess I do.

LAW. Personally, I'd say the hell with her.

BENSON [*smiles bitterly*]. The trouble is I don't mean it when I say it. [ROSETTI *enters.*]

ROSETTI. Hello, boys.

LAW [*cheerily*]. Hello, louse. Get Benson a job, will you? He wants to stay in this God-forsaken hole.

ROSETTI. Listen! I'm not handling second-hand writers. Chicken feed! Right now I'm immersed in a three million dollar deal.

LAW [*interested*]. Yeah?

ROSETTI. Yeah. With Gaumont British, and I'm underestimating when I say three million because B.K.'s turned down three million. Why should I bother with writers on the blacklist? So don't go calling me a louse!

[SUSIE *enters.*]

SUSIE [*gaily*]. Happy has his eyes open. You want to come in now, Mr. Law?

LAW. Coming, Susie. [*He follows* SUSIE *into* HAPPY'S *room.*]

BENSON. Rosetti— [*Going to him, whispering.*] Law wants to leave. He's flying in half an hour. Can you call up the studios? Can you get us a one-picture contract? We'll make you our agent for life. *He's leaving!*

ROSETTI. Sure, he's leaving. Nobody wants him.

BENSON. How do you know? You haven't tried.

ROSETTI. I've tried. I don't let my personal feelings interfere with commissions.

BENSON. Listen, I've been a scene painter, prop boy, camera man, director, producer . . . I even sold film in Australia . . . They can't throw me out of this business!

ROSETTI [*crosses to a door and throws it back*]. They won't touch you with a ten-foot pole. You, Law, or Happy.

BENSON. Or Happy?

ROSETTI. I gave B.K. a swell angle. Listen in on KNX this afternoon.

BENSON. Huh?

ROSETTI. The world is full of babies. You can get them two for a nickel. [*He opens inner door and meets* LARRY *coming out.*] Hello, Larry. I was just coming in to see you. [NURSE *pushes* LARRY *in wheel chair into corridor.*]

LAW'S VOICE. Good-bye, Happy. [*He enters with Susie.*] Good-bye, Susie.

SUSIE. Good-bye, Mr. Law.

LAW. Hello, Larry. How's every little spot?

LARRY. What's the idea?

LAW. What idea?

LARRY. What's the idea of sending me a box of dead spiders?

LAW. Didn't you like the box?

LARRY. You wait until I'm through convalescing!

NURSE. Now, don't excite yourself. You heard what the doctor said. You're going for your sun bath now. [*She wheels him out.*]

ROSETTI. I'll go along with you. Larry. I've got some great news for you. B.K.'s lending you out to Mascot! [*He exits.*]

LARRY [*as he goes out*]. What?

LAW. Well, Susie, take good care of Happy.

SUSIE. Oh, I will.

LAW. Continue your education.

SUSIE. I'm doing that.

LAW [*quickly*]. What's the capital of Nebraska?

SUSIE. Lincoln.

LAW. Who hit Sir Isaac Newton on the bean with an apple?

SUSIE. The law of gravity.

LAW. Who said, "Don't give up the ship?"

SUSIE. Captain James Lawrence in the battle of Lake Erie, 1813.

LAW. Don't give up the ship, Susie. I'll write you. [*He kisses her on the forehead.*]

SUSIE. Good-bye, Mr. Law. I've got to go back to Happy. [*Her voice breaks.*] I feel awful funny—your going away.

[*Exits.*]

BENSON [*finally*]. Well, you bastard—get out of here.

LAW. I'm going, stinker. [*Crosses to* BENSON. *They look at each other. A pause. Then* LAW *extends hand. They shake.* LAW *moves to go.*]

BENSON [*without turning*]. Say—[LAW *stops.*] I don't suppose you'll be interested—Rosetti finally admitted Paramount wants us. Two thousand bucks a week to save Diet-rich. We can close the deal in three or four days.

LAW [*turns slowly*]. My plane leaves in twenty-five minutes. And you're a liar!

BENSON. I'm not trying to hold you back. But I figured this time you might *save* your money and—

LAW. I can live on twelve dollars a week in Vermont—in luxury!

BENSON. It would kind of help *me* out— If I could lay my hands on some ready dough Pearl might listen to reason.

LAW [*casually*]. Well, we loaned out a lot of money in our time. Collect it. And send me my share.

BENSON. I thought of that. The trouble is I don't remember just who it was—and how much. The only one I remember is Jascha Simkovitch.

LAW. Who?

BENSON. Jascha Simkovitch. The fellow that came over with Eisenstein. Don't you remember? You made a wonderful crack about him. He said "There's a price on my head in Russia." And you said, "Yeah—two rubles." [*Laughs. He is flattering* LAW *smoothly.*]

LAW [*laughs with him*]. Sure, I remember him. Why, we gave that bed-bug three thousand bucks! Get hold of him and collect it.

BENSON. He's in Paris. What's-his-name came over and said Jascha was living at the Ritz bar.

LAW. Then you can't collect it. Well, I'm off. [*He moves to exit once more.*]

BENSON [*as if struck with sudden thought*]. Wait a minute! I've got a great gag for you! Let's call Jascha up in Paris—on Larry's phone! [*Chuckles, throws arms around* LAW. *Both laugh.*] Can you imagine Larry's face when he gets the bill? A farewell rib!

LAW [*hesitates*]. Have I got time?

BENSON [*reassuringly; looks at his watch*]. You've got plenty of time.

LAW. I'll work fast. Stand guard, Benson. [*He enters* LARRY'S *room.* BENSON *follows and partly closes door.*]

LAW'S VOICE. I'm talking for Mr. Toms. I want to put a call through to Paris, France. . . . I want Jascha Simkovitch . . . Hotel Ritz, Paris. . . . Listen, don't worry about the charges . . . That's right—Jascha, as in Heifetz . . . S-i-m-k-o-v-i-t-c-h.

[BENSON *closes door on* LAW. NURSE *enters with registered letter, knocks on* SUSIE'S *door.* BENSON *looks at his watch.* SUSIE *appears.*]

NURSE. Registered letter for you, Mrs. Seabrook.

SUSIE. For me.

NURSE. You'll have to sign for it. There's a return receipt on it. [SUSIE *signs.*]

SUSIE. Now what do I do?

NURSE. Now you give me the receipt back and I'll give it to the postman. He's waiting for it. Here's your letter. [NURSE *exits.* SUSIE *opens letter.*]

SUSIE [*cheerily*]. Why—it's from Mr. Friday.

[LAW *emerges, as she opens the letter.*]

LAW. The service had better be good or there'll be no farewell rib. I haven't got much time.

SUSIE. Oh, didn't you go yet, Mr. Law?

LAW. I'm on my way!

SUSIE [*reading letter*]. What does Mr. Friday mean when he says they're taking advantage of Clause 5A?

LAW. What? Let me see that. [*He reads the letter.* BENSON *looks over his shoulder.*] Well, this is the goddamnedest . . .

SUSIE. You mustn't swear so much. I don't mind—I'm used to it—but Happy might hear you. What does it mean?

LAW [*reading*]. Clause 5A—when an artist through illness—
for a period of more than fourteen days—

BENSON. They're just using that for an excuse. It's the paternity
issue!

SUSIE. What paternity issue?

BENSON. They're crazy! That kid's going to be as good as he
ever was—better.

SUSIE. What does it mean?

LAW. It means, Susie—Happy is out.

SUSIE. Out?

BENSON. Yeah. Finished—done. At the age of eight months—
In his prime!

SUSIE. Out of pictures?

BENSON [*turning on* LAW]. And there's the man who did it.
It was your brilliant idea!

SUSIE [*such a nice girl*]. Oh, no, After all, it was just like a
dream. I had to wake up some time.

LAW [*as phone rings*]. I guess that's Paris.

SUSIE. What's Paris? [*Phone still rings.*]

BENSON. Go ahead and have your farewell rib, and get out,
author!

[*Phone still rings.* LAW *enters room.*]

SUSIE. What's Paris?

BENSON [*going to door of* LARRY'S *room*]. A city in France.

LAW [*in room*]. Hello—right here.—Yes—yes—I'm ready.
Hello! . . . Hello—Jascha? Jascha Simkovitch? This is
Bobby Law. Is it raining in Paris? . . . well, it's not raining
here!

BENSON. Wonderful age we're living in!

LAW [*in room*]. Listen, Jascha, are you sober? . . . How come?
. . . Oh, you just got there! . . . You're going to London?
. . . Today? . . . Hold the wire. [LAW *enters.*] I've got an
idea! *Let's buy the studio!*

BENSON. What?

LAW. You heard Rosetti. Gaumont British is offering three
million. Let's get Jascha to send a cable—sign it Gaumont
British—offering four!

BENSON. Why be petty? Offer five!

LAW [*judicially*]. Right! [*Exits into room.*]

SUSIE. You boys are very peculiar.

LAW [*in room*]. Jascha—got a pencil and paper? Fne. Listen,
Jascha, we want you to send a cable from London as
follows: Quote. . . .

[LARRY *enters in his wheel chair.* BENSON *closes the door hurriedly.*]

LARRY. Hey, that's my room!

BENSON [*firmly shutting the door*]. A private conversation should be private.

LARRY. What's the idea of using my phone?

BENSON. Do you object?

LARRY. Certainly I object. I ain't gonna pay for your calls.

BENSON. All right, if that's the way you feel about it—here's your nickel!

BLACKOUT AND CURTAIN

Scene II

In Your Own Home. That is, if you have one, and if you listen to the radio.

RADIO ANNOUNCER. Ladies and Gentlemen, this is Station KNX—the Voice of Hollywood. At this time we take great pleasure in announcing the winner of the Royal Studios' Baby Star Contest to find the successor to Happy, who retired from the screen after his illness. Ladies and Gentlemen, the lucky baby is Baby Sylvester Burnett, infant son of Mr. and Mrs. Oliver Burnett of Glendale, California. Congratulations, Mr. and Mrs. Burnett. Contracts for your baby are waiting in Mr. C. Elliot Friday's office at the Royal Studios. Incidentally, Mr. Friday asks that you bring your baby's birth certificate and your marriage license. This is KNX, the Voice of Hollywood. [*Chimes are heard.*]

Scene III

MR. FRIDAY'S *office, the following day.* MR. FRIDAY *is sitting at his desk, dictating to* MISS CREWS.

C.F. My dear Mr. Pirandello. . . . On second thought, you'd better make that Signor Pirandello. . . . I am writing to ascertain if possibly you have something in your trunk— every author has—which would be suitable as a vehicle for our new baby star, Baby Sylvester Burnett. It can be either a short story or sketch or a few lines which you can jot down at your leisure and which we can whip up into suitable material. I am writing of my own volition as both Mrs. Friday and I are great admirers of you. Very truly yours.

. . . Now take a letter to Stark Young. [*Dictograph buzzes.*] Yes?

B.K.'S VOICE. Listen, Friday—

C.F. What, B.K.?

B.K.'S VOICE. Come right up here. I want to see you. We've got a new cable from Gaumont British.

C.F. Gaumont British? Yes, sir, I'll be right up. [*He rises.*] Miss Crews, have you the contracts for the Burnett baby?

MISS CREWS. Right on your desk, Mr. Friday. And the parents are in the commissary.

C.F. Good. I've got to go up and see B.K. [*Exits.*]

GREEN [*who enters almost simultaneously, followed by* SLADE]. Where is he? Where's C.F.?

MISS CREWS. You can't shoot him today.

GREEN. It's a wonder we don't. We're walking up and down in front of the projection room developing an idea when we hear a number—our number— We go in, and it's in *Young England*! Our song! They don't even tell us about it —they murdered it! They run dialogue over it. You got to spot a song—we ask for Guy Lombardo and they give us a six-piece symphony orchestra!

MISS CREWS. If you buy me a handkerchief I promise to cry. Lace, if you don't mind.

GREEN. Listen—play her the number the way it should be.

MISS CREWS. Must you?

SLADE. Oh, what's the use?

GREEN. Give her the chorus.

SLADE. I'm losing my pep.

GREEN. You might as well hear it. Nobody else will. [SLADE *plays.*] Will you listen to that? Ain't it a shame?

> You promised love undying,
> And begged me to believe;
> Then you left, and left me crying
> With pain in my heart, and my heart on my sleeve.
>
> I really shouldn't blame you
> Because you chose to leave;
> But one thing forever will shame you—
> It's the pain in my heart, and my heart on my sleeve.

[C.F. *has entered.*]

C.F. Miss Crews!

MISS CREWS. Yes, Mr. Friday?

C.F. Miss Crews, get hold of Benson and Law right away!

MISS CREWS. Who?

C.F. Have Benson and Law come here—immediately.

MISS CREWS. Yes, Mr. Friday.

GREEN [*as* SLADE *pounds away*]. That's the chorus! That's the chorus that you murdered!

C.F. Wait a minute, Miss Crews! Get me the hospital. I want to talk to Happy's mother.

MISS CREWS. Yes, Mr. Friday. [*She exits.*]

C.F. Miss Crews! Call my florist and tell him to send Happy a bouquet of roses. And some orchids for his mother, right away. [*He turns to* GREEN.] Will you stop that noise! [*He picks up telephone.*]

GREEN. Noise? The song that you murdered? We just wanna see if you got a conscience.

C.F. [*into phone*]. Miss Crews, call up Magnin's and tell them to send a radio to the hospital for Happy. One of those slick, modernistic sets in white. And don't forget to have my card put in with the flowers. Did you get Benson and Law? . . . Well, did you get Happy's mother? . . . Well, get them! [*Hangs up.*]

GREEN. Is that a song that you run dialogue over, C.F.?

C.F. What are you babbling about, Green? I haven't used any of your songs in *Young England!*

GREEN [*outraged*]. How about *Westminster Abbey in the Moonlight?* They wasn't our lyrics, but it was our tune!

C.F. I used an old Jerome Kern number we've had for years, out of the library.

GREEN [*crestfallen*]. You did? [*To* SLADE.] I thought you said it came to you in the middle of the night. Where? In the library?

C.F. Will you get out of my office?

GREEN [*with sudden enthusiasm*]. We got a new number you'll be crazy about.

C.F. I've got too much on my mind to listen to your tinny effusions. I told the studio to hire Richard Strauss and no one else. One great composer is worth twenty of your ilk!

[ROSETTI *enters with* LARRY.]

LARRY. Looka here, C.F., I just got out of a sick bed to see you.

C.F. What do you want, Larry? [SLADE *plays on.*] What do you want? I'm very busy. [*Turns to* GREEN.] Will you please go? I will not listen!

GREEN [*as the worm turns*]. . . . O.K., music lover! [GREEN *and* SLADE *exit.*]

LARRY. I shouldn't be here. I should be on my ranch convalescing. I'm weak.

C.F. Come to the point, Larry. Come to the point.

LARRY [*bitterly*]. What's the idea of lending me out to Mascot? I'm a star! I ain't goin' to degrade myself by playing in no undignified thirty-thousand-dollar feature.

C.F. Larry, face the facts—you're through.

LARRY. That's a nice thing to tell a sick man.

ROSETTI. Now, Larry, I told you. Your attitude is all wrong.

LARRY. Never mind about my attitude.

C.F. [*at the phone*]. Miss Crews, have you got Benson and Law? . . . Who's gone to Vermont? . . . What about Susie? . . . What? They left the hospital? [*He hangs up.*]

ROSETTI [*eagerly*]. What's up, C.F.?

C.F. [*finally*]. This is confidential, Rosetti. [*Lowers his voice.*] Gaumont British wants to buy the company intact.

LARRY. Gaumont British?

C.F. They want all our stars, including Happy. Naturally they want him. He's the sensation of London.

ROSETTI. But B.K. turned down three million. I've been handling that deal myself.

C.F. They've raised it. They've just cabled an offer of five million.

ROSETTI. They did? Say, that's marvelous. I'm in on that!

LARRY. Well, you better get me back from Mascot quick. Gaumont British wants *me*. Why, they made me an offer a year ago, only I was tied up.

C.F. They made no mention of you.

LARRY. What?

C.F. Rosetti, we've got to sign Happy immediately. Get hold of Susie and let's close.

ROSETTI. You can sign the three of 'em for a hundred a week. They're broke. And they're low. I'm going right after it. [*He starts for door.*]

LARRY. Come back here. You're supposed to be *my* agent! What are you going to do about *me?*

ROSETTI. You're all right where you are—with Mascot. I'll call you later, C.F. [*Exits.*]

LARRY [*to* C.F.]. My agent! I been distrustin' that guy for years. [*Exits.*]

C.F. [*who can balance a budget, picks up phone*]. Miss Crews, you didn't send those flowers off, did you? . . . What? . . .

But they've left the hospital. What about the radio? . . .
Well, call them up right away and cancel it. . . . Who?
. . . She's here? Send her right in! [*He crosses to greet*
SUSIE. *He is now cordial; hearty, a thing of beauty and a*
joy forever.] Well, Susie, I'm delighted to see you. You're
looking well. I must say we've missed you. I hear the boys
are in Vermont.

SUSIE [*stands in door*]. Mr. Law was going but he missed the
plane.

C.F. [*taken aback*]. Well, where are they?

SUSIE. They're in B.K.'s office, getting the contracts.

C.F. Without consulting me?

SUSIE. They said they don't trust you, Mr. Friday.

C.F. Gad! After all I've done for them!

SUSIE [*seating herself on the couch*]. Do you mind if I sit here
and do my homework? I'm way behind and I don't want to
be left back. I'm supposed to wait here until they get B.K.'s
signature, and then I'm going to sign.

C.F. I'm going right up to see B.K. [MISS CREWS *enters.*]

MISS CREWS. Mr and Mrs. Burnett have had their coffee and
now they want their contracts.

C.F. What contracts?

MISS CREWS. The parents of the other infant.

C.F. What other infant? What other infant is there except
Happy?

MISS CREWS. But what'll I do with them?

C.F. Send them away. [*Now he sees* RODNEY *looking in through
door.*]

RODNEY [*holding a large box of flowers*]. What do you want?

RODNEY. Here's the check for the milk—and other odd items.

C.F. Check.

RODNEY. I think you'll find it correct. I verified it at the commissary. And of course I included a service charge—and
interest at six per cent. The total is two dollars and eighty-
four cents. Thank you. [*Dictograph buzzes.*]

C.F. [*into dictograph*]. Hello—

B.K.'S VOICE. Listen, Friday, you might as well be here. I'm
settling the Happy contract with Benson and Law.

C.F. Yes, B. K. I'm coming right up. [*Phone rings; into phone.*]
What? . . . I never asked for trumpets in the first place. I
don't want any trumpets. I want a period of utter silence.
See that I get it. [*Hangs up. To* RODNEY.] *You* get out!

RODNEY [*firmly*]. I've something to say to Mrs. Seabrook.
[SUSIE *turns away. Softly.*] I brought you some flowers.

C.F. Give her her flowers, and get out. And don't let me find you here when I come back. Miss Crews, I'll be up in B.K.'s office. [*He exits.*]

RODNEY. I know you don't want to see me. [*Extends flowers.*] Won't you take them? [MISS CREWS *exits.*] I wrote, you know. I explained everything.

SUSIE [*still not facing him*]. Happy's not allowed to have flowers.

RODNEY. Oh, but they're for Happy's mother—from Happy's father.

SUSIE [*turning; aghast*]. Are you joking about what you did?

RODNEY. I'm not joking. Lord, no. I mean it. Look here—will you marry me? [SUSIE *stares at him.*] I've thought it all out. I owe it to you. Shall we consider it settled?

SUSIE. Did Mr. Law and Mr. Benson put you up to this, too?

RODNEY. Good Lord, no. I haven't seen them and, what's more I don't intend to.

SUSIE. Then why do you want to marry me?

RODNEY. I owe it to you.

SUSIE [*angrily*]. That's no reason.

RODNEY. My visa's expired—I've two days' grace. I must get a train this afternoon. Are you coming with me?

SUSIE. I don't think you'd make a very sensible father for Happy. I don't think so at all.

RODNEY. I'm not at all sensible. I'm frightfully stupid—impulsive—emotional—but I'm not really at my best these days. Most people aren't when they're infatuated.

SUSIE. You couldn't be infatuated with me.

RODNEY. But I am. Look here, it's no good debating. My mind's made up. I don't frequently make it up, but when I do, I stick to the end.

SUSIE. But you don't know about my past.

RODNEY. I've been through all that, in my mind. It doesn't matter.

SUSIE. But it does. I'm ashamed to tell you.

RODNEY. Please don't, then.

SUSIE. Happy's father was a bigamist.

RODNEY. Eh?

SUSIE. He married twice.

RODNEY. Is that it?

SUSIE. What did you think?

RODNEY. It doesn't really matter.

SUSIE. I didn't know he was married before.

RODNEY. But, good Lord, nobody can blame *you*.

SUSIE. His wife did.

RODNEY. Naturally.

SUSIE. How was I to know? And it wasn't his fault, either. He got a Mexican divorce and he didn't know it wasn't good.

RODNEY. Oh!

SUSIE [*drawing herself up à la Fairfax*]. So I said to him, "Your duty is to your first wife." And I ran away. I didn't know I was going to have Happy, then.

RODNEY. Have you—heard from him?

SUSIE. Oh, no. Of course, he should have told me in the first place. But he was infatuated, too, and I didn't know any better.

RODNEY. Well, have you divorced him?

SUSIE. No.

RODNEY. You'll have to clear that matter up, I think—immediately.

SUSIE. I can't clear it up. He's dead.

RODNEY. Oh!

SUSIE. She shot him.

RODNEY. His wife?

SUSIE. Yes.

RODNEY. Good Lord!

SUSIE. I hear from her sometimes. She's awfully sorry.

RODNEY [*brightly*]. Well then, you're free to marry, aren't you?

SUSIE. Oh, I'm free, but the point is—do I want to? After all, I don't know you very well, and every time we meet something terrible happens. I didn't know Jack very well, either, and look what happened to him. I've got to be careful.

RODNEY. But I'm not a bigamist.

SUSIE. Maybe not. You may be something else.

RODNEY. But the British Consul'll vouch for me. He knows my family. I haven't had much of a life, but it's an open book.

SUSIE. Oh, I believe you. But I can't listen to my heart. I've got to listen to my head.

RODNEY. Of course, I haven't much to offer you. I've just come into a little money, and on my thirtieth birthday I come into a great deal more. We can have a flat in London and one of my aunts is going to leave me a place in the country.

SUSIE. That's in Europe, isn't it?

RODNEY. Yes, of course.

SUSIE. Oh, I couldn't go to Europe.

RODNEY. But why not?

SUSIE. The boys want to put Happy back in pictures.

RODNEY. I wouldn't hear of it. That's no life for a baby. Thoroughly abnormal. And, furthermore, I don't like the California climate. Now in England we have the four seasons.

SUSIE. You have?

RODNEY [*ardently*]. Summer, winter, spring and fall.

SUSIE [*finally*]. I want to ask you something.

RODNEY. Certainly.

SUSIE. When I come into a room—does something happen to you?

RODNEY. Eh? Of course—very much so.

SUSIE [*rises and turns away*]. Well, I'll think it over.

RODNEY [*rises and takes* SUSIE's *arm*]. Look here, I couldn't possibly take no for an answer.

SUSIE. Of course, when you come into a room, something happens to me, too.

RODNEY. Does it really? [SUSIE *nods. He takes her in his arms. They kiss. Door opens and* LAW *enters with* BENSON.]

LAW. Susie, did my eyes deceive me? Were you kissing an actor?

BENSON. What's that?

LAW [*to* BENSON]. An English actor!

BENSON. What? Didn't I tell you—?

SUSIE. Boys, I've been thinking it over—

BENSON [*wearily drops down to piano;* LAW *down to end of couch*]. With what?

SUSIE. I'm going to marry Rodney and I'm going to Europe. They've got the four seasons over there, and Happy'll be normal.

RODNEY. Well put, my dear.

[C.F. *enters.*]

SUSIE. So I don't think I'd better sign the contract.

RODNEY. Most certainly not!

C.F. You're not going to sign Happy?

LAW. Susie, I've just given up Vermont for a whole year—for you. A whole year out of my life—because B.K. begged me to stay and handle Happy. I've sacrificed a great book—for what? A paltry fifteen hundred dollars a week? I didn't want it!

c.f. If she doesn't sign, we'll break that contract with you, Law.

LAW. Try and do it.

SUSIE. I'm going to Europe with Rodney.

LAW. Do you want to tell Happy he's out of pictures? Do you want to break his little heart?

SUSIE. He'll understand.

BENSON [*suddenly*]. Do you know who Rodney is? English Jack! Confidence man.

LAW [*quickly*]. Yes! Ship's gambler, petty racketeer and heart-breaker.

[RODNEY *tries to speak*.]

BENSON. Served two terms for bigamy!

SUSIE. Bigamy?

RODNEY. But that's absurd.

BENSON [*bitterly*]. I've seen hundreds of your kind in Lime-house.

c.f. So have I!

BENSON [*quietly*]. Listen, C.F., stay off our side!

RODNEY [*to* SUSIE]. You don't believe this, of course. They can't possibly believe it themselves.

LAW. Brazening it out, eh? As sure as God made little green apples—and He did—you're not coming near Susie. We'll have you in the can and out of the country by morning.

BENSON. No sooner said— [*Into phone.*] Get me the Department of Justice.

SUSIE [*to* RODNEY]. You see? Something terrible always happens when you come.

LAW [*to* SUSIE]. And you—sign that contract immediately.

RODNEY. She'll do nothing of the sort. You're not to intimidate her. Do you hear?

[*Door opens and* LARRY *enters, accompanied by middle-aged English gentleman.*]

LARRY. Come on in here, Major.

c.f. What do you want, Larry? I'm busy.

BENSON [*into telephone*]. Department of Justice? I want two of your best operatives to come down to the Royal Studios immediately. Report to Mr. Friday's office.

SUSIE. Oh, but you can't do that—

LARRY [*angrily*]. Just a minute. Major Thompson is the representative here of Gaumont British.

C.F. Oh! I'm sorry. We've been rather upset. How do you do, Major? I'm Mr. Friday.

MAJOR. How do you do, sir? I won't be a moment. Mr. Toms suggested I come down here. He told me you'd received a cable from my home office.

C.F. Yes—yes—

MAJOR. He was rather upset because his name wasn't mentioned.

C.F. Yes, yes—

MAJOR. I called my home office, and they assure me they never sent such a cable.

C.F. What?

LARRY. That's what! It was a phoney!

RODNEY [*who has been trying to attract attention for some time*]. Major!

MAJOR. Well! Aren't you— Why, how do you do? I thought I recognized you. Met up with your brother. By the way, I saw him a few weeks ago just before I sailed. Particularly asked me to look you up.

RODNEY. Is my name English Jack? Am I a ship's gambler? Have I served sentences for bigamy?

MAJOR. Good Gad, no!

RODNEY. Will you vouch for me?

MAJOR [*a bore of bores*]. Vouch for Puffy Bevan? Delighted! His brother—splendid chap— I met him first in India—he's a captain in the Coldstream Guards. His father is Lord Severingham. His sister is Lady Beasley—lectures, I believe. Now, let me see—

LAW [*interrupting*]. Did you say—Lord Severingham?

MAJOR. Yes.

BENSON. I beg your pardon, sir—*his* father? [*He indicates* RODNEY.]

MAJOR. Yes. [*shakes his head in wonder.*]

SUSIE. Is your father a lord?

RODNEY. It doesn't matter, does it?

SUSIE. If you don't care, I don't care.

MAJOR. If I can be of any further service—

RODNEY. No. I think we'll sail along beautifully now. Thanks.

MAJOR. Good afternoon. [*Shakes hands with* RODNEY.]

C.F. Who sent that cable? That's all I want to know! Who sent that cable! [MAJOR *and* LARRY *exit.*] Who perpetrated this hoax? Who's responsible for this outrage? By Gad, I'll find out! [*Exits.*]

RODNEY [*turns to* SUSIE]. Shall we go?

SUSIE. Good-bye, boys. Take care of yourselves.

LAW [*bows; bitterly*]. Thank you, milady.

SUSIE. Don't drink too much.

LAW. Thank you, milady.

SUSIE. You were awful good to me. Yes, they were, Rodney. They were awful good to me sometimes.

RODNEY. In that case, I don't mind shaking hands with you. [*Starts toward* LAW.]

LAW [*quickly*]. Don't shake hands. Just go. Dissolve—*slow fade-out!*

BENSON [*pantomiming*]. Shimmer away!

RODNEY. Eh? [*Shrugs.*] Well—come, Susie.

SUSIE [*waving a delicate little hand*]. Good-bye, boys. [*Pause. They exit in silence.*]

LAW. [*tense*]. I wonder what C.F.'s up to?

BENSON [*struck all of a heap*]. The hell with that. Look at it —it checks! Cinderella—Prince Charming—Boy meets girl. . . . Boy loses girl. . . . Boy gets girl! Where's your damned realism now?

[C.F. *enters. He looks grimly at the boys.*]

C.F. [*finally*]. Well—it's a good thing you boys are not mixed up in this! [*He goes to desk.*]

BENSON [*slowly*]. What?

LAW [*slowly*]. What happened, C.F.?

C.F. I don't understand it at all. The cable was sent from London all right. But B.K. should have known it was a fake. It was sent collect. [*He picks up phone.*]

LAW. Jascha always sends collect.

C.F. Huh? [*Into phone.*] Miss Crews, get hold of the Burnett baby immediately. . . . Who? . . . the *what* is here? [*Puzzled. The answer comes in the clarion call of the trumpets, blaring their gay, lilting notes through the windows. Ta-ra-ta-ta-ta-ta-tata-tata-tata! So much pleasanter than a factory whistle, don't you think?*]

CURTAIN